Successful Marketing Strategies for Nonprofit Organizations

Successful Marketing Strategies for Nonprofit Organizations

Second Edition

WINNING IN THE AGE OF THE ELUSIVE DONOR

Barry McLeish

WILEY

John Wiley & Sons, Inc.

Library of Congress Cataloging-in-Publication Data:

McLeish, Barry, 1956-
  Successful marketing strategies for nonprofit organizations : winning in the age of the elusive donor / Barry J. McLeish.—2nd ed.
       p. cm.
    Includes bibliographical references and index.
    ISBN 978-0-470-52981-2 (hardback)
  1. Nonprofit organizations–Marketing.   I. Title.
    HF5415.M3825 2010
    658.8'02–dc22

                                                                            2010024727

Printed in the United States of America

10 9 8 7 6 5 4 3 2 1

Other Wiley Books
by Barry McLeish

Successful Marketing Strategies for Nonprofit Organizations
Yours, Mine, and Ours: Creating the Compelling Donor Experience

For my teachers:
Winston Brembeck, William McConkey,
Larry Fuhrer, and James McLeish

Contents

Preface   **xv**

Acknowledgments   **xxxi**

Part I   Introduction   **1**

Chapter 1   A New Way of Doing Business for the
Nonprofit Organization   3

The Need for a New Marketing Orientation   4
Dealing with Nonprofit Organizations
in Flux   5
Marketing to the External World   10
Marketing Defined   10
Develop an Outline of Marketing Strategies   13
The Marketing Task   18
Marketing Tools   22
Use Distinctive Competencies to
Assess the Competition   26
Summary   27

Chapter 2   The Development of a
Marketing Strategy   29

Why a Marketing Strategy?   31
First Steps in Defining Strategy   33
The Operating Environment's Effects
on Marketing Strategy   38

	First Steps to a Competitive Strategy	47
	Breaking with Tradition to Remain Flexible	48
	Summary	49
Chapter 3	The Phased Strategic Marketing Plan	51
	External-Analysis Phase	52
	Internal-Analysis Phase	56
	Market-Development Phase	57
	Strategy-Selection Phase	59
	Presentation of the Plan	59
	Summary	60
Part II	**The External Analysis**	**61**
Chapter 4	External Analysis: Client, Donor, Volunteer, and Competitor Research	63
	The Importance of Continuous Listening and Analysis	65
	Building a Rationale and Addressing Objections to Stakeholder Listening and Research	66
	Other Research and Listening Concerns, Including Flexibility	71
	Start with Clients, Volunteers, Constituents, Customers, and Donors	72
	Segmentation as the Next Step	73
	Enduring and Dynamic Segmentation Variables	74
	Describing Clients, Donors, Volunteers, Customers, and Constituents	81
	Additional Segmentation Strategies Following an External Audit	83
	External Analysis of Competitors	84
	Positioning to Understand ``the Market''	87
	Ways to Identify Competition	87
	How Nonprofit Organizations Compete	88
	Summary	91

Chapter 5   Researching Your Nonprofit
                   Organization's Environment   93

                   The Nature of a Nonprofit
                   Organization's Environment   94
                   External Analysis, Competitors, and
                   a Nonprofit's Environment   95
                   The Actual and Potential Size of the
                   Competitive Environment   96
                   How Is the Environment Structured?   98
                   How Nonprofit Organizations Enter an Industry   103
                   How Does the Nonprofit Organization
                   Deliver Its Services?   106
                   What Is the Potential for Growth?   109
                   Relating Product Life Cycles to a
                   Nonprofit's Growth Potential   111
                   Differentiating a Nonprofit Based on
                   External Analysis   113
                   Summary   117

Chapter 6   Competition and Internal
                   Marketing Analysis   119

                   Reasons for an Internal Examination   120
                   Measuring Past and Current Performance   122
                   Dealing with Strategic Problems and Uncertainty   132
                   Assessing the Organization's Strengths
                   and Weaknesses   137
                   Looking for and Managing Long-Term
                   Relationships   141
                   Cost and Performance Analysis Helps
                   Define Success   143
                   The Internal Audit Helps Define Organizational
                   Strengths and Weaknesses   144
                   Summary   145

Chapter 7   Value Propositions and Marketing
                   Objectives   147

                   Would Anyone Miss You If You Went
                   out of Business?   147

Why Should a Nonprofit Organization
Worry about Objectives?   147
Developing Organizational Objectives   148
Using Objectives to Excel in Marketing   153
Marketing Performance Comes with
Measuring Company Objectives   155
Staying Competitive   165
Summary   166

Chapter 8   Creating Competitive
Advantage   167

Strategy Options   168
The Most Popular Strategic Orientations
and Their Application to the Organization   172
Matching the Market   176
Tactics for Achieving Competitive
Advantage   177
The Sustainable Competitive
Advantage   178
What Constitutes a Sustainable
Competitive Advantage   178
Augmenting Success   181
Market Strategies   182
Summary   185

Chapter 9   Winning through Competitive
Strategy Options   187

The Nature of Strategy and Its Uses   188
Environmental Context and
Strategic Options   191
Strategy Frameworks   193
Strategy Models   194
The Portfolio Framework   196
The Forces of Competition   198
Porter's Three Competitive Strategies   202
The Planning Process Framework   203
Summary   205

Chapter 10   Creating a Competitive Image
and Brand   207

   Brand Formulation   208
   Merging Brand and Strategy   211
   Using the Brand Strategically   216
   Reaching the Branded Goals of
   the Campaign   219
   Summary   228

Epilogue   **229**

Notes   **237**

References   **243**

About the Author   **245**

Index   **247**

Preface

Men occasionally stumble over the truth, but most of them pick themselves up and hurry off as if nothing had happened.

Winston Churchill

Who is marketing your cause? Is it you, your CEO, your board development committee, or key agency volunteers? Do they have a plan of attack or just a list of best practices? Assuming they have a plan—and many don't—the list of best practices they have may not be well suited to today's hyper-competitive nonprofit world. More is needed. Donors, customers, members of social ecosystems, and an overabundance of causes have seemingly conspired to demand that nonprofit organizations become readily adaptable and significantly radical to survive and flourish during these days of eroding tactical advantages and shrinking strategy life cycles.

The landscape has radically changed since I wrote *Successful Marketing Strategies for Nonprofit Organizations* for Wiley.

First of all, relationships are not what they used to be. We now use tools that enable us to keep in constant touch with individuals for a lifetime, whereas just a short time ago, unless people worked really hard, they would not only forget someone's name but lose their pertinent information. Now marketing directors speak of "digital friendships," which aren't really friendships at all but contacts, and organizations pretend that they can manage thousands of these new relationships and networks even though in the past they often had a hard time with just a handful of names. The good news is that the Internet has allowed research capabilities to increase proportionately, and organizations can now tailor their marketing programs according to the digital behavior of those they are following as well as that of their friends.

While it is obvious that the Internet has changed everything, what is not so obvious is that there are still few strategy and development protocols that reliably perform for organizations day in and out. What can be said is that the near-institutional transparency the Internet allows, along with massive organization commoditization, is driving mediocre agencies out of business and helping to reduce the barriers to entry for a host of new ones. These two factors have dictated that offering real value to stakeholders has never been more important and now requires not only new knowledge about those an organization wishes to serve but a common agency commitment to indeed serve them. The context the stakeholders find themselves in requires, alternatively, an immersion into their lives on the part of the agency that serves them, something that not every agency is willing to do because it places an individual's needs above those of the institution.

As such, programmatic and marketing innovation now matters more because it changes how organizations perform, creating uniqueness in the midst of agency parity, and allows differentiation to occur. Today, organization differentiation may be the most important tactic a strategist has, especially in light of the donor pullback some agencies are experiencing and the erosion of many markets.

Explaining the "how" of engaging the donors and customers an agency does have and then making them central to all the institution does is the aim of *The Elusive Donor*. Successful competitive outcomes are increasingly becoming the result of value alignment between agency and stakeholder and collaboration between the two parties. This persistent collaboration can produce institutional innovation and can also secure the loyalty and commitment of the stakeholder, who in turn locks out competitors and feeds the tendency of the organization to be involved in listening at all levels. The relentless positioning of the stakeholder at the center of an organization is not a new idea; it is mentioned at every nonprofit marketing seminar. What is new is that the centrality of the stakeholder is no longer optional. Stakeholder centrality and stakeholder listening lead to better programming, better products, and more philanthropic dollars as well as to stakeholder engagement. It is this increased penetration that creates meaning between the agency and the individual. How to achieve this interaction is the subject of *The Elusive Donor.*

Authors and philosophers have suggested that an era ends when its basic illusions and paradigms no longer make sense and have been exhausted. There is little doubt that this has become the case with countless nonprofit organizations across North American and around the world as they engage in what is for some, the most intense period of creative destruction and reconstruction they have ever seen. For many of these agencies, virtually every component that has been a mainstay of their marketing programs during the past decade has been changed irrevocably by the economic and technological upheaval they now find themselves a part of.

Oft-used advertising media, fundraising delivery systems, data base models, and "sure-fire" donation requests no longer seem to work and function as they once did for many agencies. While leaders fret over the changes occurring within their institutions, many more seem paralyzed, not knowing what to do about them. Old ways are dying hard. Margaret J. Wheatley suggests, "This is an era of many messes."[1] She may be right.

Much of today's nonprofit world seems to be in the early stages of a deeply unassailable and omni present set of changes that, for better or worse, are altering its economies, cultures, and the understanding its leaders and directors have regarding how they fit in society, what they should do, and what they should stand for. This disequilibrium is being evidenced in many ways. Donors of all classes no longer give according to the prescribed patterns they once evidenced; new constituent communication habits have upset the way many organizations converse with their stakeholders; agency supporters now expect value attainment to come in multiple dimensions as opposed to the singular "gift-giving" and "thank-you letters" of the past; and real power has shifted from institutions to stakeholders who write donation checks, volunteer, or buy organizational products (i.e., stakeholders who in turn often create self-organizing online communities around aligned interests with like-minded individuals outside the jurisdiction and control of the sponsoring nonprofit institution). As leaders try to direct and control these outcomes, a sense of powerlessness has pervaded many of them, even as the very calculus by which they have managed their organizations in the past has now changed.

The future remains an open question. What can be said is that for most institutions, it is no longer business as usual. Rather than continuing to send marketing and fundraising messages to an increasingly unsympathetic and sometimes resentful audience, many organizations are trying to engineer a different sort of social engagement with their stakeholders. New tools, new techniques, new giving patterns, and the evolution of the marketing language itself are signs of the flux marketers are in. Within many agencies the marketing function's status as the engine of causal growth and change is being derailed as over-competition has often led to service commoditization in many sectors as along with the splintering of donor bases. Stakeholders have also changed, dramatically increasing their expectations of value attainment and their sense of place within the nonprofit ecosystem.

Whereas stakeholder conversations used to be initiated and distributed by organizations that incepted, directed, and controlled their efforts to communicate with them, the new stakeholder dialog now starts in reverse order with donors, customers, and volunteers themselves providing data to the agency and stating the terms by which they would like to be in communication. Consequently agency control over content and distribution is fading. Additionally, with many audiences already highly involved in cause-related behavior and connecting with causal groups in clear and thoughtful ways, agencies no longer tactically gain anything by "shouting" their messages. Prospective stakeholders are often more knowledgeable and more interactive than ever, and more willing to trust their own recommendations. Social media provide these individuals (as well as nonprofit institutions) with a set of technologies that enable conversations, relationships, and social and knowledge networks to be built as never before. New stakeholder rules of engagement are being written formally or informally in many organizations on a routine basis.

In light of these changes, some are suggesting that marketing's role within institutions is also changing, especially with the advent of new media options. For architects of nonprofit strategy, if marketing's role hasn't already changed substantially within their own organization as well as others, perhaps the change should occur immediately. While "command and control marketing" has been changing within the nonprofit world during the past few years in favor of a marketing strategy that listens to and nurtures audience members with the goal of meaningful stakeholder and donor engagement, other changes have been more pronounced. Marketing has always been about defining targets, both individuals and markets, in the pursuit of prospective stakeholders and leveraging relationships with them to create a keen sense of belonging within their very being. Steve Yastrow, a principal of Yastrow Marketing, correctly surmises in his book *We* that the ultimate marketing challenge for marketers continues to be whether customers have a "we" relationship with the companies they do business with or an "us and them" perspective.

The need for strong causal relationships has given rise to other critical issues such as stakeholder sustainability and donor and customer retention. These tactical problems have radically increased in importance during the past 10 years as competition has intensified, with many causes now becoming commodities in the minds of their constituents.

> In an annual survey of [for-profit] CEOs conducted by The Conference Board, nearly seven hundred CEOs globally were polled about the challenges facing their companies in 2002. CEOs identified "customer loyalty and retention" as the leading management issue ahead of reducing costs, developing leaders, increasing innovation, and improving stock prices.[2]

Because marketing has always had to rely on media to deliver its messages, the presence of new communication options suggests that the various media an organization uses will need to be adjusted as to their capability to perform the tasks of retention and sustainability as well as to deliver a compelling value proposition that is supported by key value drivers. While important considerations such as brand equity and the alignment of agency values with stakeholders continue to be central issues tactically, the role the new media play may also make critical agendas dependent in part on the ongoing dialog and sustained engagement that should take place between an organization and its stakeholders. To achieve these goals, the current mindset of top-down leadership control, still popular with many nonprofit agencies, must be replaced with the relatively new design of leadership collaboration with off-line and online communities in building constructive relationships, effective knowledge networks, and strong brands.

However, for many directors these changes present an unimaginable landscape as additional managerial issues confront them. Stability and control, for example, have gone by the wayside as hundreds of institutions have had to grapple with the incessant need to respond to the discontinuous changes and financial pressures they face. Additionally, the myriad of media options stakeholders have available to them to communicate with organizations they are interested in—and if necessary, to talk back to—via web logs, chat rooms, online surveys, corporate forums, and other social avenues—now give them unprecedented moral, social, and communicative power.

Conversely, finding they can no longer turn stakeholders on and off in the same ways they once did, some nonprofit directors end up dancing between chaos and stability, retreating to what has worked in the past—more mail, more events, more cost-cutting, more top-down control—and further exacerbating the situation they find themselves in. Though there may be many different ways to "win" in the presence of new communication options (coupled with the deterioration of some of the old options), the path is not always clear.

What is clear, however, is that massive changes are taking place that affect most if not all nonprofit stakeholders:

- Television now offers 70 channels for most people, as opposed to the three or four basic ones of old.
- A substantial audience shift from prime time viewing to any-time viewing has occurred.
- Satellite radio offers listeners hundreds of channels with highly targeted content.
- Newspaper circulation is plunging, and its advertising, classified ads in particular, is being rechanneled online as news aggregations and social sites begin to dominate.
- The total number of magazine titles, along with average magazine circulation and single-copy sales, continues to drift downward.
- User-generated content on sites such as YouTube, MySpace, and Facebook is drawing millions of consumers daily.

In spite of the media renaissance occurring around them, comparatively few nonprofit agencies seem to be taking these shifts in their communication and marketing paradigms as opportunities to probe their stakeholders more deeply, learn the real reasons for their support, and become collaborators with them. Instead, many nonprofit agency marketing units continue to use the more traditional fact-based, four Ps approach (product, price, place, and promotion) to develop strategies regarding their donors and customers, letting their accumulated data—segmentation studies, response data, and purchasing habits—dictate their strategies. Some institutions, according to Seth Godin's *Meatball Sundae*, in attempting a "quick fix" by bolting on new forms of media communication to old command-and-control structures, have made clear their disdain for the ideal of organizational transparency and have created a marketing mix of incompatible ingredients.

For directors choosing the path of non-collaboration as well as ignoring the new rules of stakeholder engagement that seem to be becoming a permanent fixture, key tenets learned in the past related to nonprofit marketing and being market driven may soon become irrelevant and lost to history. For these directors and for others in similar positions, being market driven is no longer good enough; what is required is an obsessive desire on the part of an agency's leadership to create and deliver value through all of its inner workings for the targeted stakeholder. Obviously, strong relationships are a critical part of delivering this value. What are changing for many organizations, however, are the tactics of delivering "strong relationships," given that building communities of interest and providing content have now become a necessary part of the delivery systems.

While the new media usage has for some become a type of cultural experience in and of itself and for others a type of experimentation, these media are seen by almost all to be rich with information, so much so that it is almost impossible to hide anything organizationally. Unfortunately, as a partial consequence of this ease of utility many young marketing and development directors now mistakenly rely solely on social media for almost all of their promotional needs, development tasks, relation building, and consumer insights. As a result, some directors have even given up trying to engage stakeholders face to face and have tabled subsequent personal follow-up appointments and interaction simply because of the difficulty they may have in procuring appointments with members of their institution's target markets and the apparent ease of using social media. Having forgotten that individual stakeholders are still the source of most value for nonprofit organizations, these directors try to run their marketing programs "from a distance." No longer encouraging their stakeholders to be willing to talk about the organizations they are interested in online and off-line, they substitute technology for interaction in the management and communication of defined target groups who require individual care, one-to-one interaction, and personalized stakeholder concern. Jump Associates founder Dev Patnaik suggests, "Those maps are a poor substitute for actual human contact."[3]

For most marketing managers, however, much of the indeterminacy they face relates to a key tactical question with regard to the newly empowered stakeholder: How do we reach, listen to, and collaborate with our stakeholders to jointly accomplish our mutual and individual goals? Statistics suggest that many nonprofit directors have had a hard time with this and with the subsequent communication efforts required to accomplish it. One indicator of this apparent difficulty is the statistic cited by the Bridgespan Group, "[O]f the 200,000 nonprofits started in the United States since 1970, only 144 have reached $50 million in annual revenue."[4] Although the numbers of the world's wealthy are growing, their giving is not; a recent study of the world's rich reported that "the wealth of the world's rich and super rich surged 11.2 percent to $37.2 trillion last year, but the elite group gave less than 1 percent of their net worth to charity."[5]

Much is obviously at stake in finding out how to reach and collaborate with stakeholders to achieve mutual goals. Some organizations, mired in older and obsolete marketing methodologies, have become threatened by and antagonistic toward those suggesting they change. Others have mistakenly rushed headlong into massive tactical, communicative, and cultural change, giving little thought to advance planning. Some have chosen to do nothing.

In the face of so much upheaval, many nonprofit marketers would likely suggest that they themselves and their organizational strategies are currently at risk in implementing both digital and other new methodologies that are emerging as communication options. Complicating these disturbing trends are stakeholders who no longer listen to their favorite organizations in ways they once did, or respond to the advertising and public relations tools that were once the hallmark of marketing and solicitation campaigns in the same way. Dialog, while easier to do from a technological standpoint, is still critical, but it often degenerates through using new media into a series of transactions that offer little emotive content for either party.

Unfortunately an institution's marketing strategy is not the only managerial task that is in limbo and at risk during this time of upheaval. Corporate strategies and the way organizations normally process information are also being adversely affected, as are the goals the institution strives to achieve.

Although market information of all types and varieties continues to be a critically important part of communication and stakeholder dialog as well as institutional decision making, the nature of information being processed is also subject to change, even though its importance has not been diminished.

> I love the market information story author Paul Postma tells in his book *The New Marketing Era* about the major English mail order company, with an assortment comparable to that of a department store, confirming that there was no relationship between customers making a purchase from the gardening section and whether those customers had a garden or not.[6]

A more pertinent example of dealing with new market information comes from a client that is currently having a problem securing second gifts online for one of its causes following a successful online initial gift campaign. Although the research data indicates a strong brand preference for the cause, online stakeholder interest in a longer-term relationship does not seem to be forthcoming and seems to be transient in nature. Is it possible that the online popularity of this brand and its online response norms are not commensurate with the norms and popularity seen off-line, as evidenced by actual long-term commitment and multiple purchase and donation behavior? The data in this case seems to suggest that inferences drawn mistakenly from off-line media vehicles are different in nature from online media response rates. The resulting tactical questions are important and significant for marketers, because the stakeholder behavior that matters in this instance—sending a second gift to the institution—is evidencing itself differently across media in spite of similar messaging. As many marketers are discovering, not only are media changing but so are the rules for navigating them.

A number of years ago Kevin Kelly suggested in his book *New Rules for the New Economy* that networks would be the key to understanding how the economy works. Much of his prediction is being proven true, especially as organizations encounter the need to function in real time with different marketing and communication rules. With the new media serving as a means to generate and augment existing relationships, the ability to know stakeholders intimately and their backgrounds quickly allows agencies to

- Anticipate what stakeholders will want.
- Create custom-fitting programs tied to the values and interests of the stakeholders.
- Remind and help them remember what they have done in the past in relation to the nonprofit in the way of volunteering, donating, or purchasing.
- Suggest new areas to them for their involvement.

As Microsoft CEO Steven A. Ballmer told the *New York Times,*

> I think one pervasive change is the increasing importance of community. That will come in different forms, with different age groups of people, and it will change as the technology evolves. But the notion of multiple people interacting on things—that will forever continue.[7]

Though nonprofit organizations should be committed to creating value in either direction, both for the organization and for the stakeholder, creating immediate value (donating, purchasing, or volunteering today) and future value (donating, purchasing, or volunteering in the future based on the current experience) for the stakeholder requires nonprofit marketers to have a deep understanding of their audience. Having a market-centric view of stakeholders, however, becomes complicated for any organization when a stakeholder employs and is the recipient of 10 to 15 communication channels in the course of daily activities. Web analytics practitioner and author Akin Atikan notes, "Well, it is one thing to interact through multiple channels in parallel. It is quite another to fuse those activities in an intelligent way to maximize response and conversion rates."[8] Seemingly overnight, stakeholders have become multichannel users and now want to be in charge of their messaging.

Not all is lost, however. While the predominance of social media should necessarily affect how most organizations navigate and engage their audiences, how they solicit and recruit them, and how they develop an effective brand image, there are five imperatives that marketing must still deal with:

First, the human factor has not gone away. In their influential book *The Experience Economy,* authors Joseph Pine and James Gilmore suggested in 1999 the necessity for organizations to create outstanding experiences for their customers. Even though this is an important marketing tactic, in this era of many good causal choices it is simply not enough for many stakeholders. In a recently given seminar by McConkey/Johnston International, CEO Larry Johnston suggested a title closer to what stakeholders may expect today: "The Relentless Pursuit of Donor Delight."[9] As donors, volunteers, purchasers, and other stakeholders set stricter priorities for their nonprofit engagement, it will continue to be the agencies that routinely adjust their strategies and tactics to focus on engaging these individuals in the light of new response data that will thrive.

Some institutions will find that based on audience profiles and the dominance of particular media usage by them, very little in the way of tactical adjustment needs to be made. A case in point would be a client whose donor base consists primarily of older women. The agency is thriving in spite of the absence of a prolific social media strategy. On the other end of the spectrum, however, is a client that operates a camp and routinely deals with more than 20,000 grade school and junior and senior high school young people every year. A dominant multichannel social strategy is critical to this institution's communication platform. This may change in the future, but today this is the tactical reality. Engagement becomes more than what Pine and Gilmore were talking about. It must evoke empathy and allow the organization to step into the stakeholders' experience.

Second, you have to find the right stakeholders. Targeting the right stakeholders and then enticing them to try your cause is a hard task for any marketing director. There are numerous issues involved in finding the right stakeholders in today's hypercompetitive world. Homogeneity is the first tactical consideration. Marketing 101 suggests that individuals who hold similar demographic and psychographic profiles and whose value set aligns with your organization's values will have the highest participation rates with your cause. With social media being the elephant in the room for many organizations, the tactical trick is to harness the many available options along with other targeted media without either spamming stakeholders to death or ignoring them. As suggested, this is accomplished by going beyond pure demographics and looking at the values stakeholders hold. Value alignment allows intimacy, fluency, and familiarity, but first you must find the stakeholders who view your cause as you do. It is these individuals you must collaborate with.

Third, not all stakeholders are created equal. Good causal marketing must go beyond simple demographic considerations of sex, race, income, and so forth and must focus on interests as well. You must find individuals who will collaborate with you and will become bonded to your institution—and vice versa. To do so requires a closer and more sophisticated look at your organizational media mix. A close friend who is a surgeon told me that he recently got four emails marked "urgent" following three phone calls from a school, all concerning a pledge he had made to the organization. All the messages were designed to remind him of a deadline for payment of his pledge. He told me he would fulfill his pledge and then sever the relationship with the organization. The organization had violated his sense of collaboration and had told him through its actions that it did not trust him.

Fourth, the goal for organizations has not really changed. In a very real sense, in spite of social media and all the hand-wringing over how to maximize the media, the issue still remains: How do we create excitement in the hearts of our stakeholders over a cause and harness their enthusiasm for the organization by becoming collaborators with them and having their enthusiasm show up in their actions and personally generated media? Only by viewing our causes "as a bundle of processes that profitably define, create, communicate, and deliver value to its target customers" can agencies truly build their institutional brands by raising the level of their stakeholders' voices and harnessing their enthusiasm.[10]

Fifth, we have to learn to love our donors, customers, and volunteers in a way that we have not in the past. In one of my creative writing classes this story was told about poems:

There are three poems in every poem: (1) the poem the poet intends, (2) the poem that ends up on paper, and (3) the poem the reader understands.

Virtually every causal agency desires to love and nurture its stakeholders. Most leaders talk about this need routinely in interviews and in dialoging with them. Yet few actually undertake the practices necessary to accomplish this task. Douglas Akin suggests in his book *The Culting of Brands* that our feelings should be so strong for the stakeholders we serve that their well-being becomes the critical source for our well-being. This is how we begin to close the gap between what an agency wants to do and what it actually does.

The Organization of This Book

Building from the comments in the Preface, Chapter 1 notes that changes have forever altered the way nonprofit marketing must operate and that marketing and media considerations have arrived at an evolutionary convergence in how they must be perceived and utilized. The idea of "marketing" and what it means is now forever challenged.

In Chapter 2, after defining the word "strategy" in a nonprofit context, the text details why a marketing strategy is important to both the nonprofit organization and the philanthropic community, providing both of them with a sense of purpose and movement towards the achievement of organizational and personal goals.

Chapter 3 provides an overview of nonprofit market planning and research programs and lays a foundation for succeeding chapters.

Chapter 4 introduces the reader to the idea of undertaking external research analysis and the importance of such information in enabling the organization to generate strategic events as well as to make strategic decisions. External analysis of the organization's constituency is critical in determining whether it is hitting or missing its goals.

Chapter 5 picks up the discussion from Chapter 3 and continues the emphasis on external analysis as being key to an organization's ability to compete successfully. In this chapter and as part of the external analysis discussion, readers look at the competitive boundaries of the cause they are involved in and the environment that surrounds them.

Chapter 6 moves the reader from assessing his or her organization from the outside to assessing it from the inside out to highlight internal marketing, managerial, or organizational deficiencies that must be corrected to move the organization closer to its goals.

Chapter 7 is devoted to the discussion of organizational and marketing objectives, particularly as they relate to questions of why the nonprofit organization exists, what its intended markets are, and where constituent goals fit into the organization's objectives.

Chapter 8 helps the reader to take the information gathered from both the external and the internal analysis and to begin the process of melding the information into a marketing strategy for the organization.

Chapter 9 provides the reader with a number of strategy frameworks and alternatives to choose from, shows how they help nonprofit organizations in different ways, and allows the reader to merge his or her organization's past, present, and future into a coherent strategy.

Chapter 10 introduces the concept of an organization's brand and provides insight into how a nonprofit organization can manage its external image.

The Epilogue demonstrates how a nonprofit marketing practitioner can begin to think strategically and how he or she can implement strategic marketing choices.

About This Book

Who is marketing your cause? Is it you, your CEO, your board development committee, or key agency volunteers? Do they have a plan of attack or just a list of best practices? Assuming they have a plan (and many don't), the list of best practices they have may not be well suited to today's hyper-competitive nonprofit world. More is needed. Donors, customers, members of social ecosystems, and an overabundance of causes have seemingly conspired to demand that nonprofit organizations become readily adaptable and significantly radical to survive and flourish during these days of eroding tactical advantages and shrinking strategy life cycles.

The landscape has radically changed since I wrote *Successful Marketing Strategies for Nonprofit Organizations* for Wiley.

First of all, relationships are not what they used to be. We now use tools that enable us to keep in constant touch with individuals for a lifetime, whereas just a short time ago without working hard we would not only forget someone's name but lose their pertinent information. Now marketing directors speak of "digital friendships," which aren't really friendships at all but contacts, and organizations pretend that they can manage thousands of these new relationships and networks, even though in the past they often had a hard time with just a handful of names. The good news is that the Internet has allowed research capabilities to increase proportionately, and organizations can now tailor their marketing programs to the digital behavior of those they are following as well as of their friends.

It is obvious that the internet has changed everything, but what is not so obvious is that there are still few strategy and development protocols that reliably perform for organizations day in and out. What can be said is that the near-institutional transparency the Internet allows, along with massive organization commoditization, is driving mediocre agencies out of business and helping to reduce the barriers to entry for a host of new ones. These two factors have dictated that offering real value to stakeholders has never been more important and now requires new knowledge about those you wish to serve and a common agency commitment to serve them. The context the stakeholders find themselves in requires the agency that serves them to immerse itself in their lives, something that not every agency is willing to do, because it places the individual's needs above those of the institution.

Programmatic and marketing innovation also matters more because it changes how organizations perform, creating uniqueness in the midst of agency parity and allowing differentiation to occur. Today, organization differentiation may be the most important tactic a strategist has, especially in light of the donor pullback to some agencies and the erosion of many markets.

Chris Anderson (*The Long Tail: Why the Future of Business Is Selling Less of More*, New York: Hyperion, 2006, p. 2) in speaking of consumers says, "They are scattered to the winds as markets fragment into countless niches." Maximizing your organization's growth and effectiveness in light of this reality is the aim of *The Elusive Donor*. Almost all organizations face difficulties in accomplishing this and it is not easy in today's world. To achieve this type of capacity, nonprofit organizations must focus their plans, people, and programs on those areas that allow them to move ahead, offloading those parts of the agency that no longer contribute significantly. This means more than simply cutting programs and people. It means that everything an organization attempts must be justified on the basis of its significance to the institution's mission and additionally, has the metrics—financial and otherwise—to prove that this is exactly what is happening. Consequently, planning must change for many agencies in that it must become reality-based, focusing on effective strategies and programs and not simply a list of hoped-for outcomes. Likewise all programs must become synergized in how they work together to achieve a focused end result. Only in this way can effective collaborative communities be built that not only support an organization but also become empowered to serve an organization and in turn, become served. How to achieve this type of interaction and capacity is the subject of *The Elusive Donor*.

Acknowledgments

When former president John F. Kennedy suggested "Victory has a hundred fathers," I wonder if he knew how prophetic this statement was. This book grows out of discussions I have had with the many marketing directors, development directors, and chief executive officers I have worked with and am currently working with. They are heroes in my mind through their efforts towards improving society and the conditions within it for many of those they serve.

In these efforts they have served others through their work, and they have served me as well through their examples of strategic endeavors, skilled tactical assessments, and innovative marketing.

It is hard for me to overstate the crisis that I think nonprofit organizations find themselves in today. The reduction in available funds due to a depressed economy, the cutbacks in health and social services, the commoditization of many causes, and the sheer weight and numbers of those needing help have created a "perfect storm" for many agencies and those that direct and serve within them.

Successful Marketing Strategies for Nonprofit Organizations, Second Edition—Winning in the Age of the Elusive Donor is written for nonprofit executives struggling to keep pace as they confront environmental and marketplace changes on a daily basis and for marketing tacticians working to make their causes and brands viable.

I have had considerable support for this book from The McConkey/Johnston consulting group. I have also benefited from the thoughts of Bill Chickering, Cathi Woods, Pete Sommer, Bob and Phoebe Love, Ron Ward, and Kim Evans as well as from close friends Robin, David, Barbara, Roberta, Robbie, Ferguson, and Sandy.

I want to acknowledge the help of those within Wiley's Professional and Trade Group, particularly Susan McDermott and Judy Howarth, who have been with the project from the beginning and have been a constant help and a much-needed source of encouragement and direction in finishing it.

My wife Deborah McLeish is simply my best friend, and her personal encouragement lives within these pages. To all of you: "grace and peace."

PART I

INTRODUCTION

1

A New Way of Doing Business for the Nonprofit Organization

Whereas the nonprofit sector used to be regarded as a sort of back-water to the business world, as a poor cousin to the formidable public sector, it is now increasingly becoming a destination of first resort. Not only is talent flocking there—giving the other sectors a run for their money in terms of employees—but with its emerging blend of businesslike discipline and government-like compassion, the non-profit sector may yet arise to be the one the others look to.

Penn, Mark J. and Zalesne, E. Kinney, *Microtrends*
(New York: Twelve, 2007), p. 232

Could anyone have predicted some of the cataclysmic changes that have occurred in the nonprofit marketplace during the past 10 years? Nonprofit practitioners today face social, governmental, and economic changes of an unprecedented magnitude and variety. Such changes are based on the following facts:

- A global donor community has become a reality for many non-profit organizations as advertising platforms have multiplied.
- Increased media fragmentation has led donors to demand that nonprofit organizations change their methods of communication or suffer the consequences of their nonparticipation.

- Even though the world's superrich are growing numerically, fund raising has become a battlefield as nonprofit organizations compete for scarce resources.
- Data base fund raising changed the way nonprofit organizations have conducted business during the past 10 years; now the challenge is to use what agencies know about their stakeholders to customize their nonprofit experiences.
- The growth in the number of nonprofit organizations causes competition for the same audiences, and in many causal fields has led to commoditization among causes.

Not only have these changes forever altered the way nonprofit organizations must operate—requiring innovative responses that practices of the past simply cannot accommodate—but marketing and media considerations in particular have arrived at an evolutionary convergence. The ideas and actions associated with "marketing," central to many nonprofit institutional actions and counteractions in the past, are now being challenged by newer, vibrant, and groundbreaking alternatives. In this chapter, the developments that have brought marketing to this transition point are discussed, as are preliminary marketing concepts and definitions in order to lay a good foundation for a more in-depth discussion of marketing analysis, planning, and implementation.

The Need for a New Marketing Orientation

Traditionally, marketing has not been a popular subject in nonprofit circles; competition even less so. Marketing issues tend to lay our organizational souls bare and put them on trial. However, with flourishing competition in the nonprofit world, marketing and its attendant strategies *must* be taken into account to ensure the success—even the survival—of most nonprofit organizations. Today, nonprofit organizations are operating under more changes and pressures than ever before. Without closely monitored and implemented marketing strategies designed to take the organization through a particular course of action, and without the ability to change that course should the need arise, an organization risks being lost in the throes of internal and economic upheaval.

At one point in our history, it may have been possible for a nonprofit organization to achieve competitive success despite having diminished resources, increased constituent reticence, changing societal needs, and unflagging competition. Today, however, the combined difficulties associated with these "four horsemen" are leading many nonprofit agencies into financial distress. Traditional marketing responses have often contributed to these problems by being neither sufficiently precise nor innovative. How can these missteps be averted? This book explains in subsequent chapters how marketing principles can be used to develop a strong market and constituent orientation for any cause by providing a series of rational steps and arguments aimed at nonprofit practitioners who, traditionally, have not considered themselves as being part of the "marketing" team.

Dealing with Nonprofit Organizations in Flux

Consider the state of most nonprofit organizations in operation today. Many are experiencing both internal and external turbulence. Internally they are weighed down by a top-heavy hierarchy of executives; they offer little opportunity for subordinate employee advancement and are beset with numerous other human resource inequities. Externally, these same organizations are dealing with the need to reorganize, cut costs, improve collaborative communications, and involve their constituencies in more profitable ways. The need in most agencies is for their marketing units to drive change and create efficiency and stakeholder engagement within their causal ecosystem. Sadly, this is often not the case.

A Changing Domain: Constituents and Supporters Want More Control

In today's climate of clutter and fragmentation, nonprofit organizations must serve at minimum four distinct groups: *clients, constituents, volunteers, and donors.* Clients are the individuals whom the nonprofit organization serves directly and who are the immediate beneficiaries of its output. Constituents represent the consuming public that purchases some output from the organization— perhaps a book or another product. Volunteers and donors (also called *supporters* by some organizations) supply or lend the nonprofit organization various types of resources: time, money, knowledge, encouragement, or facilities.

Although each of these groups is distinct, it is not unusual to observe some overlapping of roles. A friend of a nonprofit organization may take on the role of donor, volunteer, or constituent during that person's tenure, receiving benefits from the organization at some time, providing a volunteer service at another time.

Although stakeholder insights are now more important than ever, most nonprofit organizations struggle to know how to use this information to leverage and activate their constituents. This problem in serving these groups is compounded because of their increasing lack of sustained loyalty to causes, as well as the perceived and increasing similarity of causal offerings. Given the vast number of worthy causes an individual can choose to support, volunteer for, or seek services from, nonprofit organizations can no longer assume that today's constituent, volunteer, or donor will be theirs forever. In addition, organizations can no longer assume that the primary concern of their constituency is simply to see the organization "continue as usual." Nonprofit "friends" not only want to know where their dollars are going but are also more concerned about realizing value benefits as a result of their participation. In some cases, this concern translates into asking for, or expecting, more control over or at least more say in agency operational matters.

Networking Systems Are Less Reliable

Traditional nonprofit networks are changing as well. Nonprofit organizations can no longer assume that certain individuals or corporations will supply volunteers, money, and publicity for their causes and activities just because they've done so in the past. Time, money, and the "good name" of an individual or business have become premium possessions in our society, and individuals and corporations are no longer willing to part with them easily. For example, church donations can no longer be counted on to fund many activities and causes outside of the church. Clerics of all faiths typically shy away from fundraising; as a result, many houses of worship are not in good financial condition. Organizations must look elsewhere for support. A new client has historically gained almost 50 percent of its funding from events; now individuals are less likely to attend, stores are less likely to sponsor, and loyal "friends" of the organization are harder to come by.

Hyper-Competition and the New Stakeholder Dialog Contribute to the Turbulence

External changes are also generating this growing uncertainty at an alarming rate. New restrictive policies imposed by the state and federal governments concerning tax deductions, postal subsidies, and what constitutes appropriate nonprofit activity continue to be a "nuisance" factor, affecting every organization, and are now routine. But two changes have affected the function of marketing and the very survival of nonprofit agencies far more than anything else in recent memory. First, the dialog with stakeholders has changed in ways unimaginable 10 years ago, upsetting the balance of power between agency and stakeholder. Second, hyper-competition among institutions in search of charitable dollars now threatens almost all agencies and has forced changes in the way they operate as they compete for dollars and time.

This environment and the turbulence within it have also had a negative impact on long-range planning. How does one plan effectively given these changes? Some organizations are confronting them with innovation and a renewed marketing spirit; others are floundering as work patterns, marketing platforms, and communication styles used for years no longer seem to fit. Unfortunately, marketing must constantly reinvent itself within many of the organizations in trouble. The goal of finding stakeholders and attracting them with a proposition that aligns with their values has not changed, nor has the need to retain them over time. Marketing tactics, however, often need to change, as does the role marketing plays within organizations.

The Need to Go Beyond Change Management

Nothing has prepared most nonprofit agencies for what they are facing today. With a future that looks remarkably different from what it appeared to be even three years ago, the changes being faced by executives require them to think in categories they have often dismissed and rationalized away in the past. For example, many institutions are going to see their causal business reduced, even though the needs and numbers of those they are serving may increase simultaneously. Taking action to keep their causes and relationships vibrant—in spite of circumstances—has now become "job one" for many organizations.

For some, vibrancy may mean quickly making their organizations as strong as possible, and this may necessitate off-loading parts of one's organization that no longer function at a high level. *Every* agency has this problem and needs to do something about it soon. You simply cannot become the strongest institution you desire to be and still carry underperforming units along with you. Of every part of your organization you must ask the following questions:

- Is it core to where we are going as a causal organization?
- Is there a growth demand for it?
- Are we as an institution committed to delivering value to those who will support us in this venture—particularly our most important stakeholders—as well as to those we will serve—particularly the most important segments of our service clientele?

In going through this exercise with a client, we soon realized that his causal competitors has changed in very real ways: some had disappeared and gone out of business, some were retrenching their work into certain sectors, and others were doing nothing. The client rethought both his marketing and causal service strategy in light of the circumstances at hand and what they might be in the future. In a nutshell this is what resulted from the rethinking:

- Some service areas were earmarked for more aggressive activity.
- A couple of programs were shelved to be rethought or completely disbanded.
- The marketing team was charged to reframe the organization's communication program with more aggressive analytics.

Finally, we tried to "blue sky" the organization's future. We looked at the organization's reactions when things got hard and tried to imagine what we would do if they got harder. Opportunistically, we looked at the agencies in serious trouble and wondered if there were parts of their causal business—as well as stakeholders—that we could pick up with some work. In all of this we asked how vulnerable we were in what we were planning to do, realizing that we had every reason to expect more turbulence in our path.

There are, as Peter Vaill says, "Lots of changes going on at once." Much of the way nonprofits work today, as compared with what they did 10 years ago, must be revitalized. This is no more apparent than in the way a nonprofit organization analyzes its circumstances and develops, evaluates, and implements its strategies of solicitation and service.

Every agency today has some degree of positive or negative momentum. It is going somewhere, and its mission is being decided implicitly, either through organizational drift, or by individuals and forces inside or outside the cause. A marketing strategy can play a significant role in transforming that momentum into an organization's productive direction. To accomplish this, one must relate an organization's marketing strategies to the surrounding competitive environment, melding the external world into the organization's internal operations, rather than waiting for new programs and new donors to solve all ills. Market and competitive realities can no longer be viewed as an embarrassing undertaking or an unfortunate consequence. Strategy must be set through taking into account the current reality and integrating it with purposeful research and planning to take a weak or strong organization to the next level.

Adapting to the New Reality

In light of what we see happening today, nonprofit organizations must change the way they operate, the way they view themselves, and the way they manage their resources. Rather than create programs internally and introduce them to unsuspecting publics (as has been done by many in the past), a nonprofit organization must now first orient itself to this new environment and its stakeholders and then market for the environment. The organization should first build its programmatic, volunteer, and solicitation strategies by assessing and evaluating constituencies and markets and then build its marketing strategies. This allows the organization to align its programs with values and interests of its natural constituencies, creating a mutual bond.[1] This kind of competitive marketing strategy is a broad formula for

1. How a nonprofit organization is going to undertake concentrating on its core business.
2. How it will rethink and deliver its services in a manner that gets the organization positively noticed and supported.
3. How it will identify its goals understanding the potential dangers in the marketplace.
4. How it will outline new protocols—along with as the recovery systems and policies—needed to carry them out.

Marketing to the External World

Critical to this discussion of marketing is the intended audience's point of view, which must be a part of the quality of service and attitude a nonprofit delivers. Successful nonprofit organizations should be able to bring resources together quickly after recognizing new audience needs or values. Constituent, volunteer, and donor wants, expectations, and perceptions, taken seriously, can create a competitive edge in the field in which the nonprofit organization operates.

Unfortunately—even in light of hyper-competition for resources—external points of view do not always seem important, rational, or necessary to many organization executives. Many years ago, W. Edwards Deming, the American management genius, sadly noted that American industry had become too stubborn to make the changes necessary to boost production, improve quality control, and test new management practices.[2] Today there is little choice for many agencies; they must change and adapt to the current reality. To not do so is to risk not moving an agency ahead by not focusing all of its assets and energies on the task at hand.

The financial and managerial pressures facing nonprofit organization directors in the next years will magnify these problems many times in intensity, more than any previous generation ever experienced. The nonprofit world must prepare itself for those pressures and for the competitive environment that will result. The badly needed first steps in this preparation are to

1. Define marketing and marketing strategy.
2. Define how a strategy operates in today's causal markets.
3. Ask why a nonprofit organization needs a marketing strategy.

Marketing Defined

Marketing has "grown up" in the nonprofit world. In most quarters there is little need to hide the title "marketing" behind older catch phrases such as development director or membership director. The nonprofit world, in fact, is in desperate need of good marketing directors. And though the definitions of marketing have not changed noticeably, the tactics used for developing strategies and carrying them out have changed enormously.

Philip Kotler, author of *Strategic Marketing for Nonprofit Organizations* as well as many other books on marketing, is an internationally renowned expert on marketing and is the S.C. Johnson & Son Distinguished Professor of International Marketing at Northwestern University. In the fourth edition of Kotler's text, nonprofit marketing is defined as, "the function of a nonprofit whose goal is to plan, price, promote, and distribute the organization's programs and products by keeping in constant touch with the organization's various constituencies, uncovering their needs and expectations for the organization and themselves, and building a program of communication to not only express the organization's purpose and goals but also their mutually beneficial want-satisfying products."[3]

This definition's underlying assumption is that if an organization does an adequate job of researching and understanding the needs and wants of its constituents, and designs programs and products to meet these needs, the selling job is greatly reduced. The ease of selling is directly proportional to the internal make-up of the constituent—his or her needs, wants, and values. To arrive at such a point in today's dynamic and convoluted markets, however, requires innovation, smart strategy creation and implementation, and a willingness to change organizationally.

Breaking the Status Quo

Unfortunately, the notion of nonprofit marketing for some has come to mean aggressive promotion or new web site design, as opposed to aggressive listening to constituent needs, leading in turn to strategic analysis. In the face of competition, many agencies have concentrated primarily on communicating the nonprofit's needs to the public, rather than listening to its constituents. While promotional programs are a part of marketing strategy, the strategy must first move away from the point of sale and ask these questions: *Who are our constituents, what are their needs and wants, and how do we predict what the right marketing moves will be?*

Defining the Constituents' Needs

Today's nonprofit stakeholders are more aware of what good performance means, more aware of what they want from an organization, and more concerned about realizing their own values through their support. It is here that marketing must function as the organization's "ear" in an ever-changing environment. As such, the organization moves from a "we need" philosophy to a "they need and we can provide" philosophy, based on both groups' participation in arriving at an agreed-on goal. At its most elementary level, nonprofit marketing takes place when an organization and an interested party come together for a mutually beneficial exchange or a service, resource, or idea. This is known as *exchange theory*; it is discussed further along in this chapter.

Exhibit 1.1 contains a list of questions that can help to define "marketing" as it relates to all aspects of a nonprofit organization.

Research, in the form of listening to constituents, donors, customers, and clients, allows the organization to uncover what is perceived to be special about its constituents, in both the way they think and the benefits they want from the nonprofit organization. In

Exhibit 1.1   Defining Marketing Tasks

The nonprofit organization's initial marketing plan should answer the following questions concerning markets:

1. What are the targeted markets?
2. What are the key segments within these markets?
3. What are the identified values and needs of each market segment?
4. What "business" do constituents think the nonprofit is in?
5. How much interest or awareness do the organization's activities generate?
6. How satisfied are the current constituents with the organization's output?

Concerning resources:

1. What are the major strengths or weaknesses that could either limit growth platforms or enable expansion?
2. What opportunities are being presented that will enable an expanded resource base?

Concerning business orientation:

1. What is the organization's mission?
2. Who are the key constituents?
3. Who are the major competitors?
4. What benefits does the organization have that will allow it to take a position different from its competitors?
5. Are there market segments "open" from competition that would allow the organization to excel?

Exhibit 1.2   Benefits of Research

Research allows an organization to

1. Assess new or emerging marketing opportunities.
2. Furnish information for developing marketing plans, both short and long term.
3. Provide information needed to solve problems that arise within an organization's constituencies.
4. Know which marketing decisions have been correct and which are in need of change.
5. Develop new promotional appeals and assess their success vis-à-vis competitors in the light of marketplace activities.

addition, listening to constituents produces more than just information on promotional tactics. Organizations discover whether their "product mix" (comprising an organization's causes, style of activity, or ministry) and "hard" product offerings (e.g., literature) should be maintained, increased, or phased out.

The *product mix* of an organization is the sum total of all of the organization's service outputs on behalf of particular constituencies. Research allows an organization to discover trends affecting its constituents (and ultimately the nonprofit organization), the values of different market segments, whether constituents are satisfied with the organization's goals, and the benefits they are seeking. Exhibit 1.2 lists the benefits of research.

Develop an Outline of Marketing Strategies

Most nonprofit managers will agree that marketing must become as intrinsic to the nonprofit sector as it is to the for-profit sector. However, many institutions find themselves in a marketing "pre-culture," where they have adapted the terminology of for-profit marketers without incorporating any of the commensurate systems of evaluation and procedures. This pre-culture often negatively impacts the following five arenas of thought and action in the nonprofit world:

1. The *business* or *mission* the nonprofit organization is in and the corporate values and philosophy that are transmitted through its same mission.
2. *Exchange theory*—the notion that each party in the transaction should sense they are receiving more than they are giving up; the notion of *self-interest* as it relates to the exchange.

3. The actual *marketing task* itself, which stresses the importance of meeting consumer needs.
4. The *tools* the nonprofit marketer uses (sometimes called the *marketing* or *product mix*) such as social media, advertising, fund raising, pricing, and channels of communication and distribution.
5. The nonprofit organization's *distinctive competencies*, in which the organization concentrates on doing what it does best in order to minimize any weaknesses it might have.[4]

The marketing task is fundamentally a transaction in which the self-interest of both parties is critical. The promotional tools and marketing mix available to the nonprofit practitioner has only one purpose: to satisfy efficiently and effectively the practitioner's *half* of the transaction. By further identifying the areas in which a nonprofit excels, it can strive to better serve individuals seeking competence in those same areas. The five items in the preceding list are explained in the sections that follow.

The Organizational Mission

The marketing process begins with a definition of the mission or "business" the nonprofit organization is in. The mission is important for various reasons, not the least of which is that it is the foundation on which all other marketing planning is built. An organization's mission is its purpose and reason for being, and it may also serve to determine accurately the types of services it can provide.

The task of determining the mission is especially important, because many nonprofit organizations shift their focus as the environment changes. A clear and simple mission statement composed several years ago may or may not still apply. In any case, the mission needs to be defined and redefined, or at least reconsidered.

Although "mission" can be hard to define, it must be addressed to properly develop all of a nonprofit's marketing goals and its plan(s) to meet those goals. Ultimately, mission has ramifications in three important areas:

1. *Definition of the constituent groups (sometimes called "stakeholder groups") that will be served as well as a determination of those who won't be served is essential.* If there is agreement on the

organization's mission through an analysis of constituent perceptions and feelings, the effect can be a powerful catalyst
for the organization to achieve its goals. If agreement has
not been reached—or if it has not been sought after by
leadership—then issues regarding allocation of resources,
the scope of those served, and the conservation of resources
(achieved by not making errant "scope of work" decisions)
can all come back to haunt an organization.

2. *Identification of the needs of new and existing constituents that will
be satisfied by the nonprofit organization is also required.* Typically
called the "stakeholder value proposition," what a nonprofit
agency offers in the way of service elements and relational
care helps to differentiate how it operates from others. The
organization must know what criteria stakeholders are using
to judge the success of its performance and how its value proposition successfully—or unsuccessfully—answers these needs.

3. *Absent a well-thought-out value proposition, an organization's strategy seldom achieves resiliency.* Taking into account the real and
defined assets and competencies an organization offers, its
strategy becomes a set of imperatives that are supported by
marketing programs augmented by tactical considerations.
In short, what is the strategy by which the needs of the constituency will be satisfied? The strategies and philosophies used
by the institution must be in keeping with its core set of values; otherwise there is little chance of achieving stakeholder
satisfaction.

In essence, a nonprofit's mission, when well defined, can be translated into a plan that will enable the organization to meet its goals.

The Self-Interest Aspect: Exchange Theory

A nonprofit organization is often consumed with its need for more
outside involvement in order to harvest the additional resources it
constantly requires. Marketing must answer the problem of how to
get the desired response from those groups the organization has targeted for involvement.

Imagine a simple two-sided scale. One side of the balance is
weighed down by the needs of the organization. The other side is
weighed down by the benefits that a person receives by being

involved with that organization. Which side is heavier? Which side is heavier in your organization? The two sides should basically be in balance, if not skewed towards the stakeholder.

The key to success for an organization is to bring about a certain level of satisfaction among its various constituents. This can be accomplished surreptitiously through what is commonly called an "exchange." Under the *exchange theory* an individual gives up something (e.g., time, money) in exchange for something else. The individual should perceive the return to be of greater value than what he or she has given up. *The receiving is thus the motivation for the giving.* The following explanation is offered as an example.

A sense of prestige often plays a major role in convincing people to serve on boards. Similarly, donors are often motivated not only by the feeling that they are a part of an exclusive group but by being made to feel generous, important, and central to an organization's success or failure. For a volunteer, the self-image of being essential, being needed, and belonging is often what explains why they work for no compensation.[5] Successful exchanges involve several factors:

- Activities
- Markets
- Prospects
- Costs
- Benefits
- Associated costs
- Nonfinancial benefits

Exchanges are *activities* that are engaged in by at least two parties. Each party has a goal. The organization initiating the exchange is the *marketer*, and the individual is the *prospect*.

In a pure subsistence economy, each family produces all the goods that it consumes over a period of time. There is no need to look further for other goods or services, because each family unit is self-sufficient. Marketing does not occur in this instance, because marketing involves two or more parties wanting to exchange something for something else. A *market*, then, consists of a group of buyers and sellers bargaining in terms of exchange of goods and services.

A *prospect* is someone who is likely to want to be involved with an exchange of some kind. For example, a volunteer prospect might be someone who is willing to give his or her time in exchange for the satisfaction of knowingly helping out a worthy cause.

There are *costs* as well as *benefits* for each party. The individual's costs may be money or time. These are relatively easy to calculate. There may also be costs that are more difficult to assess. In the case of a nonprofit client it may be asked, "What are the psychic costs of admitting one's inadequacy, the presumed reason for seeking help?"[6] A donor may also worry about supporting an organization with a defined or potentially controversial point of view. The organization also has *associated costs* in mounting its marketing efforts, in managing the client process, in dealing with governmental regulations, and in dealing with the positive or negative aspects of personalities in the process.

Exchanges are not always financial in nature; they can also be social or economic. Social rewards may be internal and not easily delineated or calculated. For example, by being a part of a particular nonprofit and its programs, I may reaffirm particular belief systems I maintain as to how people should be treated or how a cause should be advanced. Economic rewards, on the other hand, are usually clearly spelled out and may have some extrinsic value leading to benefits outside the exchange relationship. For example, a donor participating at a certain financial level may receive name recognition, networking possibilities, or invitations to prominent events, all of which have an indirect economic impact.

The exchange process is not always simple; it can be complex. Armand Lauffer is a professor of social work at the University of Michigan and author of *Strategic Marketing for Not-for-Profit Organizations.* Lauffer cites the following example:

> *When you make a contribution to the United Way, you do not expect thanks from the agencies that are the recipients of the funds raised or from their clients who are the ultimate beneficiaries. You may, however, experience a sense of well being at having met a social obligation.*[7]

Therefore, a less clearly defined "exchange" can still prove beneficial to all concerned.

Exchanges assume that each participant is involved voluntarily. Each participant is free to accept or reject any part of the offer. Successful nonprofit organizations view exchanges as either singular

Exhibit 1.3   A Simple Listing of Exchanges Sought between a Nonprofit Organization and Its Constituents

Exchange Partners	Type of Exchange Sought
A. Donor	Recognition, involvement, gratitude
Nonprofit organization	Resources, growth potential, service
B. Volunteer	Service, community, worthiness
Nonprofit organization	Cheap labor, lowering of costs
C. Board member	Significant contribution, access to leadership
Nonprofit organization	Wisdom, leadership, access to knowledge
D. Client	Personal benefits, services, friendship
Nonprofit organization	Fulfillment of mission, success, contribution

events or a series of events over time. For example, in relationships with donors, nonprofit organizations ultimately assign someone to manage the exchanges in order to maintain the right types of associations with donors over extended time periods.

Exhibit 1.3 lists exchanges between a nonprofit organization and various constituents that might be involved with the organization, as well as each party's reason for involvement.

The Marketing Task

For-Profit versus Nonprofit

The marketing function in the for-profit sector assumes that good marketing management creates truly satisfied consumers and, ultimately, company profitability. The world assumes a profit motive, a primary constituency (donors, clients, etc.) for the company to work with, and the ability to allocate resources based on the viability of a product or service and its acceptance within a constituency. There are intrinsic characteristics that are unique to nonprofit marketing, however.

First, nonprofit organizations do not seek to make a "profit" but often find it necessary to generate surpluses of revenue over expenses to fund unpopular or non-fundable parts of the organization.

Second, some causes do not lend themselves easily to performance evaluation. For example, a university may want to provide education for all classes of people. Although these organizations may create a psychological or social "profit," actual performance measurement is difficult.

Third, it is difficult in a nonprofit organization to determine how a nonprofit manager allocates resources without an accurate assessment of previous performance levels. Many nonprofits do not charge for services rendered. How does a nonprofit director gauge the correctness of decisions to enhance some programs and curtail others?

Finally, if the essence of the marketing task is meeting the needs of the constituent, how does a nonprofit organization do so if its mission is inconsistent with the desires of at least some of its constituents, as in the case of an anti-tobacco organization? Finally, if the essence of the marketing task is meeting the needs of the constituent, how does a nonprofit organization do so if its mission is inconsistent with the desires of at least some of its constituents, as in the case of a spiritual order with one constituent group wanting to build a grade and junior high school and another constituent group wanting to give the constituent donated money away to feed the poor?

The differences between for-profit and nonprofit organizations as they relate to the marketing task are most pronounced in the following three areas:

1. The profit motive
2. The nature of a nonprofit organization's constituency
3. The methods of resource attraction

The Profit Motive

A nonprofit organization, by definition, does not operate to produce a profit. In other words, nonprofit organizations do not have a *profit motive*. However, the profit motive gives for-profit managers a control tool that is far superior to most nonprofit control tools. The nature of the profit motive allows managers to better measure their efficiency and effectiveness in reaching their objectives. For example, relatively simple mathematical calculations will reveal what percentage of income is actually profit. The nonprofit manager must deal in the area of "services rendered," which, in most nonprofit organizations, is a nebulous concept not easily measured or evaluated. Nonprofit managers try to measure intangibles such as services provided and numbers of large donors, not the "bottom line." In essence, a nonprofit manager must establish a financial model that delineates money spent and services rendered.

The Nature of the Nonprofit Organization's Constituency

To further complicate matters, a nonprofit organization usually deals with two principal constituencies:

1. Clients for whom the nonprofit exists and to whom goods and services are provided
2. Donors, customers, and volunteers who provide the majority of resources that allow the nonprofit organization's service to take place

This dual constituency makes the marketing task even more complex.

The profit-motivated company has one marketing function—to facilitate a direct two-way exchange, which includes both resource allocation (providing goods and services) and resource attraction (obtaining revenue). By contrast, the nonprofit organization must approach these two tasks separately, because they involve separate constituencies.[8] (See Exhibit 1.3.)

A fairly common example of this difficulty is the real-life scenario many nonprofit organizations face today. The services the organization is providing, whether the client likes them or not, may not meet the expectations of the organization itself. Similarly, nonprofit organizations may also face a situation in which the resources provided by the donor or volunteer do not meet with the expectations or satisfaction of the recipient.

Nonprofit organizations may provide services to clients because of donor or volunteer pressure that the services be offered and not necessarily because management feels this is the best for either the nonprofit or the clients served. For example, one can easily give money to feed the hungry in parts of Africa without knowing *how well these services are being delivered by the nonprofits to the people who are in need of them.*

Resource Attraction

Resource attraction is the attraction of funding and other resources to nonprofit organizations. An organization's resources are typically obtained by the communication of its needs through one or a combination of the following four paths:

1. A "keep quiet about our needs" approach
2. An advertising and public relations approach

3. A mass media solicitation approach where the need is made known along with a "hard ask"
4. A strong personal selling approach

Each path, or a combination of the paths, requires a different marketing strategy, and each leads to a different outcome. This text does not attempt to cover all the possible marketing and sales approaches; there have been volumes written about what works and what does not, and "what works" for one industry may not work for another. (See the End Notes for a listing of books that may prove helpful to the reader in this endeavor.[9])

There are typically six issues that a marketer must deal with as he or she plans their resource allocation strategy:

First, there is the remarkably important issue of determining whether the cause being promoted is viable financially. This means addressing the following questions: (1) Are the operating costs excessive for the organization to bear? (2) Does the organization expect to run this program over a long period of time, necessitating the ability to lock out competitors and to be able to demonstrate some sort of competitive advantage to ensure program viability? (3) Does the program fit with what the agency is already doing, and does it provide synergy to the other programs already running?

Second, marketers must learn everything they can about the stakeholders that will be involved in the cause. This involves online research, demographic research, research on attitudes, interests, and lifestyles (also known as psychographic research), and face-to-face involvement.

Third, can the program be sold? Chief executive officers, along with program officers in particular, generally assume anything can be sold. This is simply not the reality in the marketplace. Some programs are both important to the cause and still hard to discuss and sell because of their level of complexity. Others may not have widespread "appeal" and fail to ignite the interest of the constituents.

Fourth, many nonprofit organizations are under pressure to be *democratic* in their fundraising, trusting that every stakeholder is vitally interested in all that the organization does. In countless donor and customer interviews, the participants invariably identify their favorite parts of the organization as well as the parts that they are not vitally interested in.

Fifth, most nonprofit agencies do not talk about "dollar handles" or the pricing that is going to be involved in the marketing effort. While it's not an exact science, there is still a lot to learn about smart dollar amounts to ask for. Nonprofit organizations have less variability in pricing than do for-profit organizations. The problem is amplified by nonprofit organizations that rely solely on donations and give their services for free. The agency must realistically assess how much money can be raised and how much can be charged for services.

Sixth, nonprofit organizations need to develop a resource allocation strategy. The way funds are distributed in an organization ultimately defines that organization. Some agencies undertake causes that are tangential to their mission; others undertake causes that constituents perceive as being "outside" the organization's scope of expertise. A clear definition of "mission" enhances an institution's ability to raise funds and solicit volunteers.

Marketing Tools

The marketing tools (or *marketing mix*) with which a nonprofit attracts resources, accomplishes constituent persuasion, and executes appropriate program allocation encompasses

1. The nonprofit organization's communication program
2. Its pricing policy
3. Its causes or products
4. Its distribution channels

In 1992, authors Houston Elam and Norton Paley, in their book *Marketing for Nonmarketers,* suggested that marketing can be viewed as a *systemic philosophy and approach to doing business.* It is equally important to recognize that marketing requires interacting business activities, reinforcing the premise that each area of management has a stake in the successful operation of the company and depends on every other area if it is to do its part properly. In essence, marketing tools are connected with all other aspects of doing business.[10]

The nonprofit organization's marketing mix can be expressed in two organizational formats. First, marketing can take the form of a *marketing campaign.* A campaign is usually an extended effort by an organization to reach specific financial, membership, or other resource goals within a particular time period. A marketing campaign is often evidenced by a concerted effort on the part of the organization and its supporters.

This specific effort on behalf of a unique organizational goal is in contrast to the second type of marketing, which has to do with an agency's day-to-day marketing operations and its ongoing relationship with its donors, customers, volunteers, and clients in their joint undertakings and interactions. Marketing, in this sense, is the attempt by the organization to accomplish short-term, day-to-day goals. The lines differentiating "marketing campaigns" and "marketing" can appear to be indistinct because the activities involved in both are similar. They include the following:

- Both marketing operations take into account and target appropriate audiences to accomplish goals. Similarly, target audience members (donors, volunteers, and members) are empowered to achieve their individual goals through personal involvement.
- Messages of encouragement, solicitation, and benefit are sent by those inside the organization to those outside, and messages of acceptance, displeasure, and encouragement are sent from outside the organization to the inside. These messages allow action by both parties.
- Individuals targeted by the nonprofit organization as key to the success of its efforts are given a way to respond appropriately to the offers or causes being presented by the nonprofit.
- Both the nonprofit and the individual receive adequate benefits in order to be or at least feel successful.
- Day-to-day marketing operations and more intensive marketing campaigns have clear, concise goals and objectives; the individual's partnership with the nonprofit is clearly stated.
- In every marketing effort, there is a group that fails to respond to whatever is being presented.

Appealing to the Constituency

"Marketing campaigns" and "marketing" can appear to be similar, but each must be considered separately for purposes of planning and execution, for the following reasons:

- Most people want to see evidence of some degree of current interest in the subject matter to respond affirmatively to what is being said or asked for by an organization.
- The information presented by an organization must usually be compatible with an individual's prior attitudes for that individual to be receptive.
- People respond in different ways to the same material, and their response depends on their belief and attitudes.

The Importance of a Communication Program

A nonprofit organization's marketing campaign and daily marketing operations depend on its communication program. (See Exhibit 1.4.) Most communication efforts by nonprofit organizations rely heavily on advertising media (direct mail, social media, space advertising, electronic advertising, etc.) often augmented by personal selling to accomplish specific marketing mix goals. These goals typically range from fund raising to client recruitment to volunteer enrollment.

Exhibit 1.4   Elements of a Typical Online and Off-Line Communication Program

1. Annual report designed for donors, volunteers, customers, and friends
2. A fact and/or photo book to provide a mid-year update on the organization's operation
3. Some type of routinized newsletter to discuss subjects of importance to the constituency
4. Press releases to communicate fast-breaking news of significance
5. Specialty brochures to promote different aspects of a nonprofit organization's program and to identify opportunities for involvement
6. Public meetings or gatherings to give managers and supportive constituents a chance to interact
7. Mass marketing efforts (e.g., direct mail, advertising, space ads, telemarketing and radio and television specials)
8. Highly targeted events for purposes of conveying special information to preselected audiences

Pricing

One of the principal goals of a communication program is to relay information about the nonprofit organization's *pricing* policies. "Pricing" is defined as the amount of resources demanded by a seller.

In a for-profit company, price is the direct link between resource allocation and resource attraction. A company's product price allows it to attract more resources than expended for the product's production. Some nonprofit organizations seek to emulate this system by charging for services. In undertaking such a move, a nonprofit organization relies on a single constituency—its clients—to ensure financial viability through the price it charges for its services.

Other nonprofit organizations use more than one constituency—donors and clients—in their day-to-day operations. Two constituencies usually imply two pricing considerations. Donors provide different dollar amounts—some are asked for higher amounts and others for lesser amounts. (Technically, donors in this situation are paying different fees.) Clients are also not always charged the same "price." Some nonprofit organizations have different categories of clients, charging different "prices" for services rendered.

For example, a halfway house for drug addiction might offer walk-in treatment at one price, a methadone program at another, and ongoing care at another. Other nonprofit organizations do not charge a fee *per se* for their services; nevertheless, a psychological "fee" is exacted through a "commitment" to the organization and its goals. This outward working of an organization's goals is expressed to the general public through its programs or "products."

Viewing the service as a "product" within the nonprofit context is a relatively new concept. And yet the programs—or products—offered by a nonprofit organization are its most important elements. Programs are what clients and donors accept and help fund. Program goals shape a nonprofit organization's mission.

For most organizations with two primary constituents (donor and client) "two-product" policies should also be in place. In the previously mentioned halfway house example, donors most likely feel the "product" they are buying is both helping men and women overcome a serious problem and contributing positively to a local or societal problem. The client, on the other hand, is usually buying immediate help for an urgent situation. What is the product provided to a donor? Broadly defined, a donor looks at the cluster of benefits surrounding his or her involvement—intangible items such as being a part of something being sought out or a feeling of satisfaction and pride—as the "product." The client, on the other hand, looks at the actual services provided and the clients' level of satisfaction with those services as the "product."

Program and Product Distribution

Finally, how does a nonprofit organization deliver or distribute its programs or products to the right audiences? Usually, the following key questions apply to a nonprofit organization's distribution system:

- Where is the best place for a nonprofit organization to sell its services?
- Where and how will the nonprofit organization collect its donations?
- Will the nonprofit organization place its programs in the same areas from which it is raising funds, or in different areas?
- How will the nonprofit organization access information from its distribution channels in order to improve it services?

Use Distinctive Competencies to Assess the Competition

In another effort to define nonprofit marketing practices in terms that would relate to the for-profit world, the term *distinctive competency* arises. Basically, a distinctive competency is an area of operation in which a nonprofit organization does better than its competitors. The fundamental reason to look at a nonprofit organization's distinctive competencies is to assess the presence of "competitors" offering the same or similar services to the same constituency.

In the for-profit world, competition theoretically forces an organization to better serve its consumers. How, then, does a nonprofit organization distinguish itself from competitors in order to be rewarded by strong consumer confidence and financial viability? This is done by evaluating the organization's role in terms of how it serves its clients and donors and by comparing the programs and services it offers with the offerings of other nonprofit organizations. In this way, an organization can begin to pinpoint the tasks it performs best.

To unlock a nonprofit organization's areas of competence and then "sell" those competencies, an organization undertakes an internal and external analysis of its organization, its delivery systems, the way it charges and raises funds, and the way it promotes itself to publics at large. The goal of this external and internal examination is to "audit" every system in light of the organization's mission and the service it provides to its constituents. With this information, the nonprofit organization can set its goals and develop marketing strategies to meet them.

Summary

Chapter 1 has presented an overview of how the concept of marketing functions in the nonprofit world. Chapter 2 details for the reader why a marketing strategy is important to both the nonprofit organization and the philanthropic community, providing each with a sense of purpose and movement towards the achievement of organizational and personal goals.

2

The Development of a Marketing Strategy

The great myth of marketing is that "serving the customer" is the name of the game. Many marketing people live in a dream world. They believe in the fantasy of a virgin market. This is the belief that marketing is a two-player game involving just the company and the customer. In this fantasy, a company develops a product or service designed to appeal to consumer needs and wants and then uses marketing to harvest the crop. There are no virgin markets. The reality of marketing is that a market consists of consumers strongly or weakly held by a range of competitors. A marketing campaign consists, therefore, of holding onto your customers while at the same time attempting to take customers away from your competition.

Al Ries and Jack Trout, *Bottom-Up Marketing*
(New York: Plume Books, 1990) p. 82

How do you decide what your marketing plan should be? What factors do you take into account, and how does the interplay between them help you determine the path to take? Here are some real-life examples that show how marketing decisions can be arrived at.

- A camp on the East Coast whose primary customers are young people decided to get into the winter camping business nine years ago. Positioned as an "also-ran" in a largely commodity-defined business, the camp grew slowly during its first two years while watching how the other camps did their winter programming. In the third year, the camp's directors brought in a winter camping specialist, redid their entire winter camp programming, changed the venues where much of the camping experience took place, and worked hard with local youth leaders to determine what qualified as an excellent winter camp experience. In the fourth year, they changed the type of music they used in their programming, reconfigured the daily schedule, and changed and upgraded the campers' dining experience. In the fifth year, they again changed their program and worked even more closely with other youth leaders and outlets that networked with young people to build their weekend numbers and to determine the program experience that young campers wanted. Though the camp's numbers grew, three new competitors appeared, running similar programs and themes and using similar tactics. This had the effect of diffusing the marketplace and creating a commodity market once again. In the sixth year, the camp's directors redid their programming once again, and their camp became the dominant player in the market. The camp has continued to hold this position for the past four years.[1] *What should the directors' next marketing steps be?*

- A nationally known executive training organization has been losing market share for the past five years. While never leading the market or having an affiliation with a large school or university, the organization has nevertheless developed competencies in a number of areas of leadership training, but it lacks the strength of being the number-one player in the training field. Recently, the implosion of the U. S. economy hurt the organization badly, with most—if not all—of its customers and prospective customers either cutting their training budgets in part or entirely. The training organization is down 19 percent in revenue.[2] *What should this agency's next marketing steps be?*

- A very large, well-branded nonprofit institution has just lost a fund-raising field representative responsible for generating many of the institution's very large gifts. This gentleman not only left to go to another agency but took a number of key team members with him.[3] *What should this agency's next marketing steps be?*

To develop a good marketing strategy, a strategist needs to look at taking a number of steps and answering several questions to get to the heart of what an excellent strategy looks like. This chapter enables the reader to do precisely this.

Why a Marketing Strategy?

A nonprofit organization needs a marketing strategy to provide itself, its volunteers and philanthropic supporters, and those directly benefiting from its work with a substantial sense of purpose and movement towards the achievement of personal and organizational goals. A marketing strategy is a way for all parties to see effective goal and resource attainment; it is also a way for limited resources to be used wisely in pursuit of the goals. In fact, a nonprofit organization must be an effective strategist if it is to fulfill its short-term as well as its long-term goals and mission.

Strategy in this sense can be viewed as *the managerial operation of developing and maintaining a sense of fit between the nonprofit organization and the marketing opportunities that present themselves to the organization.*

A Disciplined Effort

As illustrated in Exhibit 2.1, a marketing strategy is a disciplined effort, enacted through a management system, with the goal of developing and producing actions that help the organization to understand what is needed and to determine the marketing strategy needed to attain those goals. The ensuing strategy includes examining the nonprofit organization's output (programs, products, and the "markets" available to the organization) to determine where the organization should compete, as well as its input (from supporters of the agency and from those it serves) to help initiate sustainable competitive advantages in each market. A course of rational action,

Exhibit 2.1   The Marketing Strategy Process

- A management system develops and produces actions to enable it to understand what is needed.
- The nonprofit organization's marketing staff plan and develop a series of strategic options.
- One strategy is chosen.
- The chosen strategy either attains the goals or is scrapped in favor of another.

extracted from many alternatives, is then selected, which helps to ensure a sense of identity and direction for the organization.

Answers to "Who We Are"

A marketing strategy helps reinforce internally and externally the answers to such fundamental organizational questions as

- What is the purpose of our organization?
- Who are the people we support and serve?
- What are the methods of service we value?
- What are our goals in shaping our ecosystem?
- How are we funded and resourced?
- What business are we in?
- What are our goals in shaping the surrounding conditions?
- How will we shape the influences upon our organization?

An Environment of Cooperation

Such a strategy also builds cooperatively with the organization's funding and volunteer base, the constituency it serves and the community it resides within, and those who lead and influence the organization. The process and presence of a marketing strategy builds a common framework of assumptions and information and helps differentiate those who support the organization from those who support other competing organizations.

This sense of purpose, embodied in strategy, is especially important as this nation redefines its national and community strategies. As the three authors of *The Nonprofit Organization* put it,

> *This is a time of unparalleled opportunity and danger . . . . Without a clear sense of identity and a strategic plan, nonprofit organizations flounder in a sea of competing sorrows, always at the whim of whatever well-articulated hard luck story motivates action.*[4]

Not only has the nonprofit environment drastically changed during the past few years, it has also become increasingly interdependent with the for-profit environment. Changes in both environments have had unpredictable consequences. Those changes have included demographic changes, value shifts, shifts in federal and state funding priorities, and economic (domestic vs. international) and political factors, along with the increased cultural importance of the nonprofit sector. In addition, the boundaries that traditionally have separated public and nonprofit organizations from private enterprise have also eroded. This has ultimately led to a diversification of power.

"Sovereignty for example, is increasingly "farmed out." Weapons systems are produced not in government arsenals but by private industry. Taxes are not collected by government tax collectors but are withheld by private and nonprofit organizations from their employees and turned over to the government. The nation's health, education, and welfare are a public responsibility, yet increasingly we rely on private and nonprofit organizations for the production of services in these areas."[5]

According to John Bryson, who wrote in his book *Strategic Planning for Public and Nonprofit Organizations,*

> *This increased turbulence and interconnectedness requires a threefold response from public and nonprofit organizations (and communities). First, these organizations must think strategically as never before. Second, they must translate their insights into effective strategies to cope with changed circumstances. And third, they must develop the rationales necessary to lay groundwork for the adoption and implementation of their strategies.*[6]

First Steps in Defining Strategy

In the dozens of marketing seminars I attend, I hear words from practitioners, agency directors, and pundits like "vision," "intuition," "online communities," and "new stakeholder models." These are worthwhile concerns, but they hardly represent a summary of how an institution is to pursue its objectives. Virtually no one that I have heard speak in recent memory has first started his or her discussion by focusing on the reality of an agency's mission coupled with a realistic assessment of its ability to achieve its stated goals. This assessment is important because many stakeholders are tired of funding (to use Tom Peter's language) "world peace proposals" that have little chance of being successful or ever being completed.

How would your organization define its marketing strategy? Your strategy should be the summary of how your organization pursues its objectives. As suggested, such a strategy should start with the combination of your organizational mission and an assessment of the organization's ability to reach these goals. This assessment comes from a careful analysis of what the nonprofit organization provides and what the constituents think they are getting in return, as well as a strong sense of organizational conviction.

Quite frankly, this is hard to do and requires intense organizational honesty. Confronted by established ways of looking for solutions to problems they face, marketing directors often take on a mindset that inhibits an honest appraisal of their situation. As a result, some see no reason to do anything differently today than what they did yesterday; others want to take action but are unsure of next steps. Still others drift strategically. As Kathryn Rudie Harrigan wrote eloquently in her book *Strategic Flexibility*, "The do-nothing solution that seemed so right in the past is a difficult life preserver to sacrifice when one is afloat in the vast, cold ocean."[7]

What is needed is a marketing strategy that takes a careful look at its ecosystem and develops a response to it. Many find it helpful to build such a strategy by first defining six elements:

1. What is our mission (why are we in business)?
2. What is the value we bring to the stakeholder?
3. Who is our competition, and what is the competition's market stance?
4. What advantages do we currently enjoy?
5. What is our marketing and fund-raising budget, and is it large enough to get the job done?
6. How strong is our managerial commitment?

1. What Is Our Mission?

A nonprofit organization may have (or may be able to develop) competitive advantages, but these do not matter unless the advantages can be directed towards specific organizational objectives. A nonprofit organization must compete for a purpose, and that purpose should be its mission. Without objectives, competitive advantages are meaningless. In addition, without these same organizational objectives, constituencies and associates don't know where the nonprofit organization is going.

Consider the criteria outlined in Exhibit 2.2: All programs should be measured against these criteria, and those that do not

Exhibit 2.2   Mission Statement Criteria

Developing a mission statement requires a nonprofit organization to answer three questions:

1. What is the purpose for our nonprofit organization's existence?
2. Will the purpose change in the future if externally significant events change, such as political, economic, social, or competitive events?
3. Given the nonprofit organization's response to question 2, should it consider changing its purpose?

expressly seek to accomplish the mission should be discontinued. This is an important consideration. The services and markets an organization operates in define the scope of its competitive environment, and they, in turn, should impose limits on what the organization does and with whom. These same services and operations then allow an agency to expand not only its causal work but the number of constituencies with which it can realize involvement. Mission definition therefore, has competitive consequences, allowing a nonprofit organization to have (1) a very narrow marketing approach with just a few programs appealing to a limited audience or (2) a broader-based approach.

2. What Is the Value We Bring to the Stakeholder?

Stakeholder loyalty is no longer encouraged in the marketplace, nor is it a "given" in established customer relationships of any kind. One has only to look at the thousands of stakeholders who have migrated away from agencies that once counted on their support to see this. Why do they leave? A chief reason for the attrition of these customers, donors, and volunteers is the failure of organizations to deal with the issue of stakeholder value and the need to create and provide ongoing value and benefit to sustain stakeholder involvement. The failure to provide these "drivers" of loyalty and retention over time negates a successful strategy and precludes meaningful differentiation from one's competitors. To be both relevant and meaningful to an agency's stakeholders, the value proposition needs to be emotional and affecting, functional or purposeful in nature, communal and societal, or self-expressive.

3. Who Is Our Competition?

Being aware of other nonprofit organizations with similar missions, knowing the approach they take with their constituents, and having an approximation of the amount they spend on promotion allow a nonprofit organization to question and evaluate its own programs and eliminate areas of duplication. The process starts with asking an overarching question: How do you stand in relation to your competitors?, and continues with asking how a nonprofit competes. Follow-up questions include

- What actions are our competitors taking?
- How does our agency develop a strategic position within our field?
- Can our nonprofit organization develop a sustainable competitive advantage in light of our competitors?
- Are supply and demand in balance?
- What will our nonprofit industry look like five years from now?

Questions such as these should form the basis of a nonprofit organization's marketing plan and strategic thinking.

Any organization trying to gain a portion of consumer dollars—philanthropic or otherwise—has competition. And the competition is not only from other nonprofit institutions. It also comes from within the organization's constituency—that is, from the demands made on the dollars and time of each individual involved with the organization.

4. What Are Our Competitive Advantages?

What does your organization do exceptionally well? Competitive advantages are those qualities of programs or services offered that distinguish your nonprofit organization from other organizations offering similar programs or services. These advantages come in a variety of forms, such as

- Services or programs of the highest quality available.
- The most reasonably priced services or programs.
- The most experienced staff.
- The largest variety of services offered.
- The most highly endorsed services or programs.

Nonprofit organizations must be able to identify their competitive advantages; failure to do so puts them at a disadvantage.

How does an organization identify its competitive advantages vis-à-vis other current nonprofit agencies as well as potential competitors? Primarily, one first determines who one's competitors are (and will be) and the particular strengths and weaknesses of their causes or products, the numbers of people involved in supporting their work, the dollar amount that the organization spends on its cause, and the revenue or dollars raised that it takes in. Using this information, the marketing director of a nonprofit organization can set up a competitive analysis worksheet, listing each of its competitors' strengths in one column and its own neutralizing responses in the other. Armed with this information, the marketing director can begin to calculate strategies.

5. What Is Our Marketing and Fund-Raising Budget?

The number of dollars allocated to marketing and to the fund raising effort contributes significantly to the success or failure of a strategy. This includes not just money, but time, volunteers, and services provided. There are various formulas available to determine how much a marketing department should spend on programs and promotional considerations. Questions such as the following should be asked and the answers evaluated:

- Are some programs operating at a loss because organizational conscience dictates that they do?
- Are some programs operating profitably allowing the organization to accomplish not only programmatical objectives but other objectives as well?
- Is the organization investing in the growth of other programs, hoping they will break even in the future?
- Should some services and programs be discontinued because they no longer meet the needs they were designed for?

Certain programs may be suspect or elicit statements such as these:

- Our measures of success are unclear regarding the program.
- As an organization, we're unsure how we'll accomplish the objectives.

- We do not have enough resources to meet our goals.
- Our constituency is no longer interested in the program.

If they do, they should be carefully evaluated.

6. How Strong Is Our Managerial Commitment?

A successful competitive strategy requires a stated, financially supported commitment from top management down. Without the means and organizational commitment to support and enable its strategy, a nonprofit organization is hamstrung when it comes to necessary activities such as coordinating resources, providing a forum to work together organizationally, hiring, and developing an internal direction. Getting top-level commitment for a strategic marketing plan usually involves some or all of the following imperatives:

- Tell the absolute truth about the situation, using plain talk.
- Be able to clearly articulate the organization's strengths and failures.
- The plan must be simple.
- The plan must have "compromise points."
- The plan should be packaged in light of the organization's goals.
- The plan should take into account the audience.
- The plan should focus on key audience segments critical to the organization's success.

A strategy helps an organization to go where it has decided it wants to go. Without a conscious plan in place, competitive direction ultimately becomes a series of reactions rather than actions—someone asks for organizational help and you help; you are asked to jointly sponsor an event and you do so; another nonprofit organization publishes an annual report so you print one. Integration of these six imperatives helps deliver a systemic solution to the concerns stakeholders have about any organization.

The Operating Environment's Effects on Marketing Strategy

Every nonprofit organization is affected in some way by its competitive strategy or lack thereof. To develop a strategy, an organization must first look at the donor, constituent, and supporter environment within which it operates to determine how to proceed. There is precedent for this cautionary approach: During the New Orleans flooding, many nonprofit organizations experienced either an increase or a decrease in their funding (depending on their mission). Locally, a planned addition to the city library has to wait until the neighborhood Catholic Church's campaign is finished. The environmental impact each example shows can be as simple as diverting a stakeholder's attention or loyalty away from one favored organizations or volunteer opportunity to another. Or it may reflect organizational mail, emails, or phone calls that have gone unnoticed or unanswered. In either case—but daily in the lives of stakeholders— the environment has a great effect upon them and, hence, the nonprofit institutions they may be interested in.

The three following macro environmental forces at work today are affecting virtually every nonprofit organization in the world and upsetting their ecosystems:

- Causal industry change is now a dynamic all nonprofit organizations must deal with and master. Today, competitive advantages erode more quickly than ever before. Similarly, strategy life cycles are shrinking. In addition, there are many more excellent options for stakeholders to give to, volunteer for, and make purchases at, and many marketing and fund-raising tactics no longer work as they once did.
- Thousands of new "expert" nonprofit organizations now communicate and sell their wares because of the technological ease of doing so and the ability to ramp up new organizations more rapidly and cheaply. Leading management theorist Gary Hamel suggests in his book (written with Bill Breen) *The Future of Management* that long-standing oligopolies are fracturing and competitive "anarchy" is on the rise.
- Collaboration with stakeholders is no longer an option for most nonprofit agencies; consequently, they must now share power and control of their organizational destinies. The Internet and other social media are facilitating this change and are primarily responsible for this shift. In particular, donors, customers, and volunteers want—and are often getting—more say in the affairs of the organizations they are involved with.

The following sections focus on individual lifestyles, the situations and organizations they are involved in, and the resultant effect on the nonprofit institutions they may or may not support.

The Individual: Looking for Reciprocity

In 1990, George Barna in his book *The Frog in the Kettle* suggested that an individual's beliefs and values would ultimately undermine institutional loyalty. Today, these same individuals are exposed to 3,000 to 4,000 marketing messages per day, the vast majority of which do not create a direct and meaningful connection with them. The beliefs and values held onto tightly by stakeholders have led many to view the intrusive nature of much of marketing with contempt, mistrust, and disloyalty. This "perfect storm" of discontent poses a problem for the future of some nonprofit organizations, which assume they will achieve public buy-in for their programs as long as they continue "doing what they have done for years." The presumption of marketplace loyalty, unfortunately, still undergirds many if not most nonprofit agency marketing plans that fail to recognize the deep-rooted hostility to more clutter.

Consumers are looking for reciprocity in the messaging they attend to, for benefits that come from being involved in the cause they are engaged with. These benefits may be physical, emotional, visceral, or mental. What organizations must do is genuinely involve donors, volunteers, customers, and other constituents in all aspects of the organization and serve as an integrator, bringing these interested parties into the organization as active participants in shaping its future.

There are other signs that contribute to individuals' loosening sense of commitment:

- Marriage is no longer a preferred institution.
- Studies show that adults feel they have fewer close friends.
- Brand loyalty is dropping in most product categories.
- The proportion of people willing to join an organization as a formal member is declining.
- Fewer people are willing to make long-term commitments.
- The percentage of adults who feel it is their duty to fight for their country, regardless of the cause, has dropped.
- The percentage of people who commit to events but fail to show is on the rise.

Given some of these indicators, how does an organization build a constituency of "friends" willing to commit to join a cause?

Lifestyle and Demographic Trends

Technology has fundamentally changed how humans and organizations interact. Because of this many marketing directors now spend much of their time trying to decipher the technologies and forget that relationships are still the lingua franca of marketing. This error in strategy is even more important, because the American culture has become increasingly fragmented, with double- or triple-income families, high divorce rates, and increasingly blurred demographic lines. New thinking on the part of marketers is required.

Relationships are now the most powerful differentiators in marketing. With an overabundance of causes and causal products doing essentially the same thing, stakeholders have a hard time telling the difference between each. However, they can differentiate between being "noticed" and not being sought after.

Four trends—adapted from Mark Earl's book *Welcome to the Creative Age*—overshadow how nonprofit organizations interact with stakeholders and navigate the "new normal:"

- *First*, there are too many causal choices and not enough differentiation between them. It would be one thing if the amount of causal choice led stakeholders to give to more nonprofit organizations and buy more nonprofit products, while reducing their anxiety in the process. This unfortunately is not the case. Rather, what seems to be the case is that the explosion of choice (coupled with the 3,000 advertisements stakeholders are exposed to daily (more if you are online) seems to make it harder rather than easier for new nonprofit agencies to survive. In addition, the overwhelming number of good nonprofit options available to all leads more easily to a lack of agency loyalty, because there are few causes that are desired by stakeholders that do not have suitable substitutions.
- *Second*, nonprofit agency constituents understand the world of marketing and tactics far more than they are given credit for and are much smarter than most institutions think, and they need to be treated as such. They understand that an agency may need to raise funds or sell products. There is no need

either to hide this fact or to feel embarrassed about it. In fact, this reticence on the part of agency personnel precludes getting to really know or understand the organization's constituents, their needs, their dreams, and the reason(s) they have for becoming involved.

- *Third*, stakeholders are concerned with "winning and losing" and expect organizations they are interested in to win more than they lose. This means that a constant string of appeals that are "urgent" or scream "crisis" repeatedly have the effect of urging stakeholders to leave the agency and take their support with them. In today's new economic world, repeated "urgent" or "crisis" messaging conveys "bad management" and "continue to support this organization at your own peril." No cause has the freedom to act as it will in this economic environment. An institution has to do what it says, accomplish what it sets out to, fix what no longer works, and be candid about the associated risks and costs.

- The preceding three "givens" of the new economic environment nonprofit agencies must operate and give rise to the fourth and most important new rule: we can no longer presume on the loyalty of any of our stakeholders. This includes our employees, donors, customers, and volunteers. For most nonprofit organizations, trust is now at a premium.

Institutional Turmoil

As discussed previously, individuals today exhibit less loyalty toward institutions, governments, companies, and products than ever before, which means that there is also less loyalty toward nonprofit organizations. For example, one relatively prominent nonprofit organization has changed its operational focus three times in five years. The focus changed each time funding dried up. How can a nonprofit organization ask donors, volunteers, or clients to be loyal or to make a long-term commitment to an institution that changes its focus so frequently?

Of course during difficult financial times, many stakeholders set stricter personal rules regarding who gets funding and where they involve themselves. The organization, by changing its focus opportunistically at the slightest chance of raising more money, knew this but forsook the importance of maintaining stakeholder relationships and interest in long-term goals. In these situations, constituents began to feel expendable and not influential in the organization's future. The housing and banking crisis as well as the auto industry debacle are other cases in point. How can these institutions ever ask their customers to be loyal again given the crushing changes they continue to endure?

The distrust and skepticism of marketers' messages requires that institutions listen to their stakeholders in a different manner, especially during economically unsettled periods. During these difficult times, new market segments often emerge within a nonprofit's portfolio as stakeholders adjust their relationships; some stakeholders are fearful of the uncertainty and withhold their giving completely, and may do so for quite some time. Others can afford to give but may give multiple smaller gifts in order to spread out their personal financial risk. Some stakeholders will change nothing in their relationship with the nonprofit organization, while others will say to the organization that they are still interested and loyal but can't afford to be involved right now.

Marketing isn't optional during these periods; an agency must continue to build its brand, reminding consumers of how their relationship with the nonprofit agency matters (given that most stakeholders become less brand loyal during times when they experience financial uncertainty). In addition, institutions must continue to listen to stakeholders. Many may endure financial and economic uncertainties but may change their giving habits and priorities within or outside the agency as their incomes return to normal levels.

The environment in which a nonprofit organization operates, including the interaction between organization and constituents, is in a constant state of flux today, requiring constant vigilance on the part of the organization as it closely monitors its ongoing relationships with its various constituencies.

As the following section details, the relationship a nonprofit organization has with its competitors also bears watching.

Five Constraining Operating Conditions

There have been major consequences to the nonprofit field as a result of increased market competition. The following five operating conditions have arisen to constrain nonprofit marketers today and should be considered as operational "givens" in planning a competitive strategy:

1. Increased competition
2. New experts
3. Nonprofit organizations becoming businesses
4. Nonprofit organizations being no longer culturally favored
5. Getting rid of performance blinders

1. Increased Competition. Because of an increase in competition, principally during the past 40 years, nonprofit organizations today encounter these five operating conditions, which may not have prevailed when some nonprofits were first incorporated. Many nonprofit organizations that have been in existence for at least 10 years never expected to compete against each other. Some organizations enjoyed monopolizing their fields for many years. They were unprepared for the crowded competitive environment of today. Now there are approximately 1.5 million nonprofit organizations that account for more than $1 trillion in revenues annually. Because of the economic reality currently facing many organizations, coupled with a declining dollar and donor share, many institutions can no longer afford to specialize in a single service activity. Market and competitive demands require them to create new service programs and new ventures to maximize their competitive stance and acquire new donors and dollars.

2. New Experts. Many nonprofit organizations are now experiencing new experts as competitors who offer similar or the same services. This section refers to competitors who do exactly what the organization does, perhaps employing the same methodology.

A consequence of the increase in the overall number of nonprofit organizations is an increase in the number of organizations performing the same function. Many expert organizations are now in competition with one another. This can result in a market condition known as a parity situation, whereby the product or cause being produced is similar to other products or services being produced. This, in turn, can result in organizations with similar or overlapping constituencies. (Expert companies are those that say they specialize in one or only a few areas.)

What does this mean for the future of organizations that find themselves in a parity situation? For many, it could mean trying to determine whether they should try to survive on their own, merge with another nonprofit organization with similar goals, shut down because of a lack of funding or usefulness, or change the focus of their service.

3. Nonprofit Organizations Becoming Businesses. Many nonprofit organizations have resisted viewing themselves as businesses. However, all nonprofit organizations are similar with respect to the following:

- *Product lines.* Many nonprofit organizations, especially larger ones, are developing new causal products and services designed to appeal to only certain parts of their constituencies.
- *Donation level.* Almost all nonprofit organizations are trying to persuade their donors to give more.
- *Customer and donor convenience.* Technology-based service and receipting delivery systems, 24-hours-a-day, seven day-a-week operators are becoming the norm in order to compete. In addition, the individuals operating these systems are increasingly better paid professionals and skilled workers.
- *Marketing.* There is a tremendous "sameness" in style, scope, and delivery of nonprofit promotional materials.

What is the consequence? More time should be spent in strategies that differentiate one nonprofit organization from another.

4. Nonprofit Organizations No Longer Culturally Favored. Nonprofit organizations formally harbored a sense of being "safe," because with respect to their donors and each other, they did not view themselves in direct competition. They could expect a certain number of donations or clients each year. Because of this complacency, many nonprofit organizations failed to cultivate a performance mentality, never having had to define formally where they were going and what they were doing. Discussions of competition seemed nonexistent. There seemed to be less concern for the bottom line, less industry urgency placed on proving one's service to those in need, and less looking over one's shoulder.

But this has changed. Proliferating nonprofit organizations providing similar services and delivery technologies are forcing these organizations to think more strategically. The speed with which nonprofit services can be duplicated means that donor loyalty continues to diminish. The concept of "market" is changing. The limits to what one nonprofit organization can accomplish are also changing; many today that were formerly small and narrowly focused organizations have become nonprofit retailers of services for specific, targeted groups.

5. Getting Rid of Performance Blinders. Because all nonprofit markets are dynamic, organizations must see themselves as having to learn to serve different constituencies and not expect the opposite to happen. Agencies must be positioned as working for the stakeholder, not the other way around. No longer can a nonprofit organization solely define what its market is; rather its constituency (or lack of one) defines the market for the agency. This fact begins to force the constituent, volunteer, or donor to become more active in the organization's marketing strategy by helping to define a market and thereby more likely to become involved in the activities of the agency.

No longer relying solely on altruism and traditional notions of fund development, nonprofit agencies must look to involve and leverage the self-interest of stakeholders, creating communities of interest and becoming evangelists for the organization while learning to target other potential funding agencies. With traditional managerial and marketing methods no longer serving the third sector as powerfully as they once did, nonprofit leaders and marketers must look at the private sector's best practices (e.g., distributed leadership, unceasing innovation, strong performance metrics, and board management techniques) and make them their own.

The Stakeholder Focus

Marketing must become a stakeholder-focused and centered discipline around which reciprocity is built in both the organization and the consumer. For the past 30 years, the consumer has been gaining control, and today he or she is in control. This means that for many nonprofit institutions, traditional marketing practices are no longer viable. When Peter Drucker more than 30 years ago entitled a chapter in *Managing for Results*, "The Customer Is the Business," he was not kidding. Unfortunately, putting the customer in charge goes against the mental model many, many institutions still follow. A successful marketing strategy must be built upon the building blocks of customers, volunteers, and donors.

Every strategy must start with the individual. And the marketing effort must not stop once a person has donated, or volunteered, or purchased a product. The connection with the stakeholder must go deeper and deeper. He or she must be engaged in an ongoing dialog with the nonprofit agency. This may mean being encouraged to join a social community of donors, buyers, or volunteers to share their consumer experiences. Or it may involve brand engagement through a dynamic web site or being a part of an advocacy campaign.

First Steps to a Competitive Strategy

A competitive strategy should be built around four central theses, which are explained in greater detail in the following chapters. First, a competitive position is determined by an analysis of an organization's environment, constituents, donors, and competitors. In other words, an organization must look externally and internally to devise a competitive stance. Many successful nonprofit organizations take the following structured and managed approach to their competitive strategy:

1. The first step is analysis and data gathering of market conditions.
2. Next is donor acceptance of the organization's programs in order to arrive at a competitive position. These organizations constantly check to see where they stand vis-à-vis the competitor tomorrow.
3. The best marketing units within nonprofit organizations view marketing as a function to which every organization member contributes. They seek the advice of members of several disciplines within the organization, not relying solely on the director of development or marketing. A diversified opinion from departments such as data processing, the president's office, and accounting contribute to the overall competitive strategy. Every person and department is viewed as a member of the marketing effort on behalf of the organization.

4. Nonprofit organizations that are growing are usually more than effectively selling their organizational products to their constituencies; they are, in fact, meeting the value needs of their donors through organizational programs, and they are giving the donors, volunteers, and constituents the feeling that they are the ones who are accomplishing the good work.

The nonprofit organization is merely a conduit through which the desires of interested parties to do something beneficial to society are matched with the needs fulfilled by the nonprofit organization. Particularly the key donor and volunteer arena, value-based selling—the means by which the heartfelt needs of the individual merge with the organization's actions—becomes a priority. The concept of placing the individual's interests first and the organization's second enables the nonprofit organization to become attuned to the donor's interests. Rather than funding an organization's needs, the individual ultimately funds those areas that satisfy his or her own beliefs.

Breaking with Tradition to Remain Flexible

Finally, nonprofit organizations competing successfully break a number of time-honored traditions of nonprofit marketing management:

- They are not constrained by the annual planning cycle (their plans change as information changes).
- They develop multiple strategies that realize high potential, rather than limiting themselves to one strategy.
- They adopt a long-term as opposed to a short-term perspective.
- They stop programs that do not deliver expected results quickly.
- They measure progress on every aspect of their organization's operations.
- They reward good behavior and terminate those who exhibit bad performance.

In summary, competitive strategy is built on the constituent's needs, the belief systems and confidence-gained tactics of potential donors, the perceptions desired by the external world, and the services that are needed and are affected by their recipients.

Summary

As the reader can see, developing a competitive strategy is both time-consuming and filled with dozens of possible perturbations. However, the payback is helping an organization inch closer to realizing its dreams and objectives. Chapter 3 takes what Chapter 2 has to offer and puts it in a framework that is both actionable and measureable.

CHAPTER 3

The Phased Strategic Marketing Plan

There are plenty of conversations going on they're just not with you.
Joseph Jaffe, *Join the Conversation*
(New York: John Wiley & Sons, 2007, p. 10)

I think therefore I am.
I am because we think.
We think and so we act.
Joseph Jaffe, *Join the Conversation*
(New York: John Wiley & Sons, 2007, p. 60)

There are many ways to build an effective marketing strategy. One suggestion is to divide the task into phases so that concerns are dealt with in a sequential manner. This provides enough time for management to reach a consensus on most issues while constructing a logical framework for building a marketing strategy.

This chapter presents a six-phase process for building a marketing plan (see Exhibit 3.1) that can be scheduled in succeeding months (with the exception of the "evaluation" phase, which is ongoing). These phases include

1. The external-analysis phase
2. The market or self-analysis phase
3. The market-development phase

Exhibit 3.1   Six Phases in Building a Marketing Plan

1. *External-analysis phase*, in which the organization looks at its competitors, undertakes a SWOT analysis (strengths, weaknesses, opportunities, and threats), and identifies specific competitive scenarios.
2. *Internal or self-analysis phase*, which looks internally at the organization to determine performance levels, organizational characteristics, costs, and the level of success in different organizational ventures.
3. *Market-development phase*, where issues of market development (e.g., the organization's growth pattern, its investment level in new causal products, and the competitive advantages and disadvantages of each) are examined.
4. *Strategy selection phase*, where two or three strategies are presented in conjunction with their projections. From this discussion one strategy is selected.
5. *Presentation of the plan*, where the plan is introduced to all important stakeholder groups.
6. *Evaluation phase*, where the strategy is reviewed and judged for effectiveness.

4. The strategy-selection phase
5. The presentation of the plan to important stakeholders
6. The evaluation phase

These phases are discussed briefly in this chapter, and they are each discussed in detail in succeeding chapters. The final phase, of course, is implementation, which is addressed in the Epilogue.

External-Analysis Phase

In nonprofit marketing, organizations must consider how the external environment impacts their cause, its products, or their services, either positively or negatively. As identified in Chapters 2 through 4, an organization must first look externally to identify its clients and donors. By undertaking this action first, a nonprofit organization will understand clearly the societal segments represented by its clients, its constituents, its volunteers, and its donors. From this analysis, the nonprofit organization can develop a plan to appeal to the motivational needs of each group.

Client, Donor, Constituent, and Volunteer Analysis

As stated previously, nonprofits principally serve four distinct groups: clients, constituents, volunteers, and donors. *Clients* are individuals the nonprofit organization serves directly and who become the immediate beneficiaries of its output. *Constituents* represent the consuming public that purchases some output from the nonprofit organization—for example, a book. *Volunteers* and *donors* (also called *supporters* by some organizations) supply or lend the nonprofit organization different types of resources—usually time, money, knowledge, encouragement, or facilities.

Two critical issues are basic in client, donor, constituent, and volunteer analysis:

1. Who are the major audience segments involved with the nonprofit?
2. What are their motivations and unfelt needs?

Why are these points important? Consider the following trends taking place in the United States; how would they impact the clients, constituents, volunteers, and donors of a nonprofit organization?

- We live in a world inundated with choices. In most areas of life Americans have a wider freedom of choice than ever in history.
- Most Americans remain single for longer periods of their lives, and there are more single people than ever before. People are delaying marriage and children, and many are opting out of each.
- A new sense of individualism—powered by the Internet and other social media—is influencing religion, politics, and entertainment.
- The two great unsolved problems in America—health care and immigration—threaten to create an internal social revolt.
- In the United States, 61 percent of the population believe their knowledge of persuasion techniques is above average.[1]
- A huge growth in environmental "green" consciousness has occurred.
- Sociologists are seeing people's increased willingness to trade out incomes and material possessions for meaning in their lives

If the first step in the external analysis is to assess the impact of the market and environment on the nonprofit organization and its constituencies, what about those nonprofit organizations that do not engage in regular marketing research to monitor these trends? Unfortunately, some nonprofits in this situation simply make an educated guess.

When an organization undertakes the process of defining its audience and the trends that affect them, it should produce client, donor, volunteer, and constituent profiles. The purpose of these profiles is to determine the characteristics a nonprofit organization thinks will help it define its targeted markets. The following considerations are important in creating such profiles:

- Age
- Sex
- Race
- Education
- Family income
- Geographic residence
- Employment
- Buying behavior

Once an organization develops a profile for each group, it can begin to look at its competitors to try and determine how they fit into this market. For that, a competitor profile must be developed.

Define Your Competitors

Development of a competitor profile is an important step in the process of forming a marketing strategy, but it is all too often neglected by nonprofit organizations. In the end, lack of such knowledge costs them time, energy, money, and the participation of individuals they could have helped or reached in the long run.

Today, nonprofit organizations must *assume* they have competition and must get to know their competitors. In the process of developing a competitor profile, the nonprofit industry is addressed as a whole. The profile can serve to identify the strengths and weaknesses of those who are a part of the same industry.

The critical questions behind a competitor analysis are the following:

- Who are the competitors to nonprofit organizations today?
- Who will they be tomorrow?

- Can the nonprofit organization identify the strengths and weaknesses of each competitor?
- What are their competitive strategies?
- How many people does the competitor serve; how much money is it raising?

A nonprofit organization's marketing director should start by developing a file or list of the organization's competitors. As part of this listing and as part of a general competitor analysis, the director must consider the approximate number of people each competing nonprofit organization is serving, the types of services or products being used by each, that competitor's approximate budgets, and its likely market share.

A marketing strategy also should map out an action plan to minimize the competitive actions of other nonprofit organizations. While most nonprofit organizations do not have the resources available to respond to all "competitive attacks," remaining passive can severely limit their effectiveness. A look at the overall industry allows an organization to acquire an overview of some of the general conditions at work.

An Industry Analysis Defines Services Offered and Their Trends

As part of a competitor analysis, a nonprofit organization should assess the likelihood that other nonprofit organizations could provide the same services. In an industry analysis, ask:

- How attractive is this industry to other potential competitors?
- What trends does this industry exhibit?
- What are the key success factors the marketing strategy will have to take into account for the organization to compete effectively?
- Does this industry have a history of stability? This analysis should consider the general trends in the industry—use of technology, changes in leadership, and changes in service delivery—to help a marketing manager anticipate industry changes.

The result of an industry analysis should reveal an environment with both threats and opportunities. It should answer these questions:

- What are the evident environmental threats and opportunities?
- Does the nonprofit organization expect major shifts to occur
  in the environment during the next one to three years?

Threats and opportunities to a nonprofit organization can origi-
nate from the legal environment (new fund-raising regulations),
technological trends (more affordable technology), social and cultural trends (U.S. citizens seem to identify themselves more and
more as "environmentalists" and, as such, seem more open to promoting like-minded values), and economic trends (if philanthropic
giving is charted against population growth, it is declining; if it is
charted against age, giving is increasingly dependent on older
donors).

Internal-Analysis Phase

Having begun the process of looking internally through a computer
profile, a nonprofit organization needs to take the next step in this
process by determining how others view its work. In particular, the
organization must assess how its constituency defines what it does.
This type of *image survey* seeks to determine constituent answers to
the following questions: What work do they think the organization
is engaged in? and Can they describe it in detail?

Defining an organization this way is counterintuitive to many
nonprofits. Most directors believe they are the ones to define what
they are doing, and having done so, donors, volunteers, and clients
will follow. Wrong!

An image survey helps an organization firm up what is expected
of it in the constituents' minds. This creates more loyalty between the
two and helps to prevent the organization from trying to become all
things to all people. Similarly, knowing what is expected of it allows a
nonprofit organization to concentrate its resources, thereby saving
money that would be required in a broader market approach.

An internal analysis must begin by asking the following questions:

- Does the organization keep track of its current performance
  levels, particularly the area of service delivery?
- If the organization has a strategy, can it identify it for itself
  and others, along with a sense of how it has performed as an

organization? Can the organization identify its strategy's strengths and weaknesses as compared with the strategies of its competitors?

- What is the self-image of the nonprofit organization? How does the organization describe its culture, structure, key stakeholders, and operational systems?
- How will all of these considerations affect the organization's strategy?
- Does the nonprofit organization know its costs of doing business?
- Does it know what its competitors are spending to provide the same service and the same service support?
- Is there any advantage in one cost structure over another?
- What internal factors constrain the organization and keep it from achieving greater success in its market?

These questions are designed to access the internal "context" from which the nonprofit organization can operate. Author Geraldine Larkin in her *12 Simple Steps to a Winning Marketing Plan* wrote,

One of the biggest mistakes most people make in marketing is undervaluing the importance of context. Context is everything in marketing. That's because marketing never works in a vacuum. No one can wake up one morning and successfully go out and start selling a new widget without taking two "contexts" into consideration. The first is the company itself, i.e., your business. The second context is the world outside of your business. The more attentive you are to trends going on around you, the more successful you will be in marketing your product.[2]

Market-Development Phase

The market-development phase is the one that forces the institution to develop a direction for its services, donor relationships, volunteer efforts, and products. In this phase, competitive advantages are studied in connection with the organization's ability to deliver these benefits to clients, constituents, and donors alike. Decisions about growth or maintenance of its current marketing position also are made in this phase, as are decisions about the strategies that are compatible with the organization's objectives.

Critical issues in the market development phase are as follows:

- What is the nonprofit organization's business mission as against what it should be?
- What areas of growth should the organization consider when entering new areas of service or growth?
- What level of investment should the organization consider for each area of current service?
- What competitive strategy options are available to the non-profit organization given its service portfolio and its product line?
- Given the different strategic options available to the organization, which ones best suit its strengths and weaknesses, particularly its culture and stakeholder expectations?

The goal in looking at these questions is to aim an organization's services and products at very well-defined audiences that will be receptive to the organization's actions. This offers some distinct advantages.

The more successful a nonprofit organization is in defining its mission and the strategies needed to reach it, the easier it is for clients and donors to understand and agree to the proposition, join in the cause—or choose to support another institution. Consumers appreciate a clear approach. A nonprofit organization should not try to "be all things to all people." Many nonprofit organizations today have, in their desires to help so many people, forgotten what they do well as opposed to what they do not do well. Any organization that can focus precisely on its goals automatically separates itself from many of its competitors. Clearer goals produce a stronger client and constituent loyalty.

By taking these steps, a nonprofit organization will be in a better position to further penetrate new areas of the marketplace. Many nonprofit organizations expand their markets and marketing without having fully penetrated one field of service. As a consequence, they often do not have the benefit of knowing all of the potentialities that could arise in their marketing expenditures. By knowing required levels of investment—as well as having to deal with hidden problems that may arise—the organization will not be so likely to make an ill-advised move.

Strategy-Selection Phase

The strategy-selection phase is a synthesis of the previous three phases. This phase combines all of the strategic options that have been discussed and, taking into account the nonprofit institution's identity, goals, and capability to fulfill its vision, presents the best strategic choices. There are usually two or three "best" strategic options, from which one is selected by coming up with answers to the following questions:

- Given all of the key performance measures—clients served, sales, investment, dollars raised, donors acquired—which strategy will deliver the best performance in each area?
- Which strategy gives the best "overall" performance?

These issues are discussed further in Chapters 8 and 9.

Presentation of the Plan

The presentation of the plan provides a selected, refined marketing strategy listing all of the programs and support services, along with client and financial projections for the strategy's performance for the coming year. The presentation of the plan to all levels of management and, ultimately, all levels of employees, lists all the programs and support services, along with client and financial projections for the strategy's performance for the coming year. In this phase, the nonprofit institution's senior leadership and marketing management form a group to evaluate the strategy or strategies and then allocate resources and make timetable decisions.

In developing such a group, it is important that a sense of urgency and directions be established early, even as early as in their chartering. Chaired by a senior officer in the nonprofit organization, the group is composed of those whose skills and skill potential, rather than personalities, will help allow the organization's adoption of the plan. A group like this is represented typically by officers and employees at all levels, as well as by some individuals who might be interested outside parties, key board members, donors, or volunteers. In addition, there is often a consultant in place whose job is to point out areas of the plan that may be in jeopardy or need further refinement.

From this leadership group, the strategy plan must be communicated to various management groups and other key insiders, as well as to those who are formal members of the organization, such as key volunteers, some key donors, and some members of the board. These different management groups begin to budget for their activity as part of the plan, while key volunteers, supporters and those within the organization's "insider" network begin absorbing the new direction.

Summary

In this chapter, nonprofit executives can acquire a sense of how important it is for them to have a plan for their organization's research program. Subsequent chapters show how the gathered information will be crucial in developing a coherent marketing strategy for the organization to implement.

PART II

THE EXTERNAL ANALYSIS

CHAPTER 4

External Analysis: Client, Donor, Volunteer, and Competitor Research

Assess yourselves and your opponents.
> Sun Tzu, *The Art of War*, translated by Thomas Cleary
> (Boston: Shambhala Publications, 1988), p. 81

It is the prospect who is difficult to define and understand, not the product.
> John O'Toole, *The Trouble with Advertising*
> (New York: Chelsea House, 1981), p. 90

Concentrate on relationships, not the technologies.
> Charlene Li and Josh Bernoff, *Groundswell*
> (Boston: Harvard Business Press, 2008), p. 18

The traditional underpinnings of nonprofit competition—product (your cause), price (the amount you are asking for or the amount you are selling a product for), place (where the selling or exchange occurs), and promotion (the types of marketing communication you use)—are still useful to think through. They enable most nonprofit organizations to compete minimally at a parity level with similar causes, but seldom provide the advantages needed today for an institution to experience breakout performance. There must be more. Coupled with this need is the concurrent problem many nonprofit

marketing departments face in having to rethink how they are operating, especially given that many of them are being bombarded by

- Large numbers of low-cost competitors taking advantage
  of cheaper Internet communication, crumbling barriers to
  entry, and technological advances.
- The inability to maintain a strategic competitive advantage for
  long periods of time, because advantages erode more quickly
  than ever.
- Agency outcomes, projects launched, and institutional values
  all being altered because organizational control is now
  shared—and in some cases dictated—by stakeholders.
- Hyper-competition and the collaborative presence of stakeholders demanding results, requiring near-perfect agency
  performance.
- The shrinking of strategy life-cycles because of competitor
  imitation.

More than at any other time, causal marketing success now depends on an in-depth knowledge of stakeholders, their values, and
the strong management of their relationship with an organization.
As power continues to shift from those who run the organization to
those who support it, the retention of stakeholders' interest and
sustaining their loyalty is vital to an agency's ongoing work. Stakeholder defection, on the other hand, is both expensive and a tragic
occurrence for any nonprofit agency in the long run.

To achieve stakeholder retention and resiliency, however,
requires nonprofit agencies to organize their marketing and customer functions in a new way. Most nonprofit institutions organize
first around those they serve and then around the cause(s) they
want to promote, as opposed to organizing around stakeholders
who typically underwrite the costs of the institution and support it
in various ways. While both courses of action are important, focusing on supportive stakeholders in our economically turbulent
environment needs to be routinely rethought by any marketing unit.

Although many nonprofit directors speak of stakeholder focus
as a centerpiece of their marketing efforts, this is typically not the
organizational reality. Making it the reality, however, requires staying close to stakeholders, who are most likely experiencing

instability and uproar in their daily lives. This, in turn, furthers the dissipation of value many supporters feel in relation to the institutions they want to partner with and hinders creating resilient partnerships with them. For these remedies to occur, stakeholders must be listened to in a new way to overcome the info-stress many of them feel.[1] Stakeholder listening and analysis should take many forms and is important for

- Research of customers, donors, volunteers, competitors, and those who are served.
- Data base management and, in particular, segmentation strategies.
- Value management and alignment with key stakeholder groups.
- Listening to employee feedback.
- Building collaborative social networks.

The Importance of Continuous Listening and Analysis

Without external analysis, performed on a continual basis, a non-profit organization cannot determine accurately which marketing strategies are working, which causes should be implemented, and which products currently are appropriate for target markets. External analysis of the client, donor, volunteer, customer, and competitor allows an organization to set company objectives, raise the necessary dollars to accomplish those objectives, and attract interested clients, donors, volunteers, and other key people. Listening combined with analysis also produces a better understanding of the market opportunities, the potential effectiveness of the promotional dollars being spent, and the tactical obstacles to overcome.

"Uncover" is the operative word. Internal and external listening and analysis are essential to the process of trying to uncover opportunities and threats that could lead to strategic marketing alternatives. Clients, donors, volunteers, employees, and competitors should each be researched separately, because these groups' actions disproportionately affect the lifeblood of the organization, more so than anything else. In addition, these groups are an invaluable source of information and can provide the organization with advice on how to better reach and serve them.

Goals of Listening and Analysis

The three primary goals of undertaking a client, donor, volunteer, employee, and competitor analysis are

1. To determine whether programs being proposed truly provide the expected "payback"—in dollars, organizational benefits, or changed lives.
2. To identify the spiritual, social, psychological, and pragmatic "fit" between the market and the program to determine whether the investment of the organization's time and money is appropriate.
3. To ensure that the organization is not merely duplicating a preexisting program.

Most nonprofit organizations simply cannot afford to do research for research's sake; they need to set goals and objectives for their research. By doing this, the nonprofit organization creates a benchmark from which to judge the way it will use its research.

Building a Rationale and Addressing Objections to Stakeholder Listening and Research

In nonprofit organizations where money is targeted for very specific programs that serve the public, the idea of embarking on "research" can raise certain objections. "It sounds so expensive and complex," "Aren't there a lot of different ways to interpret the information you generate?" "Which donor has time to fill out those long questionnaires?" Redefinition is perhaps the first step to take; a systemic organizational focus on listening to stakeholders sounds both more friendly and viable than the connotations of "research." Many for-profit organizations have redefined "research" and have benefited from listening programs. They have often viewed this need as ongoing and have forced listening research to become a systemic institutional exercise (much of the nonprofit world still views research as a one-off act) that has often resulted in new organizational initiatives, including

• Making listening a central topic in leadership-development programs.

- Earmarking a portion for stakeholder listening in annual budgets.
- Vetting new programs through a variety of audiences before they are "rolled out."
- Requiring salaried employees to take an online listening course.
- Giving employees listening portals containing a compendium of ideas coming from constituents concerning organizational issues.

How can nonprofit organizations define, manage, and communicate who they are unless they listen to those who define and communicate to each other what the organization is and stands for? The definition of an organization always belongs to stakeholders first and agency executives second. "How does it feel to be a donor to your cause?" and other questions begin to allow agencies to answer specific questions regarding those they collaborate with and to gain insights into how and why they do what they do and support what they support.

There are many reasons why nonprofit organizations object to external analysis and spend little or no time in concerted listening activities. Horrendous data-collections stories abound, and the cost of some surveys seems prohibitive. Further, many in the research field have led us to believe that we must have a Ph.D. to understand the hidden dimensions of data gathering.

Those that drive nonprofit marketing strategies must be able to address their own doubts as well as those of constituents and get past them. There are some relatively easy ways to uncover the doubts of donors, volunteers, and other constituents during market analysis, and these are suggested further along in this chapter. The internal organization can process the environmental information in the form of systems, problem-solving methodologies, and competitive strategies. As a result, organizational strategies must be tied directly to donor, volunteer, customer, or client needs; otherwise, the organization will have no handle on its competitive advantage(s), on how to "sell" to specific audiences in order to raise more money, and on how to strategically help members of its target audience in their collaborative efforts with the institution.

The Need for a Focus When Conducting External Research

Another frequently cited concern by nonprofit managers regarding external analysis is uncertainty—when and how to do research and which issues should be addressed. John Lyons in his book, *Guts,* frames the issue like this:

> *I am not a friend of research. Particularly when it is asked to do what it was never intended to do: predict the future. Research can't tell us whether an ad is going to succeed any more than a critic can tell us whether a movie will succeed.*
>
> *Intuition is much more helpful. Not half-baked intuition. Intuition springs from information that triggers an idea.*
>
> *Research properly used gives me the right information. But I need it before the idea in order to trigger the idea in the first place. And to get the right idea I need research that talks to the right people so I know what they need and feel. For example, did you know that only 20 percent of the beer-drinking population consumes 80 percent of the beer? I can be friendly to research that gives me a fact like this, because now I can put my talent to work and if I'm lucky I can come up with the best beer campaign ever written.[2]*

For John Lyons, research is a means for confirming or denying suspicions or hunches about the marketplace. For a nonprofit marketing director, suspicion about how constituents or markets will act, if used as the sole governing stick, is never enough. Some additional confirmation or denial is needed, and this is where constructive stakeholder listening and marketing research comes in.

The presence of the Internet reframes how stakeholder research can occur in nonprofit agencies. Both listening and research are attempted in many ways today in nonprofit institutions—through commodity listening and research, outsourced listening and research, distance listening and research, and strategic listening and research. Exhibit 4.1 details how each of these research types can be used within an organization.

> *Commodity listening and research.* The most popular—and least helpful—way for an organization to gain some insight into its causal industry and the attitudes of its critical stakeholders is

4. Strategic Listening and Research

3. Distance Listening and Research

2. Outsourced Listening and Research

1. Commodity Listening and Research

Exhibit 4.1   The Listening Grid

to find another agency that is similar in nature and composition and identify what it is doing in its marketing and promotional efforts and to copy it. Contact with stakeholders is bypassed in favor of the quicker route of imitation. The net effect of this patterned thinking is to remake your organization in the style of the one you are benchmarking against, thereby creating a commodity situation where the donor sees no difference between your organization and another. In turn, you lose out on a chance for differentiation that may attract donors, and the donors lose out in tracking you down, assuming you are the same as everyone else.

Outsourced listening and research. When nonprofit organizations decide that they need to "hear" from their stakeholders, they often hire a vendor. Listening and research surrogates are often employed to develop a written or telephone questionnaire for an organization on behalf of a particular group of stakeholders. An outside firm may also be asked to do a series of focus groups around a particular set of questions. Using a group from outside an agency is not a bad decision—in fact, it is a popular managerial decision. You can get answers to questions you think up. What these companies cannot do is to help you find out the questions you should have asked but didn't. However, this singular research act (it is seldom part of a budgeted, ongoing series of research and listening initiatives) seldom delivers a decisive, breakthrough, long-term advantage to the agency that initiated it.

There are reasons for this. First, a research firm usually serves a number of clients and has little reason to help an agency create a compelling advantage for itself. Typically, it undertakes the job, uses standardized research systems, and delivers the information. Typically there is also diminution in the vitality of the information collected between the times it is uncovered until the time it is viewed by the nonprofit agency. Most importantly, the nonprofit's executives will not undertake the conversations themselves or interact with a constituency in any way.

Distance listening and research. Some nonprofit agencies do indeed attempt to develop an ongoing series of interactions with key stakeholder groups but do so at a distance. Those on the frontlines—individuals such as stewardship representatives—often come in contact with valuable information, but they have no formalized way of relaying it other than anecdotally. The information, in whatever form it takes, seldom travels beyond the marketing or fundraising department and is not built into the fabric and causal strategy of the organization. Rather, it provides some strategy innovation that is helpful for a time—particularly for the fundraising unit—and may help lift an organization briefly.

Strategic listening and research. Strategic listening has never been easier or more important than it is today. Your ability to find out what the market is saying about your cause goes beyond the bias of surveys and focus groups; through the Internet and social communities—and even private communities that you set up—you can hear in a new way what you typically don't hear otherwise. Borrowing James Surowiecki's "wisdom of the crowd" notation allows nonprofit agencies to divine firsthand what online chatter is saying. Your information may
  ◆ Help you pinpoint troubled spots with your brand.
  ◆ Find out what your stakeholders are and are not interested in.
  ◆ Enable you to understand how your market is influenced.

By generating insight through constant interaction, social communities can also become research communities, providing insight into all aspects of your cause. In these groups, research needs to move from a one-way dialog to a conversation propelled by a community whose interests and values are similar to your cause's, resulting in more lasting value, honest opinions, and interaction, with the additional advantage of creating longer-lasting relationships with those you interact with.

Other Research and Listening Concerns, Including Flexibility

The unvoiced fear of many nonprofit executives contemplating research initiatives is, What if the opinions of the stakeholders disagree with where I (we) want to go? In other words, most nonprofit agencies want the ability to create a flexible competitive strategy. Constituents', clients', and donors' points of view, whether perceived to be rational or not, will define the scope and quality of service and the performance goals. A nonprofit organization's marketing and competitive advantage is tied directly to meeting its donors' needs, expectations, and perceptions. When market research is not undertaken, donors and constituents themselves are forcing this responsiveness, as opposed to the organization's voluntarily making such changes by withholding gifts or volunteerism. With little tolerance for poor agency performance and a growing expectation for better outcomes and delivery of services, stakeholders—board members, volunteers, and large or small donors—are using their opinions and checkbooks to force change.

Without this type of pressure many nonprofit institutions might leave well enough alone. And because stakeholders cannot judge or see the quality of service their check, gift, or volunteerism is providing, they often make decisions to give, volunteer, or continue their involvement based on reputation, reliability, Internet presence, and even how service is provided during a donation or telephone transaction. It is these impressions—a thousand points of touch—guiding stakeholder actions that nonprofit marketers must come to know firsthand.

There is no limit to the amount of listening or external analysis a nonprofit marketer can do or the scope it can take for his or her organization. Historically, external analysis focuses upon four components:

1. Clients, volunteers, constituents, customers, and/or donors
2. Competitors

3. The industry an organization finds itself in
4. The environment in which it operates

The first element is treated in this chapter. Items 2, 3, and 4 are discussed in Chapter 5.

Start with Clients, Volunteers, Constituents, Customers, and Donors

Pragmatically speaking, most organizations begin with their clients, customers, or donors when performing some sort of constituent analysis or listening exercise in order to define the most relevant target markets through a process called segmentation. *Clients* are those individuals who consume the resources or programs the agency provides; *donors,* on the other hand, lend the nonprofit resources (money, time, encouragement, and personal access) to allow it to accomplish its goals and objectives; and *constituents* (also called customers) are purchasers of items the nonprofit may produce.

Pitfalls to Avoid

Many nonprofit organizations start incorrectly with their preexisting products and services and then use external analysis to try to enhance or mandate already agreed-on promotional decisions. Should the data not support the decisions, the data is often forgotten or put aside. Without good data that is as objective as possible and not biased toward existing causal products, marketing and fund-raising campaigns can be less than successful. Client and donor analysis should help determine whether the organization is in the right market and is providing the right products and services for that market.

Further, such an analysis helps to determine the strategic approach to take in selling the organization's values to its constituency. An organization will achieve a strategic advantage only if what it is saying and selling is perceived to be of value and use to its constituency. The more this symmetry is achieved in messages that target potential donor values, the more an organization achieves the possibility of superior competitive advantage.

For example, a nonprofit organization I work with has the desire to raise funds on behalf of those who are jailed throughout the world for their religious or political beliefs. The target audience has a desire not to see people jailed inappropriately or unjustly for their beliefs and responds with gifts to encourage the organization to continue its efforts on behalf of prisoners. Both parties achieve a type of symmetry in their communication and, consequently, are in alignment.

Segmentation as the Next Step

Having taken the first step of defining the needs, finances, motivation, and identity of clients, donors, volunteers, customers, and constituents, a nonprofit marketing team looks for natural groupings or actionable *segments* within each as a means to explore its strategy. Segmentation at its best is both art and science. Most nonprofit organizations don't have to be convinced of the need for segmentation and are quite familiar with analysis of such. Segmentation's ultimate goal is to create a difference between one nonprofit organization and the next through attributes that are important to institutional stakeholders—it is often the key to developing sustainable competitive advantage. From the stakeholder's perspective, the ultimate segmentation scheme would be mass customization whereby each stakeholder is a distinct segment and is treated as such.

At its basic level, the most common segmentation principle is first separating customers from non-customers, donors from nondonors, or clients from non-clients. This tactic, though important, typically does not sufficiently differentiate a customer base for real advantage. After this shallow differentiation is accomplished, deeper segmentation examples are the popular principles of *recency* (how recently a donor has given or a customer has purchased), *frequency* (how many times the donor has given or the customer has purchased), and *monetary* (how much the donor has given or the dollar amount the customer has purchased). These concepts are fixtures in nonprofit marketing jargon; when you ask a nonprofit director for his or her segmentation strategy, and if the director has one, you are more than likely to hear one or all three of the aforementioned concepts.

Segmentation in the sense being presented here means identifying relevant target markets that can be profiled and have adequate size, developing distinctive strategies to best reach said markets and using communication platforms to persuade, inform, and influence those targets. Historically, segmentation is a classification system born out of external analysis by which a nonprofit organization identifies viable market segments. From this classification process come promotional, fund-raising, and advertising strategies to reach each segment. Segmentation is built on the needs of constituents and donors. A nonprofit organization must equally address its donors, clients, customers, volunteers, and constituents; by not doing so, the nonprofit is assuming that all constituencies have the same needs. Differing audience segments have different needs and values and therefore require different products or services. Consequently, different marketing strategies are often required in order to get these segments to buy, use, or donate.

Henry Ford could afford to say that a customer could buy a Model T in any color as long as it was black, because he was the principal car marketer in the United States as well as a marketer of affordable cars. Nonprofit organizations cannot make such assumptions. Partnership and collaboration with donors and other stakeholders thrives on relevant communication and a sense of importance attached by both parties to what is being written or broadcast. Many tend to forget that Henry Ford was producing cars of different colors by 1928.

Enduring and Dynamic Segmentation Variables

External analysis identifies variables—enduring and dynamic—as a means to its classification or segmentation system. *Enduring variables* are constituent and donor constants such as demographics, geographic characteristics, and variables relating to personality, values, interests, and lifestyle. Enduring variables allow a nonprofit marketer to develop an a priori segmentation plan (in essence, segmenting the market based on who its constituent members are). *Demographic indicators* describe people: Are they married? What sex are they? How many children are in the household? Do both spouses work? Do they own their own home? *Geographic segmentation* has to do with where people live, not only their immediate communities but the state and the section of the country in which they live. *Psychographic segmentation* divides markets according to differences in lifestyle. It is based on the idea that "the more you know about your audience, the better you can communicate with them." These

Exhibit 4.2 Enduring and Dynamic Variables

Enduring Variables	Dynamic Variables
Age	Heavy use of product
Sex	Early use of product
Geographic location	Brand loyal
Working	Autonomous
Single	High self-involvement
Income	Hedonistic
Divorced	Awareness of product

are sometimes known as enduring variables, because they are constant within the consumer community across all causes and products (at any single point in time). In other words, these variables do not change across nonprofit classes or cause appeals.

On the other hand, *dynamic variables* are those that differ for a donor or constituent relative to each donation or act of volunteerism. Dynamic variables are often used in creating solicitation messages, because a writer is looking at how his or her organization's donors behave in certain situations. (See Exhibit 4.2.)

The following section further explores how to use each variable in a strategic manner. It is important to note that there are many ways to divide a market; typically an analysis examines anywhere from 5 to 15 variables.

Mr. and Mrs. Smith support a number of different causes financially. If your job is to raise money from Mr. and Mrs. Smith, you would first look at some of their *enduring variables.* The live in and own a house that is located in the country on 12 acres. Both have white-collar jobs—one is a doctor and the other a consultant. Both are college educated and have a combined income of $235,000. These variables are constant. However, a number of different causes, appeals, and *dynamic variables* influence their ''giving'' patterns. They support prison reform for political reasons, some hunger appeals for compassionate reasons, their church for spiritual reasons, and a religious worker for friendship reasons. With each cause, a reason for giving changes based on the variables that change as well.

Enduring Variables

The following discussion addresses enduring variables and suggests ways to uncover them and use them strategically.

Demographics.   First, consider the enduring demographic variable and its characteristics. Demographic characteristics are often used by nonprofit organizations to create a client, donor, or constituent profile. Variables such as age, sex, income, education, marital status, occupation, race, family dwelling location, regional location, and family size are indicators that help to describe potential target markets and allow a nonprofit marketing manager to pursue segments that yield a better acceptance of one's message. Demographics are particularly helpful for defining markets, because characteristics such as age affect his or her interests and activities. For example, XYZ organization's top 18 donors have the following common demographic characteristics:

- Home values exceed $500,000.
- Households have over $250,000 income per year.
- All heads of households have white-collar jobs.
- All heads of household are currently married.
- Twelve households have children; 10 of the 12 households have at least one child in college or out of college.
- Twelve heads of households have jobs in the finance, insurance, or business sectors; two are retired, two are doctors, one is a salesperson, and one is a professor and consultant.

These variables can be determined by asking the individuals about themselves, through survey research, or through syndicated studies that are relatively standard. An environmental group gathered this type of information through an online survey to begin to better understand whom they are in partnership with. The questions used were

- How long have you been a member?
- Why are you a member?
- How did you hear about us?
- Is our environmental work helpful?
- What environmental issues are most important to you?

- Are you a member of our online action network?
- How would you like to be involved?
- How would you describe your level of technology understanding and usage?
- How do you prefer to renew your membership?
- Do you read our online newsletters?
- How are you employed?
- What is your household income?
- What is the highest level of education you have had?

Some nonprofit organizations personally gather data like this through face-to-face interviews, some through online research, and some through focus groups. Focus group interviewing is one of the more frequently used forms of qualitative marketing research. A *focus group* is a small grouping of men and women (single sex or combined, depending on the cause) who are brought together for the collaborative purpose of discovering how they feel about some particular issue, trend, or product. This form of group interviewing has been around since World War II; it uses a moderator or leader who guides the group in answering questions that will provide inferential data to the sponsoring organization. (Demographic data bears mention because it can be an indicator of constant change.)

Geography.   Where a person lives often helps a nonprofit agency determine where to focus its efforts, because any nonprofit organization that has less than a national mandate for its services must concentrate its promotional resources in a geographical region. Though the presence of the Internet sometimes lessens the import of *geographic characteristics,* looking at population and geographic uniqueness and then relating these two to demographics begins to give a marketing officer a sense of how to shape the message. Noting important differences between rural populations and urban populations or between apartment owners and home owners can make the difference between success and failure in how one promotes a cause.

Psychographics.   Having first looked at where a person lives and who he or she is, a nonprofit marketer now looks at how these same individuals perceive themselves; the values they hold; their view of the world around them; the attitudes, beliefs, and hopes and fears they adhere to; and the benefits they expect to receive from being involved with the organization's cause. The goal here is obviously to go beyond demographics and flesh out people's lifestyles and values to target a fundraising or advocacy campaign more closely.

Perhaps more than any other aspect of segmentation, the values and attitudes held by stakeholders matter more than ever in a commodity-driven world. The values held by key stakeholders, coupled with the benefits they expect to receive through their partnership with the organization, can determine an entire strategy. A large youth center received a gift from a family only after discovering that the patriarch of the family had given one of the early gifts to the center *and* that the family wanted the building named after him. A marketer cannot assume that values and benefits hold constant across segments; in fact, they often change dramatically, depending on the cause and the level of the stakeholder's involvement.

Dynamic Variables

Dynamic variables are those that are specific to the relationship a donor, volunteer, customer, or constituent has with a nonprofit organization's cause or products. Not all nonprofit causes and products involve the stakeholder in the same way. The relationship with each changes, depending on the values of a donor and the cause or objectives of the nonprofit organization's programs.

Some nonprofit marketers feel that dynamic variables are the most valuable information to be had about a constituent because they help in message and solicitation creation. A number of clients currently have donor populations in which the majority of their dollars come from a small percentage of their giving universe. The relationship this small percentage has with the organization is often very different from that it has with the rank and file. Whereas enduring variables would describe these donors one way, dynamic variables indicate how to create messaging so that stakeholders consume more of your product, volunteer more of their time to your cause, or give more dollars to the projects you are promoting.

There are many dynamic variables that bear mentioning; three are examined here.

Heavy Users/Major Donors.   The heavy user concept is borrowed from product consumption terminology and refers to a major donor, also termed "affluent donor" or "key donor." Who are these people? Why do they give, purchase, or volunteer the way they do? Do they differ demographically from the rest of the nonprofit organization's audience?

How might a nonprofit organization's solicitation message change if it were trying to solicit a wealthy Hispanic couple as compared with an Anglo-Saxon couple? Would there be significantly different approaches? Depending on the product or cause, the answer can be "yes." By looking at the readership profiles of special interest magazines, one can identify distinct groupings of affluent people. This information can affect where an organization places its solicitation message to attract major donors. Success at solicitation in certain arenas may depend on face-to-face presentations, mass solicitations, or even impersonal media. The critical issue is to recognize that those who consume more of a nonprofit organizations' product or give more frequently to its cause usually exhibit peculiar sets of dynamic variables, which should then affect the organization's promotional strategy. Donors and volunteers who might be classified as "heavy users" often give to or become involved with very specific and narrow projects that do not enjoy mass followings or broad presentation.

Brand Loyal and Monthly Partners. Although the terms brand loyal and monthly partners are not necessarily synonymous, stakeholder loyalty exhibited towards a cause through giving, volunteering, or advocacy deserves a special approach as compared with those who are less loyal and give sporadically or volunteer intermittently. Those who are close partners need to be held "close" organizationally and should be reminded routinely of their importance to the organization in order to maintain that loyalty; those who are predisposed to switching their giving loyalty often need to be completely "resold' to secure each new gift.

Donor, Customer, and Constituent Motivations. Internet research suggests that there are a number of distinct shopper categories and each has a different set of motivations:

- *Newbie shoppers* need a simple interface as well as a lot of hand-holding and reassurance.
- *Reluctant shoppers* need information, reassurance, and access to live customer support.

- *Frugal shoppers* need to be convinced that the price is right and they don't have to search elsewhere.
- *Strategic shoppers* need access to the opinions of their peers or experts as well as choices in configuring the product.
- *Enthusiastic shoppers* need community tools to share their experiences, as well as engaging tools to view the merchandise and personalized recommendations.
- *Convenience shoppers* (the largest group) want efficient navigation, a lot of information from customers and experts, and superior customer service.[3]

These exhibited motivations help define strategy; are there motivational groupings within your constituency that need to be optimized? A donor to a capital campaign may want to memorialize a loved one through a naming opportunity; it is crucial to know where memorializing fits within your campaign's motivation set. The presence of social media today allows a marketing director an unprecedented ability to persuade stakeholders to discuss a cause or causal product in a systematic way, often identifying basic motives and reasons behind their involvement. Uncovering and identifying motivations allows the marketing team to assign them to different segments and assess their importance. This, in turn, leads to knowing how to develop a strategy that takes them into account. A "motivational hierarchy" allows them to be categorized as important or relatively unimportant. Some motivations lead to high impact on markets and are significant; others may be common to competitor strategies, and their use may not be advisable.

The use of dynamic variables through qualitative research to shape strategy—whether through focus groups, in-depth interviews, customer case studies used for modeling, or social network groups mobilized to be listened to—encourages stakeholder dialog, promotes collaboration, and provides the opportunity to uncover customer, donor, volunteer, and constituent experiences. Using the same tactics with former donors and customers allows a nonprofit organization to uncover problems with the cause or communication and solicitation patterns that are counterproductive. Similarly, listening to very loyal stakeholders may lead to the establishment of closer bonds as well as uncovering and identifying unmet needs.

Describing Clients, Donors, Volunteers, Customers, and Constituents

An organization's external analysis should consist of addressing four sets of broad questions:

1. Donor, client, customer, and constituent segments:
   - Who is donating to our cause (or buying its products)?
   - Who should be but is not giving to or purchasing from us?
   - Who was and is no longer (and why not)?
   - How does the market currently segment, and how should it?
   - Does the client base we're working with reflect our organization's goals and mission?
2. Donor, client, customer, and constituent financial activity:
   - How are donors and buyers stratified from largest to smallest financially?
   - What is the time frame of their giving?
   - What is the frequency of their giving?
   - Do fees for service get paid on time?
   - Is there a need for a stronger collection policy?
   - What is our lapsed rate? By media?
3. Donor, client, customer, and constituent motivation:
   - What are the primary values and motives behind donors, clients, and customers and behind constituent involvement with our products and causes?
   - What are the most important attributes of our cause?
   - What objectives and problems are the donors trying to solve and overcome by giving and the constituents by buying?
4. Donor, client, customer, and constituent needs:
   - To what degree are our donors, clients, customers, and constituents happy with what our organization is doing?
   - What problems regarding our programs must be solved organizationally to bring them in line with donors, customers, clients, and constituents?
   - What problems regarding our infrastructure services must be solved to create the ideal stakeholder experience?

Donor Profile

The following case study is a profile of a donor's involvement with an organization. The profile examines the donor in a number of ways and with different data elements to help the nonprofit marketing director make a decision on how best to pursue a relationship with this donor. To arrive at the best possible sense of how to pursue the continuing relationship with the donor, the donor must be viewed by the nonprofit organization through a number of different lenses:

Donor Demographics
The donor is over 50 years of age, living in a home that she and her spouse purchased 14 years ago in a suburban community; she vacations two weeks each year in either Phoenix or on the Florida coast, has (with her husband) a combined income of $115, 000, attends a Methodist church, and gives to three other nonprofit organizations besides her church.

Donor Financial Activity
Her financial activity shows she gave her second and most recent gift two months ago in response to a direct mail appeal on hunger in an African nation; her response was $45 (the first asked for amount in the letter), she wrote the check from a shared checking account with her husband, and she has been giving to the organization for four years.

Donor Motivation
The donor feels her personal needs and motives are fulfilled by the act of giving to the nonprofit organization. The other two organizations she supports are social service organizations. She uses the Internet to read ``special reports'' when she is prompted online but gives through the mail in an organization envelope or her personal stationery and envelope. She can readily identify the benefits she accrues by giving to the organization.

Donor Needs
Donor continues to need reinforcement via letters, e-letters, and phone calls that tell her the importance of her support. Communication should be relatively emotional, backed up by rational claims in order to maintain involvement.

Additional Segmentation Strategies Following an External Audit

On the heels of an external analysis of clients, constituents, donors, and customers, an organization has choices to make regarding the type of segmentation strategy on which it wants to embark. Any segmentation strategy depends on developing unique messaging, differentiated from competitors, that appeals to the target segment(s) being approached.

I've learned from conferences, books, and consultants that there are four basic segmentation strategies that I could use in almost every situation, namely:

1. *Homogenous strategy.* This strategy is used when an organization decides to treat its market as a homogenous whole, focusing on the common needs and concerns of all the members of the market. In essence, there is no market segmentation in this strategic choice; the goal is to deliver a standardized message, saving costs, to large numbers of prospects, hopefully resulting in new donors or customers. Today, this strategy is still a fairly common practice, especially among Internet donors, a category in which very few organizations segment their list. By definition, the media strategy for a cause that does not create different segments is as broad as possible, using many media vehicles to reach as many target prospects as possible. (A common occurrence of this type of strategy is when disaster strikes and organizations flood the television and radio airwaves, the mailboxes, the Internet, and the telephone, spreading their net as broadly as possible.)

2. *Wholly segmented strategy.* When a cause aims at the market but instead of offering one message for it targets several market segments each with a unique marketing mix, it has a segmented strategy. The goal obviously is to go after separate markets, hoping each market will yield more sales or donations through a deeper penetration. While more donations do often accrue, costs are typically higher and the marketing effort is more pronounced. The tactical dilemma for a marketing director is to run the right number of segments with enough finances to do an adequate job in each.

3. *Niche strategy.* This strategy allows a marketing director to concentrate heavily on just one or two markets, doing all the organization can to serve it well, listen to it well, build its own brand name, and achieve a strong following.

4. *The "next" niche strategy.* Very simply, if a team succeeds in one niche, it moves on to the next one, again using tailor-made strategies or projects for the market.

There is more to consider than simply choosing a type of segmentation strategy; a small marketing budget often leads to a niche strategy so that an organization can concentrate a small war chest on the best prospects. If the market is 65-year-old white women, an agency can use a homogenous strategy because segmenting the market further may not result in added dollars; the presence of competitors means looking hard at the market segments they are working in and deciding whether your offer is significantly differentiated from theirs to chance being in the same segments. If it is not, you may have to choose other segments.

External Analysis of Competitors

After focusing on clients, constituents, customers, donors, and volunteers, attention is now given to the second important external factor to consider—competitors. Believe it or not, one nonprofit organization may be competing for the same dollars as several, if not hundreds, of other nonprofit organizations. An analysis that reveals the competitors in one market will help identify whom to realistically expect to reach, in every area—donors, volunteers, clients, constituents, and customers. And, more importantly, it will help to identify a realistic market share and realistic bottom-line targets.

Baseball great Dizzy Dean is reputed to have said, "Hit them where they ain't." For some, this statement defines their view of competitive strategy: to create a product or fill a need where there is currently no product or organization by filling an unmet need or tapping an untapped market. Another tack is to build a "better mousetrap" with the hope that stakeholders will beat a path to your doorstep.

When a nonprofit director says, "We are doing better this year," perhaps the correct response should be, "Compared to what?" The understanding of where a nonprofit organization stands in relation to others offering similar services is critical. In addition, with the availability of information, a nonprofit's sales goals, recruitment quotas, returns on investment, and other key financial ratios are measured against similar categories of other companies. Success and value must be defined by the client, donor, customer, constituent, and volunteer, not by the opinions of those inside the organization. It is the stakeholders' world that should define the nonprofit organization's strategy, goals, and identification of its competitive edge.

With the donor and customer, the nonprofit institution really serves only as a "middleman" between the stakeholders' desires to do good and the client or cause they wish to help. The client—or the person for whom the nonprofit organization exists—is truly the only party who can assess whether or not the organization has accomplished its mission and objectives.

Nonprofit organizations, and the causes they promote, now live in an age where they are the only game in town. Here is a client example that illustrates that point.

Example: The Need for a Second Camp

Ron Ward is the director of a camp that routinely sells out its programs. For the past five summers he has been either oversold during his summer months or at 98 percent of capacity (or higher). His winter ski weekends, which he books for 12 weekends during the winter months, are at 104 percent of capacity, and he routinely turns away hundreds. His rental business is doing very well, as are his programmed weekends. His revenue stream is positive. His cumulative growth rate over five years is 10 percent. The camp's favorable reputation is widespread. Now Ron and his team are asking whether they should open another camp in a nearby state to relieve some of the load factor and pressure that Ron's camp currently faces and to allow a new section of the country and its young people to benefit from the camp's established program.

In thinking through the process of building a new camp, his first step was to determine a possible site and then define who his new "clients" (campers) might be and determine whether they might come to a new facility. Ron and his team plan to spend the next year and a half using many of the concepts discussed previously before the organization would determine whether to build or not.

One of the steps that Ron and his team are engaged in is identifying the organizations, institutions, and activities his new camp would competitively face. In most cases, identifying such primary competitors is relatively straightforward. Here is a partial list, noting that each entry has a varying degree of competitive intensity with Ron's camp:

1. There are three camps that Ron and his team believe will fail in the next yearly camp cycle because of (a) the far-reaching effects of Ron's programs, which are drawing away campers from the competition, and (b) the state of the economy.
2. There are four for-profit camps within 75-160 miles of the proposed new site, all offering recreational activities similar to Ron's current recreational mix, but none offering similar programming.
3. There are one YMCA boys' camp and one YWCA girls' camp within 150 miles.
4. There are three church camps within 100 miles that are small and have been small for the past eight years.
5. There are still other camps within a 200-mile radius.
6. The possible new campsite lies within an area in the state where families tend to vacation.
7. There are two major metro markets within 140-190 miles of the proposed new site.

While there are still many other strategic steps to be taken by Ron and his team (such as a fee analysis among the competitors) some principles can be drawn from the preceding list.

1. *Competition and alternative destinations.* Perhaps the most obvious one is that there seems to be an abundance of potential competition for the campers' dollars. The presence of alternatives to one's own programs is often surprising to many nonprofit directors.
2. *Direct vs. indirect competitors.* Many nonprofit organizations are not the only ones offering a service to a particular audience; there may be other organizations offering the same service. Surprisingly, clients, donors, and volunteers are often more aware of the substitute options than the nonprofit organization. The clients may be looking for the particular service

and in their search may discover alternatives. Donors and volunteers are eager to support programs that agree with their values.

In fact, the notion of substitute options is very relevant for today's marketer. If the availability of substitute products or causes is the first observation, the second observation is that despite the competition for the camper's dollar, not every competitor is competing at the same level. There are usually some *direct competitors* (those a nonprofit organization competes with on a day-to-day basis); there are also some *indirect competitors* (those a nonprofit organization competes with on an irregular basis). A pattern emerges upon analysis and leads to a deeper understanding of how this example of the youth camp market functions.

3. *Defining the key variables.* The third observation is that "the definition of the most competitive groups will depend on a few key variables. It may be strategically important to know the relevant importance of these variables."[4] With respect to the camp, important variables might include the proximity of the camp to the potential camper, the programs offered, the availability of some type of moral emphasis at the camp, some type of referral from a previous camp attendee, and so on.

Positioning to Understand "the Market"

The three principles mentioned in the case study allow the nonprofit marketer to develop a conceptual base for identifying potential competitors. The marketer tries to position the organization through the eyes of the stakeholder to understand the competitive environment. By doing so, he or she looks at competitors' performance, current and past programmatical strategies, and current and past fund-raising strategies with their strengths and weaknesses. The goal is to understand the competitive advantages of its competitors, allowing the nonprofit organization to be prepared to respond to the future moves of the competition.

Ways to Identify Competition

David A. Aaker, Professor of Marketing, Emeritus at the Haas School of Business, University of California, Berkeley, says there are two ways to identify competitors (and potential competitors):

The first takes the perspective of the customer who must make choices among competitors. The second attempts to group competitors into strategic groups on the basis of their competitive strategy.[5]

For example, a listing of all the international child sponsorship agencies that function similarly could be considered a strategic group, based on their competitive strategy. One could define this group by looking at those who use extensive mail and Internet rental lists as a source of names and income, promote their international work through magazines and network and cable television, and use the "sponsor a child for one month at $X" as their predominant message strategy.

Competitors can also be identified on the basis of their strategy grouping.

How Nonprofit Organizations Compete

Nonprofit groups compete with each other in roughly four areas: programmatical or technical superiority, quality of programs or products, superior support services, and taking advantage of market trends.

Programmatical or Technical Superiority

In for-profit organizations, research and development (R&D) activities often provide the basis for competitive advantage. Is technical superiority an advantage nonprofit organizations can use? The answer is clearly "yes," especially if the nonprofit organization engages in constant meaningful innovation.

The answer is clear from the camp case study. After years of consistently developing and improving the right programming mix, the fact that the camp's programs really work gives it a competitive advantage. The assumption that "we've got the program right where we want it" is never uttered by Ron and his team; there is a continuing commitment to produce the right innovations and to examine every activity of the camp to identify whether it contributes to the core mission. In other words, continually checking each activity against the core mission is essential. In fact, in any given programming cycle fully 20 percent of the programs are new and under heavy evaluation. If new programs do not advance the organization toward its goal, they're discarded and the staff looks for new options.

Quality of Programs or Causal Products

For a nonprofit organization, quality of programs, staff, and causal products do not simply fall into place. It takes effort to be perceived as reliable. To be perceived as such the organization must possess true quality. But what is true "quality?" Consider the following case studies.

The City Mission

The Mission first created men's housing. Then came a pronounced need to create women's housing as well. Now it has created family housing. Women who came to the Mission often had children in tow, so there was a need to create a different style of housing with larger rooms, play areas, counseling areas, and small classrooms. Now, given the economic climate, entire families are looking for shelter. While single men and women do not need the space that families need, new space is being created not only to accommodate the families but to provide job counseling rooms, on-the-job training areas, and upgraded educational classrooms for those finishing high school. Far from looking like many city missions, the Mission has given forethought to the outside appearances of the building and ''its subsequent welcome-ability.''

Selling a Small Organization's Services

A St. Louis nonprofit organization attacked the issue of communicating quality in a unique way. Being a small halfway house, it could not compete financially with the larger organizations in St. Louis that were offering similar programs. However, in an analysis of the competition and the similar services being offered, the marketing director felt his organization had a distinct programmatical advantage and could differentiate itself by saying to potential clients, "We have been in the treatment business a lot longer than anyone else," hence implying that the organization had more experience and a higher degree of success with its patients. The firm used its small size

(continued)

(continued)

as another selling point: "Since we're not part of a big hospital or organization, we can offer more personalized service." The goal of both of these "sales tactics" is to seem more humane and appear to offer a higher-quality service. By identifying the elements that were a part of truly quality programs, they began to sell themselves. Simply provided descriptions—using brochures, marketing pieces, referrals and emails sent via the Internet and word-of-mouth—resulted in strong growth and a unique market position differentiated from competitors.

Better Support Services

An organization cannot tolerate bad services anywhere. This must be a fundamental guiding principle. The expectation of "good" services is considered a "given" by stakeholders. Some organizations have worried that by growing they will have to sacrifice good services. Nothing could be further from the truth. Though products and programs are easier initially to measure than services, an agency's services say more about a nonprofit organization's ability and quality than do its programs. Simple items (e.g., quick receipt turnaround, a strong social media program, a web site that constantly improves, answering complaints and inquiries quickly, returning calls to stakeholders, and processing paperwork accurately) all speak volumes about an organization.

Taking Advantage of Market Trends

Faith Popcorn, along with Lys Marigold, suggested in their book *Clicking* that fads were about products but trends could not be created or changed, only observed. Many nonprofit institutions routinely build their marketing strategies on fads as opposed to tactics that might be necessitated by the marketplace or are inherent core competencies that provide advantages over competitors because they lack the same capacities. A case in point: it could be argued that because a web site(s) and social marketing relate to organizational fund raising, nonprofit institutions are better off using them than not. Their absence could be construed as marketplace negatives when stakeholders evaluate the organization. However, many nonprofits are spending thousands of dollars on web sites and becoming involved in social media, looking for immediate new traffic, new donors, and new dollars. Not thinking of how to maximize value over time through meaningful dialog and individualized service, these nonprofit agencies are looking for "easy, quick, and simple." Attracted by "what might be" and with a sense of a nonprofit "cultural bandwagon" effect, many institutions are spending while maintaining unrealistic marketplace expectations. Alternatively, they are dressing their web sites as old-style advertisements in new technology clothes.

In either case, rather than bringing people together they are bringing predigested information to people, hoping that technology will be the new success factor they had hoped for. Deciding not to wait to see the best strategies given the new technology, they have neither the skills nor the competencies needed to compete in the market.

Chapter 5 continues the discussion about competitive advantage by showing how to look inside one's organization.

Summary

Research of all types is valuable only if what is discovered delivers solutions and answers to issues donors, customers, and volunteers are facing. By taking this "outside in" approach in discovering the needs and values of stakeholders first, a nonprofit organization can compete at a higher level by working in the areas most important to its constituency.

CHAPTER 5

Researching Your Nonprofit Organization's Environment

The nonprofit world is less a world than a universe – vast, varied, and unexplored.
> Fred Setterberg and Kary Schulman, *Beyond Profit*
> (New York: Harper and Row, 1985), p. 2

There isn't enough money, manpower, or sympathy to go around.
> Dr. Tatsuo Hayashi, Japan International
> Volunteer Center in Tokyo

Stop racing after every new fad and focus on making consistent, emotional connections with consumers. If you stand for nothing, you fall for everything.
> Kevin Roberts, *Lovemarks: The Future Beyond Brands*
> (New York: Powerhouse Books, 2005), p. 36

On an average day you and I can expect to have contact with about 1,500 trademarked products. If we happen to go to a large supermarket the number may be as high as 35,000. How does anyone pay attention to so many products? The same thing could be asked about the nonprofit world: How can anyone pay attention to the many needs and causes that present themselves? The answer, of course, is that we don't pay attention to every need and cause, especially those that present themselves in a way we perceive as being worn-out and unimaginative. In today's hypercompetitive world, many agencies don't seem to understand what stakeholders need and want in the way of brand value and causal information. Their communication seems driven overtly by formulas (you can guess when the fall phone call will come, when the invitations to the event will be received, when the emergency mailing will arrive). What must an agency do to meaningfully connect with those who might be persuaded to be involved with its mission?

The Nature of a Nonprofit Organization's Environment

As part of a nonprofit agency's ongoing external analysis, it should not just look specifically at clients, volunteers, customers, and donors; it should also assess the larger competitive boundaries of the philanthropic community it is a part of, as well as the surrounding environment. When a for-profit company is interested in entering an industry, it performs an analysis of the industry as well as an analysis of the surrounding environment. The primary objective of the analysis is to determine the attractiveness of the industry to current and potential participants. The attractiveness potential is measured by the projected short- or long-term returns on investment that will be provided by the industry.

Other ingredients make up the "attractiveness" of the industry, including the number and quality of competitors, their strengths and weaknesses, and those distinctive competencies the company in question must have in place to succeed in its particular industry—what California Professor of Marketing Strategy David Aaker calls "success factors."[1]

The company spends considerable amounts of energy and time scanning the potential environment. This chapter shows why the same rationale needs to be applied to the environment surrounding any nonprofit organization.

Profit is *the* critical measuring stick over time in the for-profit world. A nonprofit agency, however, must measure a number of different "bottom lines" to assess its performance in the nonprofit world; it does not usually have the luxury of using one focused barometer to judge performance by. Rather, nonprofits "deal with balance, synthesis, a combination of bottom lines for performance."[2]

Peter Drucker reminds nonprofit marketers how the nonprofit world differs from the for-profit world:

Non-profit organizations have no 'bottom line.' They are prone to consider everything they do to be righteous and moral and to serve a cause, so they are not willing to say, it doesn't produce results then maybe we should direct our resources elsewhere. Non-profit organizations need the discipline of organized abandonment perhaps even more than a business does. They need to face up to critical choices.[3]

How will looking at the philanthropic community a nonprofit organization is a part of—as well as at the environment surrounding both the agency and its contributing constituencies—help in developing a marketing and competitive strategy? How does nonprofit management make the "critical choices" Peter Drucker talks about? The answer is to start by looking at the philanthropic community a nonprofit is a part of, a community that typically arrives at its marketing strategy and competitive positions largely because it works by accident.

External Analysis, Competitors, and a Nonprofit's Environment

Most nonprofit organizations live in a highly competitive environment. When an organization's managers undertake all that is involved in an external analysis, they usually confront other nonprofit organizations that are also part of their environment, have similar causal offerings (often to the same audience), and therefore function as competitors. (Competitors in the nonprofit world are organizations that offer program substitutes or the same value fulfillment to the stakeholders in question.)

A nonprofit organization and its competitors are sometimes spoken of as constituting a causal industry. Though it seems strange to speak of nonprofit organizations as constituting an "industry," this enables us to look at nonprofit agencies that compete in the same and adjacent field(s) and cause(s). The nature of the industry a nonprofit institution is part of depends on context. The definition of "industry" depends to a large measure on how a cause competes—is it competing with like-minded firms in the context of a city or state, nationally, or internationally? A nonprofit organization competing with other nonprofit organizations in the same city, all undertaking like-minded causes, usually has a much more volatile competitive situation than one whose nearest competitor is 500 miles away.

Today, nonprofit directors must begin to think in terms that have historically been outside of their normal circumstances. For example suppose you are interested in developing an international micro-finance agency. What critical dimensions would you look at to get a sense of the micro-finance field? The following questions serve as a starting point for gathering the necessary data to facilitate your decision:

1. What is the actual size of the micro-finance field and the philanthropic environment, including the potential donor universe and the number of organizations in this causal field that would function as competitors?
2. How does this environment structure itself—do competing organizations work together, or do they work separately? Should the organization be based in the United States, or should it be based internationally? Are there particular countries in which an organization such as this should not work?
3. How do micro-finance agencies obtain information if they intend to enter this causal field?
4. How does the micro-finance environment price out its services to those it helps (as well as the dollar amount it tries to raise for those services) from its supporting constituency?
5. How do micro-finance organizations ensure that the gifts they solicit and the help they provide reach those in need?
6. What are the economic or geopolitical trends that are occurring in the micro-finance field?
7. What is the potential for growth in the micro-finance community?

Each of these seven questions and a nonprofit organization's response to them will influence its marketing and competitive stance vis-à-vis other micro-finance organizations. The implications of these questions and the ultimate bearing they have on the micro-finance example and its competitive stance are discussed more fully in the following text.

The Actual and Potential Size of the Competitive Environment

The principal reason to look at the size of the competitive environment (or causal industry) is to determine how much a nonprofit will have to spend to gain a portion or share of the market for the cause it represents (in this case, micro-finance). This market share includes both those who could support the organization's mission financially as well as those the organization could care for and help. The larger the potential donor pool, the broader the philanthropic nature of the cause or appeal, or the greater the population an organization could care for, the better a nonprofit organization's chances are for success in entering a new market. However, the more narrowly focused the appeal or mission, the smaller the potential donor pool (especially one crowded with many competitors), the harder it is for the same nonprofit to be successful.

In the nonprofit world, the type of marketing and tactical information being described can be hard to come by. However, actual industry size is often available from trade associations, government or chamber of commerce publications, the financial reports of competing organizations, published financial sources, and even from donors themselves.

Continuing with the micro-finance example, the primary interest in looking at all micro-finance organizations (or the "micro-finance industry") is to determine the size of the competition, where it is located, how firmly entrenched (or loyal) donors are to particular organizations, and whether the potential micro-finance nonprofit has enough money to attract a large enough donor supply to accomplish the core goals of the organization.

Identifying User Groups

As part of this evaluation, the organization's management must also determine the potential market and how much of it is available and is not being tapped by other micro-finance organizations. This gap in a competitor's strategy—or "usage gap" as it is sometimes called—is more fully explained in the following case study:

Similar logic can be used by nonprofit agencies in analyzing the potential opportunities in entering a new industry. For example,

- Can a nonprofit organization (such as the suggested micro-finance example) find donors for its cause, or can it increase the rate or size of donations given by existing donors to the entire micro-finance industry?

Boosting Church Attendance

In a study done for a particular religious denomination in the Midwest, in certain cities it was found that attendance for denominational church services was often one-half that of other denominational churches in the same town. Clearly, church attendance for the denomination potentially could be increased by tapping into the usage gap, appealing to those either not attending church or those unsatisfied with their current church experience by

- Encouraging a greater variety of services covering a broader range of topics.
- Finding new church members by mounting a church membership campaign through various media.
- Finding new ways to reach into the community through job resource fairs, providing meals for those in need, and day-care assistance.
- Increasing the attendance of people nominally aware of the existing church services through targeted mail, neighborhood gatherings, and the like.

People might be encouraged to attend a particular denominational church if they saw it addressing a wide variety of issues and being more central to their everyday lives.

- Can the new micro-finance nonprofit agency deliver its services, products, opportunities for volunteerism, or solicitation strategies in a better way than the competition?
- Are there new ways to introduce the micro-finance cause, or are there products or variations in the way the cause is being presented to the public currently being ignored by the competition?
- Are there competitive gaps that the proposed micro-finance organization can take advantage of, whether they are gaps in the messages being communicated to the public, audiences being ignored in the marketing process, media being ignored in the marketing process, and so forth?

How Is the Environment Structured?

The ultimate goal in looking at how a causal environment or industry structures itself is to determine whether there is a sustainable competitive advantage for the entering organization. Without this advantage, any nonprofit organization entering a new market merely becomes like all the others already in the market and loses any niche it might occupy. Using the micro-finance example, the organization's management team gains an understanding of industry structure by analyzing itself along several dimensions.

An analysis of past and current marketing, operational strategies and mission objectives helps determine a nonprofit agency's stability and marketplace intentions. By looking at size and growth indicators of similar nonprofit organizations, management can begin to see how important these measures might be to the overall success of the agency's mission. An organization's culture can give a clue to constraints and potential audiences that may be attracted to the organization. Perceived accumulated costs can give a clue as to future service costs and fund-raising requirements.

Such information can be derived from annual reports made available by nonprofit organizations in the same or similar industry, talking directly to marketing or development officers of the nonprofit organizations, talking to their donors when known, and attending competitor events. The goal in this analysis is to give the public something that is not already being provided in a way that matches their existing values. Paying close attention to potential competitors' strategies and services is the best way to identify a gap in service that is not currently being filled.

Michael Porter in his book *Competitive Strategy* talks about for-profit industries structuring themselves along five basic components: competitors, potential competitors, substitute products, customers, and suppliers.[4] Porter's thesis is that each of these components has a role in helping determine how intense competition is within a particular industry.

Competitors

Ownership of the right information is often more important to a nonprofit organization entering a new field for the first time than any other resource. If an economic environment contains many competitors, increased competition among these organizations for both the philanthropic dollar and actual services provided might be expected. The nonprofit organization that is "new" to a causal field can usually expect vigorous and highly committed competitors, willing to spend money to retain their donors and other interests. A new organization can expect competitors to increase their donor services, to add new twists to existing client programs, and to tell their story to new publics through intense advertising and fundraising campaigns. Close scrutiny of possible competitors should give a nonprofit agency entering a new field a "heads up" about these possible responses.

Most likely, these competitors are also appealing for gifts or similar monthly sponsorship amounts from donors; the requested donations might be for similar amounts because of the high fixed costs the organization might have in setting up international sponsorship systems and because of a similarity of marketing styles. Volunteers might also be drawn from similar groups or pools. In addition, the individuals being helped might be from the same parts of the world or channeled through similar organizations.

Therefore, an organization entering a new field needs to ensure it has sufficient resources to mount a vigorous promotional and donor recruitment campaign and to actually get help to those it is trying to serve. If an organization cannot provide service to a group that it should truly be able to help, to reach, to fund, and to sustain, should it really be entering this industry?

Potential Competitors

In deciding to enter a causal field of service, an organization needs to look at competitors that also have the capability to enter the field successfully. What would it take for an organization to enter the micro-finance field? Most likely, it would require a combination of the following elements:

- A very strong capital investment.
- The ability to attract a large number of donors quickly.
- The ability to set up an international lending system or to work in tandem with an existing system.
- The ability to differentiate the nonprofit from other micro-finance organizations.

In addition, a new organization would have to ask whether the climate was right for new competitors to come into the field. Prevailing market factors (e.g., slow growth or a stagnant economy) may have already eliminated some of the attractiveness of entering this field?

Substitute Causes, Services, or Products

Substitute causes, services, and products provide potential clients, donors, volunteers, and customers with new kinds of value fulfillment. Normally, a substitute cause or product competes less intensely than the primary cause, service, or product but still influences the marketplace and stakeholder. The more attractive and abundant the substitutes are, the harder it is for a nonprofit new to the field to compete successfully in that field.

Using our micro-finance example, there are many forms of financial lending used by organizations. Some of these groups are international in their reach, some are tied to a particular country, and some micro-finance nonprofits are domestic, not international, in scope. Regardless of operational style, each substitute competitor poses a potential challenge to a nonprofit organization's efforts at entering a field by offering stakeholders a choice.

Just as electronic alarm systems are available as substitutes for security guards, a local micro-finance initiative could represent a substitute for a donor considering an international organizational option. A community foundation or church initiative aimed at helping local businesses could also be presented as a substitute. A city's vocational training agency might also attract potential clients. All of these organizations deal with a particular aspect of the problem that micro-financing tries to solve, and they all offer individual donors the benefit of either helping individuals currently in need or helping those who may need help in the future.

Clients and Customers

In a for-profit corporation, the presence or absence of clients and customers usually guides a company's actions. The situation is different in the nonprofit world, although the differences between for-profit and nonprofit continue to narrow. Because clients in the nonprofit world often receive services for free or at a greatly reduced price, they are not as quick to complain about their quality and are more likely to forgive or keep quiet about poor services. As a consequence, this most critical indicator of an organization's performance—its services offered—is often not an accurate barometer of performance. How do we measure the level of service provided?

Some of this forgiving attitude on the part of clients and constituents is changing, especially as other free options become available. Houses of worship are a logical example. Today they face consumers, customers, and members who demand different services, mandating different levels of quality, and who display a willingness to shop church sites on the web the way one would shop car dealerships. This makes almost any church audience a powerful consumer group because they can demand many things of the site's administration by virtue of their corporate voice and economic power.

The parish staff must continually tap into general customer "feelings" about the style and tone of services provided. Here are some suggested tactics:

1. Continually poll the membership to determine the needs of the congregation, and try to tailor services to fill those needs.
2. Monitor the "competition" to see what other churches are offering their constituents.
3. Former attendees should be questioned as to their satisfaction (or lack of it) with the services, perhaps online or through an exit interview or mail-in questionnaire.
4. Clients and former attendees should be encouraged to vent their feelings and offer suggestions on a regular basis.

Suppliers

Rather than thinking of suppliers in the traditional form as in for-profit organizations, in this case "suppliers" refers to the impact of the donating constituency who supply the needed resources to the sponsorship industry. Of critical importance in the micro-financing example is the question, Can there be enough donors to fund all the micro- finance organizations looking for help, or will donors be concentrated into smaller groups supporting a few well-known agencies?

An additional key question is, Will donors stay loyal to the organization or will they quickly change their financial support to another substitute organization working in a more attractive—or sensational—part of the world?

The following sections present five ways in which an organization's marketing staff can tap into the feelings and possible projected donations of competitors.

How Nonprofit Organizations Enter an Industry

It is relatively easy for a nonprofit organization to enter almost any causal field such as the micro-finance field. In fact, it is much easier for a nonprofit agency to enter almost any field than it is for a for-profit company to enter an industry it is interested in. Why is this? Usually two variables must be considered and answered before a for-profit company enters an industry—the start-up costs involved and the competitors it might face once it has entered the field. These two factors, however, are usually not as burdensome in the non-profit world.

Unfortunately, most nonprofit organizations look at very few indicators when they evaluate the appropriateness of entering a causal field. If they do any research in the causal environment or industry, they primarily focus on potential and real competitors, differences in marketing and fundraising appeals between groups, the similarity of organizational functions and programs in relationship to competitors, and the real or potential donor pool.

There Is No Direction without an Analysis

This lack of rigorous analysis before moving into a new field of service may be an error in judgment, because the simple reality is that *most nonprofit causes have a large number of competitors.* The more competitors, the greater the competitive forces at work and the more important an organization's marketing strategy becomes. However, unlike the situation of many for-profit industries, the presence of many competitors does not usually prevent a nonprofit firm from entering a causal field. Perhaps this is because so few nonprofits use the marketing concept or employ marketing parameters in making any decision of this type. The term *marketing concept* refers to the total orientation of a firm's resources devoted to satisfying the needs of donors, customers, and clients; it implies the presence of a single marketing executive who integrates all marketing functions and the presence of such staff functions as marketing research and product planning, with all departments contributing to increase profitable volume. Exhibit 5.1 shows how the resources of a nonprofit firm are used to satisfy the needs of various audiences, allowing each to contribute something of value.

Exhibit 5.1   The Marketing Concept

Firm's Resources	Satisfy the needs of	Allow the exchange
Funds	Donors	To give
Volunteers	Volunteer	To help
Faculty	Clients	To use services
Literature	Customers	To buy products
Mission	All	To measure progress

The major problem plaguing many nonprofit organizations is the failure to embrace a marketing orientation in what has become a marketing-driven environment. Let's take a look at how nonprofit organizations decide to enter a field of service, since most nonprofit organizations view entry into a particular environment from different perspectives.

Service or Ministry Needs Are Not Everything

Many nonprofit organizations make the decision to enter a field of service based exclusively on a perceived or imaginary need for their services. This "need" usually is determined by

- Inferential data from the marketplace (often in the form of encouragement from current recipients of the organization's services).
- Entrepreneurial "hunches" on the part of the organization's director, program director, or board that the organization should move in a certain direction.
- A "follow the leader" strategy in which the organization imitates another nonprofit organization's actions.
- Compassionate determination to address an existing societal need.
- Strong suggestions by the nonprofit organization's influential donors, who promise financial support if the organization enters the field.

In only a few cases that I have witnessed has a systematic look at the surrounding community taken place. In a great majority of these cases, the decision to enter a field of service is not predicated on an industry evaluation or up-to-date market research. Subsequent concerns about the philanthropic environment's structure, such as the realistic size of the donor pool and real or potential competition, were not systematically considered. Yet a systematic look is the key to the successful launching and subsequent viability of a new service or nonprofit product.

You Must Know What Your Organization's Competitors Are Doing

Some environments seem strategically more important than others, as measured by the amount of competition in them. For example, the child care sponsorship world is a competitive field. The microfinance field is becoming a competitive field. One would expect, given a high number of competitors in any field of service, that the competition would be more intense.

Issues that inhibit a for-profit firm from entering an industry include the concomitant high fixed costs entering (the amount of money a company will have to spend to compete effectively) and the cost to the competitors of leaving the industry (exit costs). Such costs should be considered in a nonprofit organization's decision to enter a field, but typically they are not.

Nonprofit organizations enter virtually any field of service they choose with little of the concern exhibited by for-profit firms. One reason may be the nonprofits' perception of capital investment; the investment required (or perceived to be required) is often not a major concern for an institution. Agencies seldom enter a field having decided to spend the dollars needed to do a comprehensive job in the respective field. Instead, the average nonprofit is often more interested in the public relations benefit of being able to say to its constituency that it is at work in a certain field, along with the personal satisfaction that comes with this, as opposed to the ability to do a superior job within the field as an overriding management concern. This is not as much a deliberate move as it is a journey into unfamiliar territory.

Similarly, where economies of scale are important in major industries, the issue of obtaining large volumes of business, sales, or service is usually not given the same weight within a nonprofit agency (though they should be considered). Other issues such as service differentiation or brand strength are seldom given much thought. In an industry where benchmarks or performance are not usually built into the decision-making apparatus, it often becomes more important to a nonprofit organization to be perceived as being involved in a cause than it is to excel or achieve outstanding results in the same cause. For example, in the micro-finance field it may be that the costs of delivering help of this kind require the non-profit entity to consider serving in countries where a microfinance industry and culture are already present, thereby realizing significant public relations advantages, as opposed to entering countries where the organization might feel it had to "go it alone."

Some agencies may count on the fact that donors, clients, and constituents typically are relatively uniformed with regard to the performance values of a nonprofit organization. Unlike a normal board of directors or governing body of a for-profit company, the informal board of directors of a nonprofit agency often has little interest in making the organization accountable for its viability.

How Does the Nonprofit Organization Deliver Its Services?

It is important to anticipate and cope with changes. For example, I work with an organization that builds medical clinics in Haiti. At the time of this writing, many of the organization's services and operations have been disrupted and workers killed as a result of the Haitian earthquake of 2010. Fortunately, this organization has set up channels of operation in and delivery of services from other countries and is transferring operations to help in this disaster area.

There are at least four concerns for a nonprofit organization to address in delivering its services:

- Are there inherent political or environmental problems in the channels a nonprofit uses to distribute its services?
- Are alternative channels available?
- Do trends indicate that a nonprofit could deliver services better using a different method?
- Who are the critical gatekeepers of the delivery channels or the people who influence service delivery?

David Aaker calls "access to an effective and efficient distribution channel" one of the "key success factors."[5] A nonprofit typically deals with many channels simultaneously, both in delivering services and in raising dollars. Alternative channels exist, and some nonprofit organizations sell their wares (or raise their funds) by going directly to the potential donor, often through Internet, direct mail, and face-to-face solicitation. Others use middlemen such as service organizations and churches to attract clients to achieve their distribution or funding goals. Still others count on giant nonprofit retailers such as United Way to cover the bulk of their budgets. Some larger nonprofits try to do all these things in varying degrees.

This analysis of emerging changes in distribution or funding channels can be enormously important in understanding the success factors of the causal environment. For example, for some city missions that have particular theological points of view, 20 to 40 percent of their funding dollars comes from constituencies that are either unchurched or unaffiliated with the theological stance of the mission. Research indicates that many of these new, nontraditional donors to city missions give regardless of color or creed, because the missions provide benefits to those forced onto the street as a result of circumstances. This concern exhibited by those who provide funding overrides the differences in theological stance some donors may have with the missions. A critical question in light of these new constituents is, Shouldn't the presence of a new constituency force city mission marketers to look at how they communicate with their new donor audiences?

A new audience can force new decisions about channels. The emergence of nonprofit institutions competing with for-profit agencies in the field of day care, health care, and other concerns forces nonprofit management to know who controls the decision making in certain funding channels, how services are chosen, and how this may change in the future. The presence of Internet-only donors should compel an agency to look at its communication plan and provide suitable adjustments.

What Are the Trends in the Environment?

As a nonprofit marketer, you must learn to understand and appreciate the trends occurring in your organization's environment, and you must act on that information. Without doing so you, may settle for prevailing theories of competition and strategy that may not explain the environmental effects your organization finds itself a part of. A correct analysis of trends is essential to achieving a sustainable competitive advantage for any agency. Without it, your cause and its resulting services may lack necessary differentiation and become a "commodity" that mirrors other agencies and their services.

What economic, environmental, or geopolitical trends are suggesting new growth directions or change for the future of your nonprofit and its causal environment? One trend may be the new-found legitimacy of the nonprofit sector and its growth rate during the past 15 years. Another trend is the phenomenon of nonprofit agencies partnering and sometimes merging with other nonprofit agencies to benefit more individuals through their work while fighting the financial pressures many find themselves dealing with. Still another trend is the emergence of social media as an important communication and solicitation tool in times of emergencies—witness the oversaturation experienced by U.S. stakeholders, many of whom receive thousands of marketing messages a day. Although there are no hard and fast rules for analyzing one's environment, consider using the following questions as you evaluate your environmental space:

- What technology trends are affecting your organization? For example, if you are operating a camp for young adults in junior and high school, you need to be well versed in social media.
- Are there demographic trends affecting your work? For example, a number of mission agencies have aging donor bases, and many are not successfully replacing them with younger donors.
- How are economic trends affecting your donor and client base? Has your strategy changed to compensate?
- What significant threats and opportunities is your organization facing?

It could be disastrous for a nonprofit organization to enter a new causal industry without taking a look at current trends. For example, consider the men and women I talked to who wanted to build a horse camp in Colorado for young people. This sounded like a good idea until they found out that Colorado has more camps per capita than any other state in the nation and many of them are not operating to capacity. These facts alone should have a bearing on the proposed camp's competitive stance, its strategy, and its potential for success.

What Is the Potential for Growth?

There should be a direct correlation between the potential for growth in a particular causal industry and the attractiveness of that industry to the nonprofit organizations considering entering it. The potential for growth usually indicates greater opportunity for a company. Today many nonprofits are seeing the upper plateau of their client and financial growth curves. Their ability to grow translates to their ability to continue and to expand the causal services they exist for; lack of growth leads to curtailment of services and less success in raising money.

To answer questions regarding the future, a nonprofit agency must know whom it is currently attracting to buy its products or support its cause. By answering this question a nonprofit agency can begin to address how its client services and causal products are being perceived and being compared with those of its competitors. (See Exhibit 5.2.) Given an accurate knowledge of client, donor, and customer perceptions, a nonprofit cause can determine where there are gaps in the competitive strategies it is using within in its causal environment. This type of perceptual mapping allows the nonprofit marketer to look at market niches not occupied by the competition and gives an organization the opportunity to create new products or causal thrusts to fill these voids. An example of mapping is shown in Exhibit 5.3.

Often used in tandem with perceptual mapping is another growth strategy—repositioning the existing client services or causal products to enhance growth, sales, or donations and extend the

Exhibit 5.2   Who Supports Your Organization and Why

Monthly partners	They like the cause and have budgeted an amount to spend on a monthly basis. They don't need to be resold on the program's importance but only reminded on a regular basis that what they are doing is important.
Major donors	They give for ``strategic'' reasons. They also are attracted by who else is giving to the agency. They like to interact on a regular basis with the chief executive officer of the agency and some influential members of the board.
Small, infrequent donors	They give primarily for emotional reasons and in response to an appeal that they can identify with.

Exhibit 5.3   Perceptual Map of Industry and Competitors

Which Organizations Receive Support (using monthly child sponsorship as an example)

Organization A	Organization A is the oldest child care organization in the field and has the largest number of sponsored children throughout the world.
Organization B	Organization B is half the age of Organization A and is not well known. However, Organization B has decided to center its operation on only three continents, therefore not offering as large a choice for constituents as Organization A.
Organization C	Organization C imitates almost everything that Organization A does, including how it operates organizationally and how it conducts its sponsorship campaigns.
Emergency Intervention as a Primary Appeal	
Organization D	Organization D is specifically geared to work in highly visible troubled areas of the world. It establishes a network of operations and then begins to slowly transfer the operations to local governmental agencies.
Combination of Monthly Sponsorship and Emergency Appeals	
Organization E	Organization E undertakes both disaster and famine relief and engages in child care sponsorship as its core mission.
Organization F	Organization F is similar in nature to Organization E except that it draws its financial support primarily from one denomination, though the organization is not denominationally specific as to whom it works with.
Hard to Determine	
Organization G	Organization G seems to have entered the child care business more for its marketing potential to the organization as a donor acquisition device than for its missional qualities.

nonprofit's life. For example, Arm & Hammer baking soda repositioned its product for the swimming pool market; while still promoting the traditional applications of baking soda, the company repositioned the product as a remedy for eyes that have been exposed to chlorine. Using marketing research, the Girl Scouts of America saw growing numbers of "latchkey kids" and created the Daisy Scouts, a program for preschoolers.

Relating Product Life Cycles to a Nonprofit's Growth Potential

Knowing one's audience and positioning a nonprofit organization for the future are both a part of the same issue—the product life cycle for a nonprofit's client services and causal products. For years for-profit companies have talked about life cycles as they relate to their products. It is a useful discussion, because it is folly for marketing, fundraising, and nonprofit management practitioners to assume a never-ending supply of money and interest in the services, products, and causes they are promoting.

There are four generally recognized stages of development that a for-profit or nonprofit product or cause goes through. Stage 1 is market development, when a cause or product is brought to market before there is a proven demand for it. Stage 2 is the market growth stage, where demand for what the nonprofit is doing increases and the market as a whole tends to grow. Stage 3 is market maturity, where there are a number of competitors in the causal environment and product area concerned and demand begins to level off. Stage 4 is market decline, with the cause or product beginning to lose appeal for the client, donor, or consumer.

How do these four stages pertain to the nonprofit world? The question is important, because there is little discussion of life cycle theory relating to a nonprofit's causal product planning in the nonprofit marketing literature. Perhaps a nonprofit organization's service and economic viability in a causal market would be improved if the organization would project the life cycle profile of its proposed services and products. To consider such a scenario early on could guard against inappropriate causal market entry choices and enable a nonprofit to make wise potential competitive moves in advance of market entry.

> *Stage 1—Market development.* The most critical nonprofit issue in market development is the recognition that demand often has to be "created" for the cause being promoted and sold. This creation of interest has a lot to do with (a) how a causal product or service offering fits with the potential client and donor constituency, (b) the equity (or good will) associated with the nonprofit's previous performance in the client's and donors' eyes, and (c) the availability of substitute causes

for the potential client and donor constituency to be involved with that provide the same psycho-emotional rewards.

Most for-profit companies spend millions of dollars and hundreds of work hours trying to orchestrate new product programs that fit with their consumers. Most new products simply don't make it. According to Theodore Levitt,

> *The fact is that most new products don't have any sort of classical life-cycle curve at all. They have instead from the very outset an infinitely descending curve. The product not only doesn't get off the ground; but also it goes quickly underground—6 feet under.*
>
> *It is little wonder, therefore, that some disillusioned and badly burned companies have recently adopted a more conservative policy—what I call the "used-apple policy." Instead of aspiring to be the first company to see and seize an opportunity, they systematically avoid being first. They let others take the first bite of the supposedly juicy apple that tantalizes them. They let others do the pioneering. If the idea works, they quickly follow suit. They say in effect, "We don't have to get the first bite of the apple. The second one is good enough."*[6]

Stage 2—Growth. During the growth stage a nonprofit jumps into a causal environment or market, using Levitt's "used apple policy," to try to persuade the client, donor, or consumer to prefer its particular type of causal service or product, as opposed to building demand for the services and products as is usually the case in Stage 1. As clients, donors, and consumers accelerate their acceptance level, the number of competitors increases. This "feeding frenzy" can give the appearance of much more client and donor acceptance than is actually present, thereby luring even more nonprofit companies into the mix. A prime example of this behavior occurs when the national media pick up on a particular tragedy or famine. The number of nonprofits claiming to help those in distress increases in proportion to the perception of donor acceptance and interest in the crisis.

Stage 3—Maturity. The presence of many competitors often leads to market saturation and intense competition. Usually this competition centers on the promoted cost of providing the new service to the donating or purchasing constituency; the existing services that are actually provided to the clients, donors, and customers; and other promotional practices aimed at establishing a company, name, or brand preference. In this stage there are usually intense attempts to acquire new audiences, to explore new ways of coming face-to-face with the donating audiences, and to create differentiation from the competition, often using only marginal differences to appeal to distinctive markets.

Stage 4—Market decline. Market decline is often a result of over-saturation of competition, client dissatisfaction with the level of services provided, donor or customer boredom with the cause, or some nonprofits leaving the causal environment because of their inability to maintain adequate donor acquisition levels or income-to-expense margins. During the stage, the delivery of services falls to just a few nonprofits.

Differentiating a Nonprofit Based on External Analysis

Having discussed how nonprofit agencies make decisions to enter a field of service, we now see how they can differentiate themselves from each other within a given causal field or environment once they have entered it.

Because the concept of strategy is an abstract one, not only is there room for interpretation but there are many definitions of strategy at work in the marketplace. However it is defined in your organization, the definition should include at least two issues: (1) how you deal with the resources you have inside and outside your organization and (2) how you deal with competitors and rivals in the marketplace. The strategy chosen will inherently involve the organizations that can be considered competitors. Some competitors will be direct, running programs similar to yours, working with similar audiences, and trying to effect similar change. Other competitors will be indirect—for example, summer school is an indirect competitor to summer camps.

Dealing with competitors is where the concept of differentiation fits in. The resources you have in your organization and the activities and programs you engage in theoretically enable you to look different from others in ways that matter to your core constituents. If you didn't, there would be no need for your organization. You would be a commodity just like everyone else. Running programs that are different and unique as well as running programs that others are running but doing so in a different way allows you to compete successfully.

As I have suggested, not all programs, taken at face value, appear to be different. The less differentiation your programs have from those that they compete with, the less stakeholder loyalty your organization will experience. Nonprofit institutions with similar causes typically distinguish themselves from others through one—or combinations of—the following:

- The degree to which they specialize in their cause, their product line, or the audience segment they work with
- The degree to which they try to impress their name and their purpose on a given market through advertising, sales force, and fundraising field reps
- The way they try to accomplish their core mission, either working through a middleman such as a church or service group or going directly to the consumer or donor
- The quality or characteristics of their causal product(s)
- The leadership status they claim in the development and endorsement of their causal products, using phrases such as "new technology" and "cutting edge" programs
- The cost position (usually a low cost) they have in delivering their service to clients
- The donation amount they request on behalf of client services, which is usually but not necessarily tied to their cost position
- The amount of leverage they command—often financial, political, or name recognition
- Their relationship with a parent company and the objectives, resources, and reputation handed down from the parent

The area of specialization of a nonprofit provides "market signals"—or competitive information—to other nonprofit institutions. The market signals can be used to develop a reactive approach by one nonprofit towards another and to develop not just a competitor analysis but a strategy formulation. It is the characterization of these strategies by the nonprofit agencies in question that allows them to be grouped by their specialization.

A curious thing happens when an organization undertakes a group analysis: the individuals undertaking the analysis immediately notice that some nonprofit institutions employ the same client specializations and compete with each other in a similar manner. Others employ different strategies altogether. Jeff McLinden, a vice president of McConkey–Johnston International, Inc., speaks of "specialty or positional mapping" as a way to reposition nonprofits by looking at their market signals. Agencies having trouble gaining significant market share, especially those grouped into similar areas and methods of specialization, can undertake this exercise to arrive at a strategy for the marketplace.

This strategic "look" allows one to view the market as a whole and provides the necessary ability to look at the nonprofit individually as it relates to the whole. It becomes clear in doing this evaluation that there are often significant barriers to competing successfully in a market; they may result from the lack of money the institution can spend to attract an audience, the scarcity of programs the nonprofit can afford to offer, or the presence of a very small potential donor base. Just as these barriers limit what an institution can do, they also serve to protect organizations in the causal environment by keeping other institutions out of the competitive arena.

It is the presence of many competitive groups in a causal environmental analysis that leads to the rivalry and intense competition many in the nonprofit world are experiencing today. There are at least five significant factors that determine how strong the competition may be in the causal group or industry a nonprofit organization finds itself a part of:

1. The amount of overlap that occurs with donors, customers, and in some cases, volunteers.
2. The sameness of the programs being offered and, alternatively, the differences being exhibited by the programs.
3. The number of competitors, their size, their donor universe, and their brand strength.
4. The marketing strategies the groups are using to promote themselves—their similarity and their degree of success.
5. The size of the marketing unit each competitive group has, their experience, and the scope of their activities.

Some nonprofit groups choose to enter a causal environment by announcing their entry through market signals. Two examples from clients show how. The first example regards a college.

- A college engaged in a capital campaign to build a new facility. Early in the campaign, the college announced to the financial community that it was contemplating a building fund initiative. The campus goals and plans were put in the hands of a network of financial and political movers and shakers within the city. In addition, the college made a substantial effort to network with other institutional heads to determine whether the proposed timing of the campaign would put it in competition with other, unannounced campaigns or major fund-raising plans. Similarly, substantial efforts were made through the use of focus groups with donors to help determine the viability of the campaign from their perspective, as well as to assess donor support.
- Each signal was designed to send a different message to a portion of the city's potential donor constituency. Each action or market signal was also taken by the college to provoke a response from other competitive institutions to assess their response, to assess donor response to the announcement, and to let other institutions evaluate their own financial plans, given the college's announcement.

A competitor to the college could have responded to the campaign information in a number of ways. It could have viewed the announcement as a threat to its own programs; as a stimulus to respond to the building program by announcing a bigger, more elaborate building program of its own; or as a gentle prodding for it to ensure its own donors' continued support of the institution given the potential excitement of the campaign. It could choose to advance or delay its own financial initiatives or to determine which key donors in the community had already committed (or could commit financially) to the college's project. Each competitive response depends on the position an institution feels it is in with respect to the college that announced its campaign.

A simpler example of how market signals are used involves a number of nonprofits located in the same city. All are planning fundraising banquets within a similar time frame and all have overlapping constituencies. In past years, the announcement of banquet dates by the respective organizations to their constituencies was made increasingly earlier in the year; invitation committees were recruited almost the week after the year's previous banquet, and advance announcements of banquet locations were made well in advance of the event. All of these actions were taken to move a competitive step ahead with the constituency in question.

The multiplication of these fundraising banquets began as the nonprofit agencies in question developed similar fundraising tactics; now they are trying new marketing tactics with banquets being held in new locations with different causes being promoted. Each new marketing signal is provoking a mirrored response from a competitor.

How a nonprofit competes is the center issue in these scenarios. How it views itself internally and assesses its competitive and strategic capabilities is also an important feature of competitive strategy. Chapter 6 continues this discussion by looking at how a nonprofit can turn each of its operations into a competitive unit by focusing on its own strategy development.

Summary

A nonprofit organization successfully enters a cause-related field by knowing as much about the environment as possible. Then, by discovering both the environment's receptivity to the agency and its ability to differentiate itself from its competitors and attract both existing and new donors, a nonprofit organization can successfully enter a new area of work. In a nonprofit world filled with many good choices, the option of differentiating an agency from others is moot. Factors such as what your external analysis is saying to the organization along with the life cycle stage your programs are in all contribute to a successful marketing strategy.

Competition and Internal Marketing Analysis

At first, increasing information leads to better decisions, but after a while more and more information has less and less effect. There even comes a time when further information makes it difficult to sort out important information from the rest. There is confusion and information overload. Yet, as most data processing departments will confirm, executives faced with difficult decisions simply ask for more and more information in the hope that somehow the new information will do their thinking for them.

Edward de Bono, *Sur/Petition*
(New York: HarperBusiness, 1992), pp. 12–13

Without baiting the question with loaded prefaces, ask assembly workers or managers, "Can you tell me, in your own words, where are we trying to take the company?" Then compare the response with the official version.

Tom Brown, *Industry Week*, May 18, 1992, p. 11

One of the great hurdles in nonprofit marketing is getting from the phase of looking outside the organization to looking inward. Achieving closure on the process of looking at an organization's environment requires taking this external information and constructing internal marketing systems to evaluate and use it. This requires discipline. It also requires that an organization create an internal evaluation system to help determine whether it is ready to deal effectively with the environment it inhabits and to answer the question, Should our existing strategic platforms be modified and altered, replaced, or worked even harder?

Just as it is important to examine a nonprofit organization's external marketing elements, as discussed in Chapter 5, now the nonprofit marketing practitioner's gaze must turn inward to the inner workings of the organization itself to develop a strategic marketing plan. This look at the internal environment must take into account all the important organizational issues that contribute negatively or positively to the organization's marketing strategy. There are many important reasons to undertake this analysis, as we will see in the following section.

Reasons for an Internal Examination

One important reason for this internal examination is the fact that constituents are becoming increasingly sensitized to the need for nonprofit organizations to demonstrate performance and efficiency in both their fund-raising and their overall service operations. Given the influx and years of media-reported cases concerning the misuse of funds, lack of governance, excessive salaries, and the like, these instances—though not prevalent—nevertheless present all nonprofit organizations in a bad light. In addition, these reports send clear signals to agencies that there is a need for excellence and cost-effectiveness in their financial performance along with the satisfaction they provide stakeholders. Excellent performance is also needed in how they handle threats and opportunities that come their way and how they maximize their organizational strengths while minimizing their weaknesses.

There is however, another more important reason for this internal examination. Nonprofit constituencies are changing in their relationships to nonprofit agencies in how they buy, how they give financially and support the institution, and how they purchase nonprofit products. Some of this occurrence comes as a result of the destabilizing nature of the Internet and other forms of social media; similarly, constituents as a group are becoming increasingly sensitive to the need to support only nonprofit institutions that demonstrate increased performance and efficiency in their service offerings and in their marketing and fund-development practices.

Stakeholders are also changing the way(s) they choose to be involved with nonprofit organizations. As a consequence of this stakeholder movement, donor loyalty and retention must become leading concerns for the nonprofit marketer, often taking priority over reducing costs, developing staff, or improving the quality of the organization's service.

At this point in nonprofit agency history, the need for a true marketing and service orientation has never been more apparent than now. For example, rather than pretending to have a marketing culture, as so many agencies do, now is the time for all within nonprofit organizations to be involved in marketing and be vigilant in their desire to provide value to those who are involved with the agency. In the final analysis, it will be only demonstrated donor, volunteer, customer, and client value that will ensure an organization's survival. This means, for example, that departments that have traditionally not been involved in marketing (e.g., accounting) need to begin sending out donor-friendly receipts and to be gracious to donor and customer inquiries on the phone, via mail or the Internet. Human resources departments must learn to hire staff that can actually excel at customer service as well as fight for better pay for employees, and marketing departments must move to thinking and strategizing about how to retain donors and customers for longer periods than ever before in their agency's history.

Nonprofit entities must understand the intelligence of their consumers and must also endeavor to ensure that the services of their nonprofit organization are of extremely high quality. The assumption of "blind allegiance" that so many nonprofit organizations seem to operationalize strategically as it relates to their clients, volunteers, customers, and donors simply is not present in today's market.

Is this retrenchment by constituents merely a sign of the times? Perhaps, though the truth may be that these times are the "new normal." Some studies have shown that many of the wealthy are shifting in how they give money away, often choosing to leverage their funds as opposed to donating them. Other giving groups that traditionally have been the backbone of U.S. philanthropy have been hurt by recent economic downturns, and many have curtailed both the size and the scope of their giving. In harsh economic times, an internal analysis becomes even more important to nonprofit organizations as the necessity to pursue the correct marketing strategy to an agency's various constituencies becomes manifest.

An internal analysis (which goes by many names, including but not limited to *environmental audit, development survey, opportunity analysis,* and *marketing audit*) uses both historical data and performance metrics to arrive at a sense of seasonal fluctuations and operating patterns in an organization's income and service patterns. These are used also to identify historical strengths and weaknesses, institutional efforts to fix these issues, current marketing and communication strategies that are working (or not), as along with financial issues and constraints.

After doing an external audit (the subject of the previous chapter), why do an internal audit? If an external audit looks at markets served, the nature of the client, donor, customer and volunteer matrix, and the competitors and competitive environment an organization wrestles with, an internal organization analysis uncovers the following key issues:

1. The past and current performance of the organization with respect to clients, donors, and customers, their level of satisfaction, brand strength and causal product quality.
2. The strategic problems that need to be faced by the organization and the opportunities that should be taken advantage of.
3. The organization's ability to overcome its weaknesses and its ability to maximize its strengths.
4. The organization's fund-raising and financial performance, its costs and its strategy.
5. The organization's strategic strengths and weaknesses.

Exhibit 6.1 spells out all the key elements in an internal organization analysis in detail.[1]

The first step in the organization's internal analysis is to look at its past and current performance.

Measuring Past and Current Performance

In simple terms, an internal analysis starts with what worked in the past and what didn't. Because an articulated strategy sometimes evolves or turns out differently from what was planned, the goal in this internal examination is to determine whether a nonprofit agency's strategy for its clients, donors, and customers needs

Exhibit 6.1   Checklist of Key Elements in a Nonprofit Organization's Internal Analysis

1. *Past and current performance*:
   A. What type of institution does the organization think it is?
   B. Does the organization have a plan?
   C. Does it measure the plan's performance?
   D. Is the board of directors helpful in this process?
   E. Is the company's location a burden?
   F. Can the organizational culture be described?
2. *Strategic problems*:
   A. What is the organization's image in the marketplace?
   B. What is the organization's history of marketing, especially in the areas of fund raising, donor and customer retention, and acquisition?
   C. How does the organization discover new prospective donors and customers?
   D. Does the organization have a branding strategy?
   E. Does the organization have a social media strategy?
3. *The organization's ability to overcome problems*:
   A. Does the organization have access to
      - Prospects for service, volunteers, and fund-raising?
      - Existing donors, those needing to be upgraded, and former donors who need to be renewed financially?
      - An adequate budget for service and fund raising?
      - Professional service, marketing, and fund-development counsel?
      - A constituent, client, and donor relational service mentality?
4. *Fund-raising, service, product costs, and performance*:
   A. What is in the organization's service portfolio, and what causes, concepts, and services is the organization currently trying to sell to various audiences?
   B. What financial constraints is the organization facing in achieving its goals?
   C. What is the organization's productivity as to
      - Rate of financial return?
      - Average gift size?
      - Average cost per gift?
      - Service success rate?
      - Program cost percentage?
      - Bottom line cost percentage?
      - Lifetime donor value?
   D. Is the administration involved in fund development and how?
      - How much time does the CEO spend in customer and donor relationship management?

(continued)

Exhibit 6.1   (Continued)

- How much time does the marketing director spend in donor and customer relationship management?
    - E. Is there adequate computerization?
5. *Organizational strengths and weaknesses:*
    - A. What are its strengths?
    - B. What are its weaknesses?
    - C. What are its opportunities?
    - D. What are its threats?
    - E. What is its action plans for each of these.

---

adjustment. One of the more difficult aspects of this measurement concerns longer-range plans and strategies, particularly those involving funders, customers, and some client populations. Because most measurements are short term in nature, it is often hard to find indicators that convincingly represent long-term prospects. As part of measuring past and current performance, the focus should be on those competencies and programs that serve as a baseline for future strategic actions.

Most nonprofit institutions discover after awhile that some parts of their work are more heavily supported than others. This discovery allows an organization to review its strategy and determine how much it will spend to promote these areas of work in the future and then to contrast these decisions with its spending objectives in other areas.

Likewise, an internal analysis rests upon the organization's objectives. The implication is that objectives need to be both specific and measurable. Objectives, along with their impact on marketing strategy, are discussed more fully in Chapter 9, which looks at different types of objectives, how they relate to a nonprofit organization's marketing strategy, and where they fit in the overall marketing structure. Suffice it to say the pursuit of objectives allows an organization to more readily and ethically attract sufficient resources and, having done this, take these resources and create the programs, products, and services the awaiting public desires and expects. In addition, objectives provide a measuring stick of sorts, allowing a nonprofit organization to measure its progress toward its goals.

Unfortunately, most nonprofit agencies do not have stakeholder satisfaction and brand loyalty on their list of current objectives. Because the presence of donated dollars is a more readily available measuring stick, objectives such as these often dominate planning efforts. While undoubtedly helpful, short-term financial measures do not necessarily measure how stakeholders view an organization. To accomplish this, one helpful measure is to interview disaffected customers, donors, or clients to find out why they have stopped supporting or frequenting an organization. Another helpful measure is to interview existing stakeholders and find out which parts of the organization they really like, to determine levels of dissatisfaction.

The Importance of a Plan Cannot Be Overstated

With marketing budgets being squeezed to get more for less, along with the need to strengthen donor, customer, and client retention, the importance of a relevant strategic plan cannot be overemphasized. Given a crowded economic marketplace, high stakeholder turbulence, and donor and customer belt-tightening, strategic plans must ensure that an agency's marketing and service operations stand out and deliver excellence in all areas. This simply means that the plans must deliver value in all areas of donor and customer involvement and must be relevant to the goals of the organization. Because in many organizations planning is assumed and not actually engaged in, it must once again be a formalized process, neither forgotten in the crush of day-to-day activities nor delegated to outside groups such as the board of directors. A good marketing strategic plan often has the following four attributes (though it is not necessarily constrained by them):

1. *First*, a plan must take into account what donors or customers consider of value; it then must ensure that all the interactions that take place between the organization and individuals over the course of their life cycles with the organization reflect this relevancy in connection with their involvement at any point in time. This assumes that an organization will do all in its power not to allow a stakeholder relationship to stagnate. Instead, dynamic relational techniques and strategies will evolve and be employed over time.

2. *Second*, a plan assumes that communication will take on an integrated approach. Communication silos can be neither tolerated nor encouraged. Online and off-line communication channels—according to their strengths and weaknesses—must work together to achieve an end result that is satisfying and of value to both the organization and the stakeholder. All media—online and off-line—must be evaluated and used only in conjunction with targeting, and their ability to deliver the organization's message in an appropriate manner must be assessed.

3. *Third*, a plan assumes excellence in execution in order to maximize return on investment, ensure satisfactory delivery of messages, and appropriate listening to stakeholders. Conversational marketing—incorporating stakeholder listening and extended conversations—is still, by and large, one of those marketing ideas that is talked about by everyone and not implemented by many. Nearly all the marketing and development officers I have worked with over 30 years spend less than 15 percent of their time engaged in conversational marketing. While brilliant execution can help nonprofit organizations to stand out from the crowd and deliver the necessary returns an organization needs, there is a tremendous need for community, dialog, and collaborative partnership with stakeholders. Given this, metrics need to be developed around agency protocols and need to be benchmarked to reveal the best way to deliver ongoing stakeholder conversations.

4. *Fourth*, a plan assumes that leadership at all levels understands the relevant needs of the organization's stakeholders and uses this intelligence to ensure the most profitable relationships with donors and customers, the ongoing relational nurturing that should take place system-wide, and long-term advancement of the organization's objectives. For some organizations, paying attention to where the plan is taking the agency may have the result that many ingrained ways of operating are redefined and jettisoned.

Regarding board members in particular, if persistent predictions of shakeups in certain environments hold true, nonprofit administrations will see a continual thinning of the nonprofit ranks in industries that do not develop and articulate a separate board of directors' strategy. Especially for organizations contemplating capital campaigns or major donor efforts, a strong board is often the key to success in such endeavors.

In addition, given that much of philanthropy boils down to conversations and connections, coupled with the fact that almost 83 percent of all gifts are made by individuals, it makes sense that the ideal candidates for nonprofit boards are those that give, purchase, or volunteer already to an organization, come from backgrounds that lend themselves to connections in their professional and personal pursuits, and are not shy about promoting the organization's cause. Having effective board leadership—the kind that holds organizations accountable for their actions—is one of the best ways for a nonprofit organization to outdistance its competitors.

Location Is an Issue, Too

Of course not all nonprofit problems are the fault of marketing, nor can they be solved solely by marketing. A major problem can occur with the location of an organization in relation to its services and supportive constituency. A marketing strategy must take location into account; read the following case study for an example.

Tapping Into the Right Location

A large nonprofit organization is based in a small town in Michigan. The city's population is under 4,000, yet the organization is very successful financially. How can this be? The organization has strategically set up funding offices in key metropolitan centers in Michigan. In addition, these cities are where the nonprofit agency draws the majority of its clients as well as donors. Although the satellite cities are more than a few hours away from the base office, they contain the bulk of the philanthropic dollars that are raised. The organization, by way of its regional offices, has overcome a seemingly bad location. In a perfect world, a rural community would not be a good market in which to raise needed funds and draw in the desired client population as would a larger metropolitan area. Fortunately the organization could adapt and prosper.

The demographic profile an organization works with should be an important consideration in its market planning and strategy and ultimately in the location of the organization. While much is made of the power of the Internet, many regional organizations must first look to location as a means of defining its brand and enabling it to raise important community donations. Larger communities as well as small ones should not be exempt from the same type of scrutiny.

There is a limit to how many charities a community can support. One town I am aware of has a population of about four million residents, one million of which are students. In the town there are close to 100 colleges and universities, 65 hospitals, and there are some 35,000 charitable organizations in the state. It may not be possible for all of these worthwhile organizations to receive adequate support.

Should a nonprofit organization that finds itself in an undesirable location leave and search for new surroundings? For many nonprofit agencies this is far easier said than done. In fact, most nonprofit organizations in this situation need a marketing strategy to redirect their marketing efforts in the short run in order to cater to both their ideal client population as well as to the national philanthropic population. In the long run, they need to consider a move of some type to a more appropriate setting.

Redefining the Organizational Marketing Culture

What is at the heart of the turbulent changes our culture and society are experiencing, and how are these changes affecting nonprofit organizations? What should the nonprofit response be? Should it go further than suggesting that without aggressive marketing strategies agencies will experience more financial problems than those with strong marketing programs?

A nonprofit agency's response should start with the question, How does the organization define its 'marketing culture'? It used to be enough to say that an organization defined its marketing culture when it had someone in charge of its marketing efforts. Now, much more is required. Marketing can no longer be isolated inside an organization; it must be dispersed across its entirety in terms of its processes. For example, how many departments are involved in receipting a gift? Six immediately come to mind: those that provided training for the fund development staff, the staff that ultimately solicited the gift, the mailroom that opened the mail, the accounting team that credited the right department with the gift, the data entry people who processed the gift, and the individuals who sent the acknowledgment. The donor should receive the outcome of cross-functional teams working in sync, each with a marketing and customer assignment.

Although there are more conversations about marketing than ever before, most nonprofit agencies tend to operate in a "marketing pre-culture," in which their executives have not yet established a true commitment to marketing. A fear of change is often at the heart of this and is rooted in resistance to new ideas and ways of doing things, particularly in helping their organizations think through how they must operate together in a networked fashion to achieve excellence in donor loyalty and retention.

How does an agency go about achieving a strong marketing culture that literally transforms the organization? How should it look operationally?

1. The organization should first strive to create within itself a structure that is highly suitable for the needs of its donors, constituents, and clients, as well as one that is able to carry out the competitive tasks of the marketing enterprise. Marketing calls for more than creating brochures and implementation issues. A marketing department must learn how to deliver value to its donor, customer, and volunteer population in such a way that its demonstrated expertise creates positive results in every field of endeavor it operates in. As part of this value deliverance, marketing units must also create differentiation between their organizations and those that are competitors. Without differentiation, organizations become commodities. This calls for more than the popular branding conversations that many organizations are having, with their extended conversations about logos and color schemes. This is a differentiation that is grounded in the organization's actually demonstrating to its constituents that it is fundamentally different from other organizations that are operating in the same field; the organization must use this differentiation in defining who its donor base is and the value that donors can receive by being a part of the organization.

2. Second, the marketing team's culture must have as a basic
   tenet the desire to serve the organization's various constituencies in a way they want to be served. In this context, for
   profit marketing phrases like "Be the customer champion"
   need to be applied to the donor world. For example, most
   nonprofit segmentation strategies are stagnant and fixed;
   they do not evolve with the donor as he or she changes their
   relationship with the organization over time. In this light
   segmentation strategies as they are typically taught in most
   seminars are not tactically strategic. You cannot be the donor champion with a fixed segmentation strategy—or a
   strategy of any kind—that always treats the stakeholders the
   same way.
3. The nonprofit marketing culture must desire to see objectives met through implemented marketing strategies. In
   particular, these strategies should be of a style and structure
   that the organization can tolerate. Perhaps an easier way of
   expressing this is that the nonprofit agency and its marketing
   team must be seen as providing solutions to problems stakeholders would like to see resolved as opposed to being
   seen as solely raising money or selling agency products.
   Because all stakeholders have more options to support than
   they either need or want, a nonprofit entity must position itself as providing maximum value to individuals in exchange
   for their support or purchase. An agency achieves this type of
   value in the stakeholder's eyes by appearing as someone who
   is concerned about the needs the stakeholder holds dear and
   impartially holds out the organization they serve and its programs as a possible response. What stakeholders most want to
   see are the problems and opportunities they are interested in
   either solved or taken advantage of, respectively, by an organization they trust and believe in.
4. There should be a balance between planning and operating,
   between long- and short-term goals, and between growth and
   income goals. Without constant causal and program innovation, nonprofit organizations often risk their future viability,
   market and donor position, growth and profitability. Recently I visited an organization in Canada that told me one of
   its programs had not changed in more than 20 years. Though
   the organization was seeing annual slippages in program

attendance and profitability, it would not tolerate any discussion of change.

Though program change in this example is probably necessary, innovation must be more than mere program change. It must be part of how you do things, part of your organizational and marketing culture. I have a friend who says, "You can never be satisfied." This notion must carry through in how you market your organization. Many nonprofit marketing directors allocate most of their financial marketing war chest to short-term fund development goals that will help them "win" at the expense of building long-term investments in stakeholder relationships and subsequent organizational and brand equity. In the distribution of their marketing resources, they try to be democratic in how they promote the breadth of their agency's causes, selling weaker concerns the same way they sell the organization's primary concerns. Breakthroughs are almost impossible to achieve. As previously mentioned, customer and donor retention goes by the wayside when not enough dollars are allocated to this agenda.

5. An organization's marketing culture should facilitate communication and decision making among its members and demand that communication be integrated throughout the rest of the organization. Marketing is generally mistrusted by the public, and bad fund development, poor customer service, and manipulative advertising are no longer tolerated. Marketing can no longer be perceived as a one-way, unidirectional, exercise controlled by the nonprofit agency; rather, markets have become conversations.[2] They are fluid and continuous. What's more, the roles of marketing and the consumer have reversed; whereas marketing used to expect all consumers to follow its lead, today marketing must fit into where a stakeholder is going.

Into this mix have come the new social media, which are remarkably different from other media. In particular, they have encouraged not only connectedness but collaboration and community. They have enabled long conversations to take place between organizations and stakeholders and have allowed stakeholders to become producing consumers and content providers, or "prosumers" as Alvin Toffler called them in *The Third Wave*.[3] This has resulted in further empowering stakeholders who are not only skeptical but can be very intelligent and demanding regarding an organization.

6. Such a culture should have agreed-on evaluation points and benchmarks of performance. Cost is an obvious point of analysis for a nonprofit organization and is an important one when a marketing strategy is dependent on achieving a cost advantage (or cost parity) over competitors and then demonstrating this advantage to future or current stakeholders. Cost advantage can be important in order fulfillment or service delivery. This applies to other commonly discussed financial performance indicators such as acquisition cost, average gift size, largest gift size, donor value, and donor migration. What is often not discussed and evaluated is new product and service innovation. Equally important with other measures, innovation helps ensure new stakeholder value. Marketing metrics must also be benchmarked, especially for linking financial performance with stakeholder value.

Dealing with Strategic Problems and Uncertainty

Problems are nothing new to nonprofit organizations. In fact, most nonprofit executives are overwhelmed by short-term tactical problems on a daily basis. However, some of these problems are of a higher profile within the company and, as such, require both dramatic and response strategies and programs. It is these problems that an internal organization analysis seeks to uncover.

Not Considering Stakeholder Satisfaction and Brand Loyalty

A backwards analysis of many nonprofit organizations would reveal that a high percentage of them "jump" into their environments, trying to promote themselves with little thought given to the potential acceptance of their service or solicitation message by the community. "Jumping in" efforts may confuse marketing with advertising, and the overall goal is typically community recognition rather than acceptance of the group or its message. This approach is counter to creating a stakeholder-driven mission in which the organization's market research and conversation in the new potential environment are laden with strategies that focus on the needs and wants of stakeholders. "To make the Center

City Nonprofit a recognized name by letting people know we're at work in a certain area" is a typical organization mission statement. In reality it is an undifferentiated marketing strategy, hoping to be able to attract anyone to its cause without separating marketing from image relations. Where does the constituents' voice fit in? In this case it doesn't.

Client, donor, and constituent analysis would reveal two major problems with this lack of constituent-based strategy. First, in attempting to attract everyone with one campaign—client and donor alike—a nonprofit organization stands the chance of not attracting anyone. No organization can meet everyone's needs adequately. Further, such a strategy costs more than most nonprofit agencies can afford because it is too general. It is typically strategically smarter and financially wise to target carefully defined audience segments by asking some or all of the following questions:

1. Are there potential stakeholders not being served at all, or are they being served in such a way that our organization could provide value to them?
2. Is what our organization brings in terms of value to stakeholders sufficiently compelling—either through better client solutions, new innovations, or at a cost substantially lower than other competitors—for them to consider that partnering with us represents a strong benefit to them?
3. Can what our organization provides strongly impact the causal industry so that our organization could be an industry leader?

Every institution that is interested in long-term prospects must assess how its "self-image" fits with the needs of the target markets it currently serves as well as those it wants to serve. A failure to impact the client areas it was created to serve will hurt a nonprofit organization in areas it might not think about initially, including the ability to attract volunteers, to gain community recognition and support, and to attract good local services. Long-term prospect viability and health must take into account the organization's assets and competencies when both current and future strategies are looked at. Which strategic direction is most important? The problem with the examples previously cited is that the loyalty of the customer base is either being assumed or is considered not critical. Current dollars raised and/or nonprofit sales are the only indicators examined. How can an organization assess its self-image? The following checklist outlines some basic areas of self-assessment for a nonprofit:

1. Regarding the organization's donors, customers, and other constituents, consider
   - Their opinion of the agency, its policies, and the solutions the organization offers its clients and donors.
   - Their acceptance or rejection of the services offered and their perception of how unique they think the services being provided are.
   - Their regard for the way the organization serves them and their feelings of collaboration—or not—with the organization's staff.
   - The fulfillment of their expectations—or not—in their involvement with the organization.
   - Their feelings towards the organization's media, fund raising, communication programs, and the level of media service they receive.
   - Their motivations in supporting the organization, its service products, and the fee- or fund-raising costs for them.
2. Regarding markets, consider
   - The organization's size and attractiveness in comparison with others.
   - Its coverage, cost structure, and client size compared to others.
   - Its capability for market expansion and increased organization size and scope of service compared to others.
3. Regarding the competitors, consider
   - Its service products as compared with those of others.
   - Its perceived quality of brand as compared with competitors.
   - Its level of innovation in the causal industry.
   - Its current marketing strategies as compared with others, including the degree of copycat marketing strategies.
   - Its customer, donor, and client support services provided as compared with those of others.

Tracking Marketing History Is Important

Most nonprofit institutions lack experience in putting market theories into practice. They also typically have an even shorter history of tracking their results. Consequently, nonprofit organizations cannot really accurately advertise how effective their programs are. Nor can they say with any real certainty which areas of untapped monies in the marketplace they are ignoring by using their traditional fundraising methods but not using others. Sometimes strategies simply evolve into something they were not meant to be.

Many nonprofit organizations are successful today because they run marketing programs year in and out, constantly measuring their outcomes, and never growing tired of improving these programs. Once one marketing program is honed to near perfection, another should be started. Strategic problems may occur, but successful institutions cope with these issues over time by adjusting their strategies and expectations. Good results in one area do not necessarily lead to good results in another, however. Marketing requires constant attention to detail and performance. It also requires deciding which programs to keep and which to abandon.

Given the difficulty many nonprofit organizations may have in their marketing culture, staff and systems, as along with providing adequate budgeting for marketing ventures, a historical record can reveal both strategic strengths and weaknesses. Organizations can develop systems over time that become strengths and sources of competitive advantage based on historical needs; similarly, they can remember managerial errors of the past in order to strengthen management teams in the present. Internal constraints of the past can also be purposefully remedied in order to implement strategies of the future.

Discovering Prospects

Rigorous internal analysis is also important when organizations seek to expand their constituencies and initiate new relationships. Few organizations can rely solely on volunteers or a few highly committed donors to meet their service goals and their growing budgets. In fact, one of the key criteria for many nonprofit organizations considering moving their organizational headquarters is the issue of whether the new location will yield better prospect discovery. In deciding to move or to aggressively pursue new prospects and potential donors, an organization needs an accurate understanding of who it is most likely to attract as a service client, volunteer, or donor. This decision must be based on research, experience, and an understanding of what value or solution the organization can provide the prospect, as opposed to stereotyped prospect targets or out-of-date notions about who will give to the cause that do not resemble the target at all. For many organizations operating today, the doctrine is still taught that the only guaranteed donor prospect in America for almost all nonprofit organizations is a white woman, over the age of 50, coming from a middle-class environment that has demonstrated an openness to emotional appeals.

Today, many nonprofit constituencies, especially in the donor arena, are a very different type of target prospect in age, income, education, color, and sex. Organizations that take the time to develop a profile of their users or other stakeholders and then use this new information strategically in their marketing often find an immediate improvement in their service, volunteer, and fund-raising programs.

Defining a Rehab Center's Clientele

A major university hospital is interested in expanding the number of clients its rehab unit serves. One group within the hospital is advocating an expensive, strong public relations focus in the city. Another is advocating an equally expensive advertising campaign. A third option was finally chosen.

The hospital took the time to discover where its patients were coming from and which doctor they wanted to see. It found out that the majority of its patients came because doctors within a 150-mile radius constantly recommended this hospital and one rehab doctor in particular because of their specialized service and strong patient care. What's more, the doctors who served as referrals for this hospital's rehab unit generally came from smaller metropolitan areas and worked within smaller medical practices.

This information allowed the rehab center and its marketing team to construct a marketing program and strategy that benefited from the information acquired.

How does an organization uncover the same types of strategic information about its markets? What steps should an organization take to accomplish this? Some answers to these questions are given here.

1. A nonprofit organization must first formally establish steps to gather marketing intelligence information on a regular basis, including formulating a budget for gathering the information, appointing a person to run the process, and securing a commitment from senior management to use the information strategically on a regular basis.
2. The organization must then establish "sources" of marketing information and continually cultivate those sources. These sources could include competitors (which would require continuous attention), donors and clients (monitor their opinions on a wide range of issues), and members of the nonprofit organization who should regularly contribute their impressions of how the organization's systems of marketing and service delivery are functioning.
3. Third, the organization must collect, interpret, and evaluate the information in order to make use of the data.
4. Information must be interrelated with ongoing organizational procedures using the relationships between research elements.

Assessing the Organization's Strengths and Weaknesses

To create an effective marketing plan, an organization must be able to differentiate between its strengths and weaknesses, particularly as they relate to the competition. There are usually four areas in which this type of evaluation is critical: service delivery, methods of raising money and communicating a message to the various publics of the nonprofit agency, methodology of creating new services, and overall marketing.

The Power of Service Delivery

The delivery of services can be a very powerful medium through which to maintain a competitive presence because it can provide an inherent intense stakeholder experience and involvement.

Stakeholder intimacy, built on an understanding of what stakeholders need and want and then delivered in a personalized fashion, strengthens an agency's brand and strategic direction in the stakeholder's mind. While the vast majority of nonprofit directors believe they deliver a superior nonprofit experience, clearly the numbers are turned when customers, donors, and volunteers are asked their version of their experience with the same nonprofit agency. An organization cannot pretend it provides great service when it uses an automated receptionist, takes four weeks to send out a receipt, and does not police its various functioning staff and units to ensure their standards are up to par.

The following questions must be answered for an organization to ascertain its strengths or weaknesses in this area:

- Is the organization delivering its services at a higher or lower than normal cost as compared with similar organizations?
- Does the nonprofit organization possess a service array that is distinct, or are its services being duplicated by others?
- How does the organization respond to inquiries, questions, and complaints?
- Does the organization possess flexibility in delivery of its services as compared with others?
- Are there alternative ways to deliver the agency's services?

Communication: The Key to Stakeholder Retention

Anyone who views a sale as a transaction will become toast down the line. Selling is not about peddling a product. It's about wrapping that product in a service—and about selling both the product and the service as an experience. That approach to selling helps create a vital element of the process: a relationship. In a world where things move at hyper-speed, what was relevant yesterday may not be relevant tomorrow. But one thing that endures is a dynamic relationship that is grounded in an experience that the organization has provided.[4]

Marketing communication's basic mission is to create a difference between what one nonprofit agency offers and what another agency offers in servicing a similar cause and to do so using values and attributes that appeal to and are important to the stakeholder. The biggest frustration most nonprofit agency heads have with their marketing and communication teams is that what they produce shows little difference from what their competitors produce. This has become decidedly true in the Internet age where the tactical pressure that most marketing and communication units feel is not so much to differentiate their cause but to use all of their marketing mix options to provide messaging. Unfortunately, this ultimately limits their level of differentiation from others, creates a commodity situation among competitors, and results in communication efforts that almost universally avoid detailing the benefits that attract the stakeholders in the first place.

For example, I am not having a lot of success in using the Internet to raise a lot of money in normal fund development situations or in getting a second gift from some audiences. The Internet is helpful in times of organizational emergency, in year-end giving, and with some high-profile causes. However, there is typically tremendous pressure from development and marketing people to "use the Internet." Ok, for what purpose? To send some white-collar knowledge worker another e-mail blast that he or she is not going to read? You have to know what certain media can deliver and to ask yourself, Will consumers win if I send them another solicitation?

Jack Welch, former CEO of General Electric noted, "The winners will be those who deliver solutions from the user's point of view. That is a big part of Marketing's job."[5]

On this point, the communication of some nonprofit agencies often ignores segment differences and presents variables that are used commonly across all segments rather than segmenting and re-segmenting to arrive at segments that feel they are valued customers or donors. Increasingly segmentation strategies for many organizations appear to be undifferentiated strategies that target all stakeholders with the same marketing mix and message. Instead, communication departments should struggle with how to deliver unique value options across different segments.

Communication efforts also suffer from a tremendous lack of research as to what stakeholders want in the way of communication. The result is an influx of copycat strategies, where to read an agency's copy or see its video or look at its web site often seems to be an articulation and listing of company features as opposed to a portrayal of benefits within a value proposition that are meaningful to the reader or viewer. Marketing communication strategies must always ask

- Can we describe the audience in detail?
- Does our audience differ from competitor audiences in what they are expecting from our communication?
- What are the core needs our communication and value strategies are trying to address, and is there a tailored fit between segment, message, and benefits?
- Does our value proposition reflect and strengthen our brand position, and can it be defended against competitor attacks?

Competitors

Determining whether an organization has a particular advantage helps to define its tactical rules when engaging in competition. As more and more organizations see their services being duplicated by competitors, the marketing function often become the critical area in which an organization can establish its strengths at the expense of a competitor's weaknesses. Since there are few initial barriers to entry in the nonprofit world, overcrowding seems to be everywhere, and market shakeouts are routine; disappointing market share expectations are the norm for many organizations. Competitor intelligence is important, because new nonprofit products superior to one's own can easily enter the market. As a consequence, capabilities not necessarily important in the early days of operation can become more so, requiring the organization to be nimble and fearless. For example, customer experiences are far more critical than they were 10 years ago; creating a "transformative experience" for a constituent is far more easily said than done.

Many hope the new social media technology will become a competitive asset in their marketing arsenal as they face competitors; they want to know how best to use it. Here are some answers:

- Use social media to improve the experience your stakeholders have with your organization.
- Make sure you know how your competitors are using the media to determine whether you can see competitive advantages in the way your organization uses media.
- Don't be afraid to change your marketing mix if you are seeing disappointing returns in your marketing and fund-development efforts.

- Find out whether submarkets occur from individuals who signal they want to deal with your organization only through social media.
- Make sure you have the skills and competencies needed to compete in the social media market.
- Make sure you have clear goals for your social media usage.
- Use social media only if they improve your value proposition to your stakeholders and provide them with clear benefits.
- Rigorously test social media's strength in procuring gifts, and know how best to use them in your fund-development tactics.

Looking for and Managing Long-Term Relationships

Vigilance in the management of constituent relationships is the first precondition for marketing success. For example, many nonprofit marketing administrations presume that a second gift from a donor will occur automatically or that a volunteer will return. Unfortunately, this kind of assumption is no longer realistic. Instead, long-term relationships with a variety of constituents require constant attention to the needs and wishes of the constituents, meaningful and collaborative communication, and effective use of marketing strategies designed to renew the relationship on a regular basis. The goal in using this variety of tactics is a stable relationship with the constituent. In the case of a donor, the benefits of this type of relationship may include a series of gifts over a period of time, including some with upgraded dollar amounts, as well as the potential for future gifts of both capital and estate.

Further, a stable relationship with a volunteer can yield hundreds of hours of donated time and effort, thereby reducing the financial stress associated with hiring additional employees. A successful relationship with a client gives the nonprofit institution both an opportunity to exercise its service to successful completion and the opportunity to receive referrals for its services from satisfied clients.

In each of these instances, access to the appropriate individual with whom the nonprofit organization can partner is often the key. Without a supportive community, an organization will have to downscale its service expectations and growth plans. The ability to recognize and thank clients, donors, and volunteers adequately is an integral criterion for stakeholder success. No internal analysis would be complete if it did not ask how constituents are being treated and thanked. For many individuals involved in a campaign, personal recognition is becoming increasingly important in their concept of philanthropic involvement. They are interested in seeing their names on buildings and behind initiatives. How does your organization not just thank its constituents, but how does it build long-term relationships? In that connection, here are 10 significant guidelines to keep in mind.

- *First,* a good marketing team looks for people already interested in the cause or issue at hand. Finding someone who is already convinced of the appropriateness of the nonprofit organization's talks allows for that donor's values to be affirmed more easily when they give. Always remember the findings of the two Stanford Business School professors, James Collins and Jerry Porris, who found in part that the key to great companies is the creation of a web of shared meaning and values around common metaphors that abide and guide the company into the future.[6]
- *Second,* the courtship of a donor is the most important part of building a long-term relationship.
- *Third,* fund development in the form of a value proposition is ideally personal in nature. The soliciting organization must always try to be as personal as possible in the structuring of its solicitation.
- *Fourth,* you must learn to ask for the gift. This simple action allows donors to know exactly what you are expecting of them.
- *Fifth,* you must frequently thank your constituents.
- *Sixth,* always report on the progress at hand, even if it is negative. Be transparent. Donors, customers, and volunteers want to know the truth, and they usually assume the nonprofit organization will encounter some discontinuities in getting its job done.
- *Seventh,* don't exaggerate or lie in your communication. The supporter will never forget this if you do and are subsequently found out.
- *Eighth,* don't take "no" personally. In other words, your supporters cannot say "yes" every time you ask. Some parts of your organization are more appealing to them than others.

- *Ninth,* let your constituents know where the money is going. Always have a budget written in plain English with nothing hidden.
- *Tenth,* assume your job in marketing is always to build relationships. Make sure your strategies reflect this philosophy.

Cost and Performance Analysis Helps Define Success

A nonprofit organization undertaking a performance analysis must understand how much it costs for the organization's monies to be raised and how much it costs for the various parts of the services to be performed. Costs and performance can become an advantage or a disadvantage for the nonprofit entity. Determining the biggest costs and the best and worst performing projects, as along with projecting these trends into the future, allows a nonprofit organization to improve its own performance and to develop strategies vis-à-vis its competitors.

Analyzing the Service Portfolio

Most nonprofit organizations undertake different activities on behalf of their supportive constituency and those they serve—activities such as providing shelter, counseling, medical services, food services, job retraining, and so on. These "service activities" make up a nonprofit agency's service portfolio. A portfolio analysis is useful for determining the attractiveness of some parts of the organization's operations, the cause's ability to generate cash or to simply spend it, and its comparative strength against competitors' services and portfolios. In essence, organizations are trying to evaluate both the financial viability and the attractiveness of the parts of their service work as well as the strength of the organization's position within that market.

The determination of how much money and time the nonprofit organization should invest in each service is one of the key elements in any organization's strategic marketing. This analysis leads naturally to resource allocation decisions and the amount of effort to be placed in each service area. Which service areas should be expanded and which should be curtailed or stopped altogether? This decision is most crucial for organizations that are involved in multiple causes that aren't necessarily related. Nonprofit management teams cannot be "experts" in every area, and they must determine what is worth focusing on (investment to penetrate the market successfully) and what is not according to the level of assets and competencies needed to excel in the service areas (divestiture). In those service areas that are growing fast, organizations should expect competitors to enter these same areas; therefore, their investment in these areas may be defensive in nature.

These areas of service emphasis become important decisions, because most nonprofit agencies are already not spending enough money or maintaining enough relationships to achieve dominance in areas they are interested in. The willingness to measure, monitor, and rethink how the organization is undertaking its many work roles and to organize its systems to best meet constituents' needs usually puts an organization into conflict with those who use financial constraints to oppose new ideas. In an increasingly competitive environment, the future success of many nonprofit organizations lies in developing the necessary controls to monitor their expenditures as well as to master the strategy of marketing their cause or purpose. Every nonprofit institution ought to have a budget as a first control, and this needs to serve as a financial plan for the organization. A second means of control is for the organization to have a projected budget practice in place—a process that allows the organization to analyze the income and expense of its various activities on a project-by-project basis. Third, every nonprofit organization ought to have a contingency or reserve fund where money is put away. This fund may equal as much as 5 percent of the organization's total budget.

In making decisions today, many nonprofit organizations rely more on financial data than on information of any other kind to help address their allocations on behalf of services, fund-raising strategies, and long-term investment decisions. While financial data is important and cannot be minimized, some institutions would be well served to measure their service outcomes as closely as they measure their financial outcomes. Though there are industry guidelines that nonprofit agencies can follow in addressing their cost issues, cost averaging typically ignores organizations that undertake programs for ethical or organizational reasons and may knowingly incur higher costs.

The Internal Audit Helps Define Organizational Strengths and Weaknesses

In a very real sense, everything discussed concerning the internal organizational audit has been about "strengths and weaknesses." Organizations prospering on a daily basis take their strengths and weaknesses very seriously. In fact, they are often desperate to get rid of their weaknesses at all costs. They will plan and staff to accomplish this task. They concentrate on their strengths and doing those activities they know how to do best. Marketing issues are evaluated and, ultimately, become issues of value proposition, cost, and time. A discussion of a nonprofit organization's strengths and weaknesses becomes the summation point in the internal analysis and provides the staging point for the development of a marketing strategy. Nowhere is the issue of strengths and weaknesses more pronounced than in the articulation of a nonprofit organization's objectives. This is the subject of Chapter 7.

Summary

Rigorous honesty is important when analyzing an organization's strengths and weaknesses. Glossing over agency programs that are not performing well does not help an organization in either the long or the short term. Nor does the assumption of stakeholder loyalty. To deliver superior value, an organization must not just be flexible in meeting needs; it must first know what those needs are and whether the organization can indeed meet them without changing some part of its operation. Organizational honesty is hard, but it will allow an agency not only to survive but to thrive.

Value Propositions and Marketing Objectives

The value decade is upon us. If you can't sell a top-quality product at the world's lowest price, you're going to be out of the game. . . . [T]he best way to hold your customers is to constantly figure out how to give them more for less.

Jack Welch, Chairman of General Electric,
as quoted by Philip Kotler in *Kotler on Marketing*
(New York: Free Press, 1999), p. 54

Would Anyone Miss You If You Went Out of Business?

What are the best ways for a nonprofit organization to market itself and enjoy success in fund development? A great many still believe that the best way to accomplish both the raising of money and the positioning of an organization to the public is by hawking and selling their needs, regardless of donor or stakeholder interest. Even in today's economy, many organizations still believe that donors, volunteers, and customers will come flocking in. Unfortunately, the American public no longer gives this way, if they ever did. Stakeholders must buy into an organization's goals, values, and results before they buy into the organization's needs.

Why Should a Nonprofit Organization Worry about Objectives?

Very simply put, "We often talk better than we act." There is little doubt that most nonprofit institutions understand the need for marketing; however, what they mean by implementing "it" must

147

be examined more closely. This chapter continues the inward organizational look at how a marketing strategy is initiated, beginning with the organization's objectives, its value proposition, the resulting way(s) it measures and assesses its past and current performance, and the steps and approaches it uses to reach these objectives.

Developing Organizational Objectives

''Objectives'' are those levels of performance labeled by the organization as areas that are critical to the evaluation of the organization's overall effectiveness. The internal assessment is more difficult than the external assessments discussed previously, because an institution, in looking inwardly at itself, evaluates those organizational areas that constrain it—its strengths as well as its weaknesses—and determines the need for new action to improve its marketing and service sector activities. Further, this inward analysis is richer with data and information than the previous preoccupation with competitors and the operating environment The outcome of this inward journey allows an organization to determine whether its competitive strategies are working, based on its objectives and the support it is receiving.

A nonprofit analyzes its objectives by asking a variety of questions.

Competitive Performance Starts with Asking Why We Exist as an Agency

It is helpful to remember the nonprofit director who asked the following question when considering her nonprofit organization's objectives: "Who would miss us if we were gone or didn't exist?"

Without identifying major constituencies or knowing which services offered are most effective and widely received, there is really little reason to undertake strategy considerations. And even though this chapter is not about planning, nonprofit leadership must first look at the planning process. To assess the role of objectives in competitive strategy, the leadership must first look at the planning process. In particular, this beginning look encompasses the market the nonprofit is in, its purpose, the way the future looks, the strengths and weaknesses the nonprofit brings to bear on the market, and the areas it can excel in.

For a nonprofit to develop its mission statement and objectives, the first goal for any organization is to decide whom its agency services and nonprofit products will serve. In essence, what are the markets that will be served, and what are the services that will be provided by the nonprofit organization in question for each of these markets in order to meet some need? This vital step also allows the organization to look both backward and forward at its markets and assess its service (or projected service) performance within each.

Defining the Nonprofit Organization's Purpose

Sometimes embodied in a finished statement that planners call a "mission statement," the definition of the nonprofit organization's purpose must include the following:

- A statement describing the environment the organization is currently in and where it wants to be in the future—in essence, the reason for its existence.
- The statement is results oriented and not activity oriented; it should be realistic and not project a "dreamed of future" with little bearing in reality.
- It should state not what an organization can do but the reason(s) for doing it.
- Mission is the purpose for which an organization exists, although the techniques it uses for reaching its mission may vary by circumstance.
- Mission is outward and oriented to clients, donors, customers, and volunteers, as opposed to being inward and organizationally bound.
- Mission is the essence and the "sine qua non" of organizational activity—the last purpose to be abandoned.[1]

By developing a mission statement, an organization also develops boundaries around its objectives, requiring the nonprofit to function within a defined universe of activity aimed at a particular outcome. A mission statement is most forceful when it can be reduced to one sentence; however, some organizations use several paragraphs to describe their mission. If your organization has a mission, you should review it. If it does not, you should start developing one.

Trends and an Uncertain Future

An organization cannot think about its mission statement without also thinking about its future. In developing organizational objectives, however, some assumptions about markets, the future political environment, geo-demographic changes, economic realities, and competitors must be made. In developing these assumptions, the nonprofit organization must also measure the impact of its assumptions against the reality around it and make the necessary changes in operating style and procedure. This is done to ensure that the organization is on the right course, its resource allocation is correct, and its staffing is adequate for the job it is attempting. Leaders of nonprofit organizations must be skilled at trend spotting, absorbing polls on relevant subject matter, and reading important literature as it relates to its cause.

How does an organization investigate its future?

1. The first step is to define the nonprofit agency's objectives; this allows the organization to assess performance and company direction. In this process, some objectives may be changed and others set.
2. The organization then moves on to past, current, and future strategies that allow it to meet these objectives, paying particular attention to the value propositions that have been used.
3. The third step involves the organization's strategies. Strategies are worthwhile only if they reflect the costs to the organization in both personnel and dollars, the resulting problems and challenges that may have erupted with constituents, and, of course, the successes. Are the organization's strategies the correct ones for this time and environment?
4. Finally, the organization looks at areas where donors, clients, and customers may or may not be in agreement with where the organization is headed, as evidenced by the support and agreement with the direction or lack of it.
5. This process also involves noting new consumer and lifestyle trends in society. Trends can represent either a threat or an opportunity to an organization. My camp clients are noticing a substantial increase in the number of families that want to vacation at the camp. This allows them to have a low-risk vacation that saves money and still lets the family escape some of

the pressures of their day-to-day lives. Another trend is the increase in donors and customers who want to know how "green" are the new buildings that agencies are putting up as part of capital campaigns, with the obvious desire to see buildings that are more environmentally sound. Still another trend is the substantial shift in how society views some parts of the nonprofit world, making some causes harder than ever to raise money for.

6. Also involved is looking at new nonprofit products and their introduction. For their long-term health and viability, most organizations must undergird their future marketing strategies with innovative new products, systems, causes, and plans that allow stakeholders to feel alive within the organization. There are two major problems that limit the innovative capabilities of nonprofit organizations: First, they don't want to fail, particularly if they are using donated money. This has lead to overly conservative cultures that are risk averse. In many organizations this culture has a crippling effect. Second, many nonprofit agencies do not move fast—in fact, they don't even know the word "fast." They have become masters of committees and formal reviews.[2]

7. Studying demographic shifts is a must, especially as they relate to the family. The predictability of demographic studies helps marketers when they look at birth rates, marriage and mortality rates, and age. For example, the nuclear family constitutes only about one-quarter of our society, yet many religious nonprofit organizations operate as though it will return to its earlier status. Hispanic people are well aware that they are becoming the dominant ethnic group in America, yet I do not see many Hispanics on boards of directors. Women continue to outlive men, and much of the undifferentiated nonprofit marketing is aimed at older sections of this audience. Demographics should matter tactically to virtually every nonprofit marketer in this country.

8. Seeing how the economy is running and the mood of the nation toward it is another must. As I write this at the end of 2009, the country is scared, unemployment is somewhere between 10 and 12 percent, giving to many groups has dwindled, and strategic uncertainty is rampant. There is inherent unpredictability as to where the nation is going.

Philanthropic giving is unequally distributed across many groups; when news is bad, some groups of consumers reduce their giving. Other groups, often religious or strongly compassionate in nature, increase theirs. For the moment, it makes sense for most nonprofit organizations to consider reducing their expenses and budget to find out what "normal" may come to mean in our society.

9. Organization leaders must observe how new technologies are affecting their stakeholders. Organizational and consumer response to technology issues varies. For most nonprofit agencies, social media have represented a technological disruption that they are now dealing with tactically and strategically. Some agencies are trying to deliver the new media in an easy-to-use form and are positioning the media as a benefit to those involved in their organization.

Strategically Using Strengths and Minimizing Weaknesses

The importance of a nonprofit organization's strengths and weaknesses—as well as those of its competitors—is often trivialized in day-to-day operational reality. Part of the problem is a practical matter; it is not difficult to talk about the functions an organization does well. It is far more difficult to talk openly and honestly about weaknesses, and for many organizations it is almost impossible to reconcile the areas of weakness with the solutions that are proposed. Another problem is that nonprofit management teams are not used to thinking about and exploiting competitors' weaknesses as they relate to strategies. Ideally, the key strength of a nonprofit organization should be pitted against the key weakness of a competitor, resulting in a strategic advantage.

Organizations have weaknesses and strengths—all do. More important, though, than castigating one's organization is to know what strengths are needed to succeed in particular fields of service. To accomplish this, the following questions should be asked:

1. Will the strengths that our organization possesses lead to superior performance within this service industry? Or are our organizational weaknesses so dominant that they will ultimately lead our organization to poor performance?

2. What do donors and customers want from a nonprofit organization in this field? What values will they most highly prize, and can we deliver a strategy that will appeal to these values?
3. Do our competitors possess more of the industry strengths needed to succeed than we do?
4. Will other factors—our product line, our brand, our donor base—enable us to succeed in this service field?

Some organizations resort to an anonymous survey to achieve a more accurate reading of their weaknesses. Others hire an outside consultant who, through interviews and personal and group observation, develops an assessment of organizational strengths and weaknesses.

Regardless of method, agreement on what an organization's strengths and weaknesses is an important ingredient in setting both objectives and goals.

Using Objectives to Excel in Marketing

The category called *objectives* differs from an organization's strengths. Unlike strengths, which measure what the organization is currently doing well in such areas as leadership, fiscal responsibility, constituent loyalty, and the organization's visibility in the community, the area of objectives deals with issues that the nonprofit agency must perform well in connection with just to survive.

It might seem rather pedantic to say that a discussion of a nonprofit organization's marketing prowess must start with a discussion of the need for clearly defined institutional objectives. Yet marketing practitioners cannot talk about marketing performance in isolation from objectives, because performance and its measurement depends primarily on the direction an organization takes and the progress it makes towards that end. The simple task of setting objectives allows a marketing director to decide who the organization's clients, donors, customers, and volunteers could be, what kind of marketing strategy is required for them, the dollar amounts that will be needed to reach the goal, and the level of marketing expenditure needed.

There are three major tasks that occur within a marketing unit as it relates to the objectives an organization sets.

First, organizational objectives give a client a reason to be involved with the agency, and they give donors, customers, and volunteers a reason to give or serve. Most clients avail themselves of a nonprofit's services to realize objectives of some sort, often in their own lives. Similarly, most volunteers and donors do not just give away their time and money; they give also to realize objectives of some sort. Usually, objectives for clients, donors, and volunteers are personal in nature, tied to personal beliefs and value systems that mirror some or all of the nonprofit organization's goals.

How can an organization tap into these constituent goals? The best way is for an organization to ask its constituents what their goals are, either through research vehicles (e.g., online or off-line questionnaires or telephone surveys) or through face-to-face discussions between organization and constituent. This seeking out of constituent opinions must be an ongoing, interactive process between the nonprofit organization and those it serves and draws upon for resources.

Second, an organization's objectives help to determine the types of volunteer and community support it receives, as well as to determine the financial gifts the organization will ask for and from whom. Objectives allow the nonprofit agency to judge the various levels of support it will require from both the service side and the financial side.

Third, according to Thomas Broce, objectives help us "sequence" gifts—that is, large gifts should be secured before our efforts are directed to smaller gifts.[3] Objectives help the organization know the level of support it will need, especially in connection with gifts at the higher level of financial support.

Objectives also provide the basis and rationale for nonprofit management to make allocation and resource decisions and to impose fiscal controls. In addition, they often provide the motivation an organization or department needs to meet its targets. From an institution and a donor perspective, objectives allow the nonprofit agency to communicate across departmental boundaries for purposes of planning and evaluating, and they allow communication to intelligently pass to a donor and vice versa.

Nonprofit executives often feel their objectives are clear when in fact they are not. One organization had as its objective, "To provide mutual understanding and acceptance between the races." Another nonprofit stated its objective was to "Assist mankind in its search for God." These may be worthwhile as dreams and missions, but to develop the yardstick by which these organizations might measure their progress in accomplishing these objectives proves to be another matter.

To be effective, objectives must be both specific and measurable. Otherwise, an organizational mission plays no major role in performance. Without the establishment of a benchmark measurement, it is impossible to measure results. Without this measurement, who is to say whether the organization has been successful or not. With clear objectives, however, an organization can access substantial funds that might be available from donors who give in a thoughtful manner, who need to find out whether they are helping to accomplish the objectives the receiver of the grant so forcefully stated in its solicitation. Without a strong clarification of believable and saleable objectives understood by development staff and volunteers alike, the likelihood of attracting new prospects who can give large sums of money to a cause is diminished.

As I write this chapter, I have two management reports on my desk from other consulting groups that a new client has given me. I represent the third consulting group they have hired. What strikes me about these reports is that apart from being very professionally done, neither consulting group mentioned that the nonprofit in question has no written plan for the year, no measurable fundraising or service objectives, and no sense that this is an important omission. I fear many organizations are in a similar place.

Marketing Performance Comes with Measuring Company Objectives

If marketing performance starts with having objectives, then certainly the measurement of the organization's ability to reach these objectives becomes necessarily important. This is true for both a nonprofit organization's image and donor equity. All of these factors become more salient as the necessity and difficulty of the measurement process increases. Information, particularly as it relates to stakeholders of all kinds, is more important than many other organizational resources.

What this means practically to a marketing manager is that the specific purpose of an organization's service programs or fund-raising campaigns must be clearly understood before being implemented. Unclear programmatical objectives—whether for fundraising objectives, attracting volunteers, social media communication programs, or branding—translate into unclear research objectives and unclear responses to measurement questions. As a consequence, campaign or program objectives are altered retrospectively to fit the results.

Measurement as a Necessity

The most common for-profit measurement used to measure objectives is *profitability*, commonly referred to as the "bottom line." Measuring income versus expense allows a nonprofit organization to test whether its nonprofit services or products, fund-raising campaigns, and nonprofit marketing tools are applicable to their constituencies and viable within the competitive environment.

"Profit" within the nonprofit context is measured many ways. Many nonprofit leaders measure their fundraising teams only because this part of the organization works with an easily definable commodity—money. In fact, however, there are many systems a nonprofit could and should measure, including

- Growth
- Employee welfare
- Brand strength
- Web site traffic
- Donor movement and financial responsiveness
- Management development
- Financial stability
- Nonprofit service product quality
- New service program investment
- Donor acceptance of programs

How does a nonprofit leadership team measure all of these items? Peter Drucker suggests that all business organizations need objectives in key result areas—areas where performance and results directly affect the survival and prosperity of the business (or non-profit organization). These areas have value by virtue of the contributions they make to the organization.[4]

In an informal phone survey of 15 marketing and development directors, the respondents named the following key result areas as being important for purposes of measurement:

- *Marketing and/or fund raising.* This area includes donor satisfaction and stakeholder expectations, as well as traditional tracking of donor financial activity.
- *Programmatical growth.* Traditionally this measures the ongoing programs of the organization. Of equal and sometimes more importance are decisions about programs that are not performing as expected.
- *New nonprofit service programs or products.* New programs can come as the result of new in-house capabilities, data gleaned from constituent research (donors or recipients of service), or in response to outside competitive activity.
- *Internal operations.* This area includes the systems an agency mounts to handle its office management, its donor relationship programs, its staff and organizational policies, and the distribution of information to donors and clients.
- *Financial resources.* Is the organization in debt, or is it planning for and building revenues for the future?
- *Physical plant and resources.* What capital will be needed to finance the projected growth of the organization and its resultant physical plant needs 5 to 10 years from now?
- *Internal productivity.* J. Donald Weinrauch says that to neglect defining what makes an effective marketing person in one's industry is to make a colossal management and marketing mistake.[5] One of the harder tasks nonprofit organizations are confronted with is finding well-trained marketing people who can transition from the for-profit to the nonprofit environment. Training a marketing staff is an activity that an organization must plan for, and the process must be guided by clear objectives.
- *The effectiveness of particular media.* With the advent of the Internet, directors are worried about how to successfully use the media available to them in an effective way.
- *The costs associated with each program and the manner in which programs are funded.* What type of input is required for the

organization's programs? What work-hours, dollars, investment, and so forth are required to deliver the current services and products?

Measuring Success and Failure

How do mission-driven organizations measure success and failure?[6] Many for-profit organizations have a straightforward means of measuring marketplace success or failure in terms of financial profit and loss, but for the most part, nonprofit organizations have not developed a uniform rigorous methodology to do so. In some organizations, program growth is measured and discussed as much as money. In others, there are intervening objectives that are required and serve as a link between the necessities of short-term everyday operations and long-term objectives. Dr. W. Edwards Deming understood the difficulties of purely numerical evaluation and often quoted the director of statistical methods for the Nashua Corporation, Dr. Lloyd Nelson, who stated, "The most important figures needed for the management of any organization are often unknown and indeed unknowable."[7]

Success and failure can be easy to measure, depending on an organization's reason for existence. For example, an organization that provides meals to those needing them may choose to measure the number of meals they serve and the dollars they raise to cover the cost of providing the meals. This commonsense approach allows the organization to tally numbers as basic indicators. This cost rationale and utility approach, however, may not go far enough for some of today's stakeholders, who may be looking for mission and progress indicators. When Albert Einstein noted, "Sometimes what counts can't be counted, and what can be counted doesn't count," he was most likely not talking about nonprofit success or failure or stakeholder strategy and value creation.

Still, sophisticated donors, customers, and volunteers have become preoccupied with value creation and other important strategic issues. Nonprofit strategists have had to take into account their need to measure the stewardship of their organizations as well as the changing notions of what success or failure means to many stakeholders. Unfortunately, some notions of success and failure have come into conflict with the definitions many organizations still hold on to and use. When asked, for example, to define what a successful strategy should look like, nonprofit leaders often have little to say about the subject as it relates to donors, customers, employees, and volunteers. For many of these leaders, measures of strategic success are typically about achieving the core goals of the mission as expressed in financial terms and not necessarily about serving or satisfying stakeholders or being concerned about the tactics employed to achieve the mission.

This lack of exactness about what success looks like for an agency may help explain why short-term objectives often dominate nonprofit organizations' strategies. They often become the principal criterion in determining whether a marketing strategy is working or not, at the expense of long-range concerns. Frequently changed tactical plans as well as routine emergency appeals and a crisis fundraising management culture are also signs of fuzzy measures of success.

This, of course, is where the strategic rub occurs in some agencies. Success as defined by the stakeholders is generally different from the way the organization wants to define it. Stakeholders' perceptions of strategic success may be connected as much with the organization's affirmation of values the stakeholder holds most dear as with the areas its mission is focused on. Providing this understanding of the stakeholder's need for duality can become an important distinction in the life of an organization and even its most important strategic marketing weapon. When a stakeholder's supportive concerns are truly listened to and acted on by an organization, they become the means by which an organization begins to break through the communication noise that surrounds most stakeholders and begins to establish a strong brand.

Knowing what success looks like for both the institution and its stakeholders becomes important in this equation. Having a family of measures that concern not just revenue tied to institutional progress as well the progress being made toward fulfilling the mission is key. The clearer the goal being discussed and the narrower its mission, the easier it is to have stakeholder discussions centered on measurement. What's more, the nonprofit agency is often rewarded by the stakeholders when they are presented with clear-cut goals and success measures; stakeholders often stay with these agencies for longer periods of time, perceiving a safe haven free from the typical bombastic claims that abound in the marketplace.

Intervening and Intangible Objectives

How does a nonprofit develop objectives that state where the organization needs to go in the future (long-term success) while retaining a short-term, day-to-day operational performance mentality? Obviously, for many nonprofits long-term goals simply do not work for day-to-day operational decisions. Intervening objectives can be developed that link long-term objectives with current operations. Intervening objectives project a nonprofit's operations forward a number of months while linking its current operation to future success. Exhibit 7.1 gives an example of how different objectives fit into a cohesive whole.

Exhibit 7.1   How Different Objectives Fit into the Whole

In this example, a direct-mail manager for a nonprofit organization has a number of objectives, some short term, some intervening, and some long term. (In the example, the intervening objectives provide the stair-step linkage to achieving some of the direct-mail department's long-term objectives.) The manager may be concerned about the following objectives:

Short-Term Objectives

- All direct-mail copy is done according to editorial calendar and dropped on schedule.
- All online copy is done according to editorial calendar and dropped on schedule.
- All legal and managerial approval of copy is done according to schedule.
- All list requests are done according to schedule.
- All copy is sent to design 10 weeks before drop date.
- All mailing house materials are given three weeks for production.
- All drop dates are observed.
- All receipting is done within 72 hours of receipt of gift.
- All online and off-line responses are tracked 16 weeks from date of first response.
- All response data is done for the weekly managerial summary.

Intervening Objectives

- All direct-mail personnel are put on a yearly training schedule.
- Incidence of input receipting error is reduced by 25 percent per year.
- New monitors for all copywriters will be installed within the next six months.
- Management is apprised of direct-mail strategy through quarterly meetings.
- Instigate research project for online donors who gave at fiscal year-end.
- Inquire and do research for new software data base management system.
- Test four potential rental lists every quarter.

Long-Term Objectives

- Maintain overall direct-mail department income/expense ratio of 4.5 to 1.
- Install new data base management software within 18 months.
- Hire additional writer within 12 months.
- Hire additional designer within 18 months.
- Grow active donor base by 6.5 percent.
- Increase internal capacity to handle 2,500 receipts per month.

As explained in Exhibit 7.1, nonprofit marketing management can use both short and intervening objectives to achieve long-term growth concerns. And while most objectives in the nonprofit world project growth, intervening objectives allow a nonprofit entity to structure competitive actions in the form of objectives in a realistic and timely manner to help build a strong competitive position should conditions warrant it.

Not all objectives—short term, intervening, or long term—are tangible in that they can be measured easily. Many nonprofits also have intangible objectives. For example, they might want to change the public's mind about some issue, they might want clients to feel better about themselves, or they might want to improve the world's condition somehow. How does a nonprofit measure these intangible objectives so as to chart its progress towards its goals?

Objectives become meaningless unless there is a measurement tool behind them that translates the objectives into realizable goals. What then of objectives that do not lend themselves easily to measurement? This is obviously not a problem if the goal is easily measurable. For example, a college needs to build a gymnasium, and the financial goal is either met or it is not; a missionary raises his or her deputation support or not; an environmental group buys the 16 acres of land or not; a family of four is given a box of food or not.

In each case the measurement for achieving the objective is easy. It is in areas of intangibility (such as how donors feel about your brand or its reputation among a certain group) that measurement becomes difficult. An organizational objective may be to encourage conservation thinking, or it may seek to persuade groups of people regarding a specific issue or political stance.

Although this type of measurement may be difficult, it is usually not impossible. Many of the same research techniques used by for-profit corporations to measure the marketability of their products can be used in the nonprofit "intangible cause or product" arena.

Five Critical Measures

There is a need to manage "beyond the numbers"—but how?[8] To build a more effective marketing strategy, there are five critical issues a strategist must address through his or her information systems.

1. Organizational leadership must decide what will be measured within the organization and what will not. Given that few organizations have the resources to measure everything that is important, this becomes a critical decision. As part of this decision, leadership should decide to measure both the initiatives that lend themselves to easy measurement practices (such as with money—donations, gift size, number of gifts, etc.) and the intangible areas that are often harder to measure (how the program directors are delivering the organization's product to the clients). Having determined this, management must create a list of key indicators in descending order, capturing the most important information first. Without doing so, an organization that has not done much measurement will find itself quickly stymied by trying to measure as many things as possible without necessarily having the wherewithal to make the information actionable for management.

2. Who in the organization will see the measurements that are made? If information gathering is assigned to all department heads without managerial "teeth" in the directive, meaningful information gathering will not happen. Increasingly, larger and more complex nonprofit organizations within some causal industries are hiring information officers to manage their organization's information flow and the security behind the dispersal of key data, to help determine the timeliness of the information dispersal, and to help prioritize what will be measured and in what sequence. At the very least, a marketing support system should be created that represents a coordinated collection of data, systems, and diagnostic tools that enable those making marketing decisions to better use the information on stakeholders.

3. How will the information-gathering process be used to create more value for key stakeholders? It is not wise to implement the first two steps and then forget this third step: Will it find its way into annual reports, into quality control charts for program leaders, or into donor data that helps field representatives do their jobs? Will the information be actionable enough that the parent organization can change its strategy should the data dictate it? Clear and actionable data tied to measurable goals will move stakeholders and secure their support in a way that lofty mission statements will not.

4. Data that is gathered in an organization must be timely, as specific as possible, prescriptive, and presented in a financial framework. Data must be timely if it is to have an impact on an organization's actions. Strategies are imitated so quickly in the marketplace by competitors that the cycle time for data does allow it to become old. In addition, data that is collected must address specific parts of an organization if the information is to be acted on. The more specific the data being gathered, the more the data can be looked at by managers and become a guide to decisions they have to make. The absolute best guide that data can provide takes the form of a clear-cut recommendations—for example, "By taking this step as opposed to that step, we will deliver more value to our donors and should retain them on an average of 11 months longer than we are currently."

5. Peter Drucker observed, "All the data we have so far, including those provided by new tools, focus inward. But inside an enterprise—indeed, even inside the entire economic chain—there are only costs. Results are only on the outside."[9] For a nonprofit organization to benefit from the information revolution, it must both create an internal data footprint and work to integrate this information with continuous, real-time market information. In fact, forward-thinking nonprofit organizations are looking at their competitive plans in terms of the need to allocate funds so that long-term stakeholder creation can occur. Internal data, created in isolation, does not help focus an agency externally, whether the issue is funding sources, financial markets, employee markets, or customer segments.

Looking at the issues of institutional objectives and gathering information about stakeholders follow from two assumptions. First, all nonprofit agencies must assume they are in the market research business; second, to handle the information collected, all nonprofit agencies are also in the data base management business.

No matter how large or small organizations are, no matter the causal service they're in currently, or even the services they eventually want to offer the public, nonprofit organizations must listen and talk to their constituents as though the future of their organizations depended on it. This is mandatory if they intend to build organizations that merit clients' and donors' support and continue to grow. In addition, the data base that this information yields must be used to direct and manage all parts of the organization and, specifically, the marketing plan. Of great importance is not only the stakeholder or customer data base but the causal or product data base. It is essential to have all the necessary information about one's own cause, gathered from online sources, industry sources, or competitor sources, in order to regularly review product features, new causal trends, product benefits, and persuasive arguments.

Collecting the information efficiently is also essential. Philip Kotler, the S.C. Johnson and Son Distinguished Professor of International Marketing at Kellogg School of Management insightfully suggests, "Information carries both a cost and a value. A company can spend too much on information acquisition, leading to comments like, 'We are drowning in information and starved of knowledge.' There are vast differences between data, information, knowledge, and wisdom. Unless the data are processed into information, which is turned into knowledge, which becomes market wisdom, much of it is wasted."[9]

Data collection involves organizational listening and is accomplished in many ways; the following three methods seem to be the most popular:

1. Stakeholder observation and engagement is often accomplished through marketing directors, field representatives, chief executive officers, and program officers, all of whom can have extended conversations and contact with key stakeholders. Visiting them, talking to them about the cause they are interested in, observing how and where they live, and

noting what they like and dislike about the nonprofit organization, all contribute greatly to the knowledge base of the nonprofit organization.

2. A camp client benefits greatly from a study done by his association concerning trends in the camping world. This example of secondary data (data gathered for another purpose) is of great help to this camp director and allows him to make marketing and managerial judgments without having to gather primary data.

3. Primary data is often the most benefit-laden data that can be gathered and typically the most expensive. It is gathered through extensive face-to-face interviews, focus groups (small groups gathered to discuss an issue or product with a moderator who guides the process), and online and off-line surveys (often best suited for descriptive research).

Staying Competitive

Most nonprofit organization understand the marketing necessity that says, "Pay attention to the individuals who enable your organization to be viable." Many of these same organizations have embraced a marketing "pre-culture" that embodies all the trappings of the marketing culture with the exception of actually implementing many of the systems. Others have embraced a full-blown marketing culture as a meaningful and collaborative exchange between the nonprofit agency and client, customer, or donor and have translated this orientation into action. One important step in helping nonprofit organizations move from a non-implementation culture to one of implementation is for them to critically examine their operations to find out what they did strategically from a marketing perspective in the past and what they hope to do in the future. Specifically, it is important to do this from a client, customer, volunteer, and donor perspective. This process involves asking the following questions:

1. What has been the past marketing performance of the organization, and what might this mean for future marketing performance?

2. Was a marketing strategy used in the past, and is there a current marketing strategy the organization hopes to use?

3. Were there problems that occurred inside the organization, such as implementation problems that may have affected the marketing performance?
4. How much did the marketing campaigns in the past cost? Did the projects come in under budget, over budget, or at budget? Did the organization spend enough money to accomplish its marketing goals?
5. How are other, similar causes doing right now financially?

Summary

Internal nonprofit analysis first identifies the organization's needs and then determines what clients and constituents want and what donors and other stakeholders will support. These findings are turned into programs and services. The goal is to help the nonprofit organization determine its strategy for achieving a strong client, customer, volunteer, and donor perspective. To accomplish this, it must look at internal variables that are either positively or negatively affecting this stakeholder orientation. This information then contributes directly to developing a nonprofit organization's strategy, which is also the subject of Chapter 8.

8

Creating Competitive Advantage

*Strategy has come to discuss the objective of competition as sustained
competitive advantage. That is, the successful firm is one that
demonstrates long-term advantage over its competition.*
Professor Stephen Tallman, University of Richmond,
as quoted by Rich Horwath in *Deep Dive*
(Austin, TX, Greenleaf Book Group Press, 2009), p. 37

How do we make the best choices strategically? What advertising
should we use, which audiences should we target, and what will be
our value proposition? This chapter has a built-in assumption: very
successful nonprofit companies either intuitively or explicitly have a
strategy. At issue is not whether an institution has a strategy operating; every nonprofit organization has a strategy operating whether it
is explicitly stated or dictated by chance. However, to improve their
strategic positions, nonprofit organizations usually need to develop
their strategies explicitly. The "how" of doing this is what the next
chapters are about.

Unfortunately, marketing management language can be very
imprecise. Within the nonprofit community, words such as *strategy,
policies, objectives,* and *planning* often have meanings that vary,
depending on the organization. For purposes of clarity, the chapters on strategy adhere to the following definitions:

- *Objective*—the end measurable result the nonprofit organization must accomplish.

- *Strategy*—a summary of how objective(s) with major financial or programmatical implications will be pursued.
- *Planning*—predetermining a course of action to which a non-profit organization anticipates committing resources (financial, human, and otherwise).
- *Policy*—a decision regarding how an organization will conduct its affairs.

Strategy Options

Some nonprofit organizations are successful without having a specific, well-worked-out strategy. They see a need and go about fulfilling it. Often riding a series of breaks based on luck and intuition, these organizations come up with a formula, a marketing and branding strategy that fulfills the value needs of their supporters; a strategy of sorts is born. More organizations try this tactic than we might think. However, the impact of stakeholder values and their combined marketplace "voice" have become a driving force within the nonprofit culture and the environment surrounding it. Coupled with other nonprofit voices such as foundations and corporate giving, institutional strategies have become too substantial to ignore. The rules of philanthropy have shifted as a result. It is no longer possible to ignore the need for organizational strategies that take stakeholders into account, give them real benefits, and serve them by listening to and collaborating with them. These spillover effects have also enabled better nonprofit products to be available in our society.

There are other real benefits to having an explicitly stated organizational strategy. Central to these benefits is having both internal and external stakeholders united in knowing where the organization is trying to go. Further, a strategy allows all employees to know what the central value proposition is to external stakeholders and enables them to live it out in their daily jobs. In these organizations, strategy is not the same thing as planning. Many nonprofit organizations have long-range plans but have no strategies to achieve the goals of their plans. Benjamin B. Tregoe and John W. Zimmerman—senior leaders and management consultants with Kepner-Tregoe and authors of the book *Top Management Strategy*—noted that strategy is a continuing process that must be separated from normal operations. In their opinion, there is often confusion in management's mind between

Exhibit 8.1   The Adverse Effects of Long-Range Planning on Strategy Formulation

1. Long-range plans are typically based on projections of current operations into the future.
2. Plans that companies make determine their direction, as opposed to letting a clear sense of direction determine their plans.
3. Where long-range plans exist to guide planning, they are invariably set in financial terms.
4. If top managers do not have a clear strategy with which to assess the plans that percolate up from the organization, they become locked into allocating resources on the basis of these plans.
5. Long-rang plans are often overly simplistic.
6. Long-range plans are often inflexible.
7. Long-range planning is actually more short range than anyone cares to admit.

strategic thinking and long-range planning, the outcome having an adverse effect on strategy formulation. Long-range planning alone—while important—is inadequate for strategy formulation. (See Exhibit 8.1.)

Nonprofit organizations that purposefully fail to build strategy or seem to operate by chance ultimately do have an operating strategy. Although it is generally not recognized or explicitly stated, this de facto strategy usually fits into one of the following categories:

- A strategy of hope.
- A strategy determined by crisis.
- A strategy that is status quo in nature.
- A strategy that continues to run while its associated costs or impact are not measured.

Strategy of Hope

This is far and away the most popular method of setting a strategic direction. This methodology lets events control the outcome. Perhaps this is such a popular method because of the lack of certainty in today's economic world. Strategy by hope is often the eventual outcome of the pressure some nonprofit executives feel today that freezes them into inaction. One thing is clear: Strategy by hope is certainly the easiest strategy to come up with, with no pressure to perform or associated deadlines.

Doing nothing strategically is a kind of "life preserver" for some nonprofit executives. In a sea of competing courses of action, doing nothing may seem like the safest method of survival, and for the rare nonprofit executive, doing nothing may work for a while. However, for the majority of nonprofit organizations, embarking on a particular strategic course of action proves to be the most effective tool for organizational growth and for maneuvering through a competitive environment.

Strategy Determined by Crisis

This has become a remarkably popular strategic mode during the past three years of economic turmoil. For some organizations, this strategy is used to gather quick dollars and sympathy from unsuspecting donors, who respond to an emotional appeal only to be approached again and again with a crisis approach. This type of ongoing crisis, sometimes fabricated by the organization, takes the place of ethical fund raising. A crisis strategy of sorts is also employed frequently in small organizations where there is what Bill McConkey, Chairman of the Board of the consulting group McConkey/Johnston International Inc., calls "founder's fever." In this state, the director or founder spends his or her days dealing with "crisis after crisis" as opposed to allocating line supervision and responsibility. By keeping busy, feeling needed all the time, and having the organization revolve around them, directors feel gratified and have an ever-present reason (or crisis) to explain why objectives are seldom fully reached.

Unfortunately, because so many nonprofit executives are not only competent but work exceedingly long and hard, they can often go for quite long periods of time relying only on themselves. In doing so, they ensure the organization will grow according to the limits of their time and energy. In addition, they guarantee that the organization will suffer when they leave, get sick, or simply tire out.

Strategy by Status Quo

Simply stated, most nonprofit managers and marketing directors are risk averse, and because they are, it becomes much easier for an organization to allow people to do what is right in their own eyes. They avoid upsetting the apple cart or departmental peace by imposing their ideas or by suggesting that there should be a jointly agreed-on strategy with an agreed-on destination that will require people to work collaboratively for the common good of the agency. Without such a mandate, employees can be content with their own progress, working in a relatively risk-free environment the way they have always worked. These employees typically work hard while going strategically where they think they should go, implementing their outcomes and doing what they think is right, without the slightest bit of coordination or pre-thinking of where their colleagues are going or where their personal strategies are taking them. As a result, dysfunctional operations often occur, internal department competition can flare up, and accelerated burn-out of employees is sometimes a by-product.

Because employees never arrive at an institutional objective or destination as a group, this process can destroy the trust among employees needed to ensure an organization's success. A brand of unproductive, splintered attention can develop in this kind of organization. Managers at the top of many for-profit companies work hard to direct themselves and fellow workers towards a goal, with the end goal often bringing some kind of value to stockholders. A large number of nonprofit organizations do not practice this degree of concentration, engaging instead in activities that carry little value in the eyes of key stakeholders. If an activity cannot be justified in the eyes of a stakeholder, it should be reconsidered.

Although splintered attention is not a favorable condition, some nonprofit agencies actually thrive in this environment for a while. Organizations in this strategy mode rely on salesmanship, from the top and in their supporting media, to help ensure trusting donors and nonprofit friends that the organization is embarking on new programs to meet new challenges, while avoiding discussion of how existing programs are faring.

Investing in a Strategy While Not Counting the Cost

Loyalty towards programs, regardless of how well they are performing, is a problem within the nonprofit world. Users of this strategy go on doing what they have always been doing, keeping in mind that tomorrow will be exactly like today. This strategy presents itself as steady and rigid, but the reality regarding its performance may not be so positive. Some of the reasoning that allows this strategic problem to continue relates to the notion of risk and of individuals not wanting to appear wrong in their judgment.

The inherent problem in this type of operation is that it is distinctly aimed away from the needs of clients and donors and is instead focused on the organization's desire not to upset the balance that it is enjoying. Managers routinely punished for missteps and errors often find themselves employing this strategy to find protection and peace at all costs and push accountability away from them.

The Most Popular Strategic Orientations and Their Application to the Organization

All successful nonprofit strategies must involve themselves in one of two issues: (1) the cause's services or (2) its products in relation to clients and donors (which, together, ultimately constitute the organization's markets). There are many articulated strategies for organizations to use; some are designed to enable a defensive posture in light of strong competitive forces at work, while others are designed to allow offensive posturing to take place. Still others are aimed at giving an organization a defendable position within its cause-related field. There are many approaches, each successful one ultimately involving a unique construction specific to the nonprofit organization in question. At the broadest level, though, there are some distinct strategic postures that any nonprofit organization can take in coping with its environment and those forces it identifies as competitive.

Three generic marketing strategies, in one way or another, fit every nonprofit marketing situation. These three postures are

1. No strategic change
2. A product strategy
3. Sustainable competitive advantage

A part of these three strategies is to look at how strategy relates to competition. There can be little doubt in the for-profit world that the goal of strategy is to beat competition. This sentiment is not always true in the nonprofit world. In fact, some nonprofit organizations are embarrassed at being the strongest within their cause-related field or having clients and donors think their programs are the best. "Keeping up" with the competition is not enough. The key to long-term success is getting ahead of the competition. Allowing oneself to be defined by competition is only a small part of strategy. The effectiveness of a strategy is ultimately defined by the value the client or donor feels he or she receives, not by the posturing of nonprofit organizations vis-à-vis other nonprofit organizations.

No Strategic Change

No strategic change (or the concept of staying where a nonprofit organization finds itself strategically) may sound like a terrible strategy to some, but it is a viable strategy when conditions suggest that the cost of change is too high. Although many business periodicals document an endless parade of companies that folded when they did not change to meet changing environmental conditions, some companies feel they flourish by not changing, and, in some cases, by waiting until environmental conditions change. Consider this example: the executives of a large nonprofit in the East Coast came to the conclusion that to continue their programming the way they did it, more revenue—either raised or generated by fees—would be required. They felt that such moves in the current economic environment would drastically alter their relationships with their donor and client populations. As a result, they decided to alter their expectations and favor other objectives that better reflected their personal and professional judgments. The board agreed with the leadership's decision, as did the donors and clients. No change in strategy was initiated.

Although no strategic change is a viable marketing strategy, there are few instances where it is a good strategy. A "good strategy" is usually thought of not in terms of short-term changes but as involving long-term construction whereby the nonprofit organization, over time, places itself in a position that can be improved over the same time period. Too often in the minds of nonprofit executives, a no-change strategy translates into "no improvement" in the way things are done. Organizations that adopt a no-change strategy usually do not attempt to raise the standards, cut costs, or maximize their resources. In addition, little thought is given to how the nonprofit organization might defend its market position should a competitor come in and offer the same set of services—perhaps more cheaply—to the same constituency. Quite literally, "no strategic change" often becomes a euphemism for lack of managerial thinking and focus.

Most nonprofit organizations run very hard just to stay in place in terms of dollars brought in and maintaining their service share of market and their return of their fund-raising investment. In times of increased competition in an economy that is very volatile, most non-profit managers would find a do-nothing marketing strategy as neither attractive nor wise. In addition, this strategy seems to ignore a nonprofit organization's needs to strategically self-renew in light of donor and client demands. The lack of strategic choice often causes organizations to focus inward, becoming fixated on long-range planning while ignoring donors, clients, the market at large, and competing nonprofit organizations. The ability to sustain performance is lost. There must be a connection between long-term strategy and client, donor, volunteer, and constituent needs.

If a no-change strategy is adopted, the organization must not lose sight of its donors and clients. This is where the definition of the client/constituent and the donor/volunteer becomes important. Clients and donors are iconoclastic, making and breaking patterns every day, often showing very little loyalty to any group. As donor and customer behaviors change, so must the marketing strategy of an organization. Constituent values change and migrate in different directions. A no-change strategy ignores such value migration and relies on hunches and stereotypes to navigate in the marketplace.

It makes sense to move away from a no-change marketing strategy when analysis indicates that the nonprofit organization can no longer meet its objectives the way it intended. Organizations need to look ahead one to three years and project where they will be at the end of the measurement period, as against where they think they should be. If the two are not reasonably within striking distance of each other, the strategy of no change should be reexamined.

One way to move into a more competitive strategic mode is by looking at the causes, services, and products a nonprofit organization offers.

A Cause and Product Strategy

Nonprofit causes and products are items or programs offered to markets that provide service to clients and provide an organization with financial support, volunteerism, and a sense of goal accomplishment. A nonprofit organization's program is that which ultimately benefits or satisfies a particular segment of society. Its products can be more than physical, tangible items. They can also be embodied in a person, a service, an event, an idea, or an institution. Sometimes a nonprofit organization's products are defined individually, such as a book on a particular recovery program; sometimes they're defined as a part of a particular grouping, such as a line of recovery books; sometimes products are defined in broader categories, such as a "book publishing division."

Most nonprofit organizations have used a product strategy, knowingly or not. The primary reason for this has been historical. It used to be that all a nonprofit organization had to do to be financially successful was to produce some type of program and a supportive constituency would immediately fall in line with money, enthusiasm, and volunteerism. And while a product strategy can still be a very wise competitive strategy, much has changed during the past several years, as shown in the lack of loyalty exhibited by donors, volunteers, and customers toward nonprofit causes and products, and in the proliferation of causes that mirror each other's operational, promotional, and service activities—what could be termed as generic causal product approaches.

The point was well made by Theodore Levitt, among others, that people, when they purchase, buy more than products.[1] They buy the expectation of benefits. It is this cluster of benefits—or the value alignment that donors, volunteers, customers, and clients gain by being involved with any organization—surrounding the organization that is missing from many marketing strategies. An organization, simply put, must provide more benefits for constituent involvement than other nonprofit organizations that provide similar service. That, ultimately, will make a difference.

This augmented view of what a product is and the hidden aspect of competition, forgotten by most nonprofit agencies, has had significant consequences. As the need for different benefits changes among donors, clients, and constituents, one shift that should occur in the nonprofit marketplace (and should affect every nonprofit strategy) is the need for stakeholder analysis to determine why people will or will not support a cause, and the benefits that accrue to them from their decision to do so.

An organization that opts for a product strategy says, in essence, that the causes, services, and products it produces will be key to the retention and expansion of its supportive constituencies in the future. Its causes will define its markets of clients, support, and help. In a broad sense, every nonprofit organization that adopts this strategy also adopts the notion that its competition will come primarily from other nonprofit organizations that are producing similar services and products for similar audiences.

A nonprofit agency facing this generic onslaught will try through differentiation to create a cause, service, or product that is perceived as unique and different from the offerings of its competitors. This differentiation allows it to create interest among its constituents for the way in which it is pursuing its goals. Differentiation can occur in many ways: through targeted audiences, through the quality of the service offering, through the way (technology) in which the service is delivered, through the donation amounts that are asked for to support parts of the operation, through the quantity of services given back to the supportive clientele, and even through the alliances the nonprofit institution has or the endorsements it enjoys.

Typically, there are a number of practical decisions a nonprofit entity must make when employing a cause and product strategy. They are discussed more fully in the following section.

Matching the Market

The cause, service, or product needs to match or align with the correct market. There is an interrelationship between what a nonprofit organization offers and what the market wants to buy, support, or become involved with. Ignoring this interrelationship can be detrimental to nonprofit organizations, because they may be producing services or products that the market simply does not want. Alignment must be created between donors and customers, the organization's strategy, the processes it uses, and the environment the cause is a part of.[2] In particular, the cause cannot be viewed in isolation. Everything affects its perception in the marketplace including what your competitors are doing, the economy, and the prevailing social trends.

As a consequence, an organization cannot just send out a positioning or branding message and expect it to have resonance apart from the environment. The organization must work with the environment to differentiate and position its products and cause. It must understand who the market influencers are, what the religious issues are, what people are thinking, what their prejudices are, what their likes and dislikes are, what they want to hear. Then companies must position their products to fit the attitudes of the marketplace.[3]

Tactics for Achieving Competitive Advantage

A nonprofit marketer must understand basic rules of performance and how they influence the strategic competitive advantage a non-profit institution seeks. Certain generalizations about nonprofit causes and products prevail, and understanding them can lead to better marketing decisions. Ignoring them can lead to disaster. Here are some:

1. The pursuit of organizational stability can be the antithesis of strategic renewal.
2. A small number of causes and products can often bring in the majority of clients, donations, customers, and volunteers.
3. The more marginal a cause, service, or product is in terms of client interest and financial and volunteered support, the more likely it is to drain the organization's finances and the managerial time of its leadership.
4. The more marginal a cause or product is, the more likely it will take excessive expenditures to achieve marketing success.
5. Usually, an increase in management time and in fund-development expense cannot turn around a cause, service, or product that clients, customers, and donors alike perceive as defective, inferior, or unattractive.
6. An inferior service, cause, or product can tarnish the reputation and image of other products.
7. Product and service accountability on the part of the nonprofit organization as along with performance measurability enhances resource allocation decisions for individual nonprofit products and service.
8. Modifications and repositioning tactics can extend the life of a service, cause, or product.
9. Competitors are constantly looking for ways to acquire competitive advantages over others' services and products.
10. Client and donor product and service perceptions may be more significant than superior or inferior product performance.
11. Very successful nonprofit products and services achieve the highest average gift size or possess superior qualities as compared with competitive causes and products.
12. Faddish, fashionable, or popular causes can be like Roman candles—quick to light the skies and quick to fizzle out.
13. Under most circumstances, donors prefer growth over stability.

The Sustainable Competitive Advantage

Sustainable competitive advantage is an element (or combination of elements) of the business strategy that provides a meaningful advantage over existing and future competitors.[4] The goal in talking about a sustainable competitive advantage is for a nonprofit institution to establish a difference between itself and its competitors that is consequential, meaningful, and sustainable by the agency.

- To be consequential, the competitive advantage must be perceived by stakeholders to be of an unusually high quality. It must show superiority and mastery.
- To be meaningful, the advantage must be understood by stakeholders as not just important but important enough that they feel compelled to be involved with the nonprofit's cause.
- To be sustainable, the competitive advantage must be more than a "flash in the pan" and must be supported and enhanced by the nonprofit agency over time.

What Constitutes a Sustainable Competitive Advantage

In previous chapters, an organization's assets and competencies were noted and talked about simply because they form the basis of a competitive advantage—specifically those that are difficult to copy or compete against. For example,

- A client has a leadership team that has worked together for almost 20 years; the team's members know each other and the organization so well that it is hard for others to match their collaborative skill mix.
- A client has reengineered its camping program so extensively and with such strong talent and credentials that competitors have not had any success in mirroring the capabilities of the camp.
- A client has a very strong marketing culture and outspends its competitors' combined marketing budgets.
- A client's CEO spends more than 70 percent of his time in relationship management with the organization's donors and prospective donors and has gained a national reputation for donor management.

In each of these examples, any competitor can try to imitate the strengths that are noted—and many have—but no one has succeeded. Whether personal competencies, corporate relationships, corporate culture, the amount of time and energy expended, the quality of managerial leadership, or the budget that is available, none of the competitive advantages have been duplicated by competitors.

A Competitive Advantage Hinges on a Value Proposition

Strategic competitive advantage depends on the four components that constitute a value proposition:

1. Where you compete
2. The capabilities you bring to the market
3. What you do in the service markets
4. What the donor, customer, volunteer, and client realizes in value

What you offer as an advantage to your constituents ought to be of superior value, based on your organization's assets and capabilities and how you use them tactically. In a crowded market place, delivering enduring value to a stakeholder may be one of the most important attributes of a competitive strategy. Further, it may be the hardest for a competitor to reproduce.

Where You Compete.   Whom you compete against and where you compete are two sides of an important tactical question. Your knowledge of the competitive forces in the marketplace and the value options they are offering various markets helps you tactically in your choice of a possible target market. The decision is important precisely because of your organization's need to create relevant value and strategies for your prospective stakeholders that will be so appreciated by them that they will, in turn, lock out competing offers of value by your competitors. To offer prospective customers and donors the same value constellation as your competitors leads to marketplace redundancy, to competitive parity, and ultimately to lowest-price scenarios involving your products along with a lack of vital donor loyalty in your fund development. Knowing the weaknesses of your competition and aligning those weaknesses with the strengths and capabilities your organization possesses allows you to assess how and where your strategy will be most valuable to stakeholders and where your competitors will be most vulnerable, not only immediately but in the long term. Likewise, knowing your organization's weaknesses allows you to steer away from markets where you cannot deliver strong and unique brand associations.

The Capabilities You Bring to the Market.   The goal in creating a competitive advantage is to offer capabilities and programs or activities that allow you to create superior value for the stakeholders involved. What your organization is—its core competencies and resources—allow you to compete at an advantage. Capabilities come in two flavors: (1) those your competitors will be able to imitate and use to steal your market away from you, and (2) those they will try to imitate but will be unable to.

Capabilities that cannot be imitated are invaluable simply because they help determine what the competitive rules in the market will be. The more distinctive your organization's capabilities are, the bigger the competitive advantage you will have in the marketplace. If two organizations have the same capabilities, it will be much harder for either to gain marketplace advantage. If all competitors have access to the same capabilities it will be hard to gain an advantage. It is when your organization has a distinctive capability or capabilities (e.g., in marketing expertise, programming competency, effective leadership and managerial culture, or intellectual property) that allows superior programmatical innovation or impenetrable brand recognition and strength, that true competitive advantage occurs and supports the organization's value proposition.

What You Do in the Service Market.   What you do in the marketplace matters increasingly in today's transparent society. Your programs, when built around your agency's capabilities and selected for distinct markets, become the visible portion of what stakeholders know and see concerning your organization. How you resource these programs (people, money, infrastructure) ultimately helps you achieve your corporate missional goals and becomes the evidence that enables stakeholders to judge an organization's performance and value set.

Many organizations run more than one program at a time, and this can help an agency's competitive advantage; each program typically targets a select group of stakeholders and presents each group with a unique value set tied to the program being offered. As programs become bundled together, working in unison and leveraging each other, the organization drives success in a more advantageous way than the organization that promotes only one program.

What your organization does—or does not do—in the marketplace becomes the part of its strategic advantage that is presented to the public at large. According to Rich Horwath, founder and president of Strategic Thinking Institute,

> *The challenge most executives face trying to determine their competitive advantage is that they look at the entire organization or product as a whole. It's not until the organization or product is broken down into individual activities that a clearer assessment of competitive advantage emerges.*[5]

What the Donor, Customer, and Volunteer Realize in Value.   Stakeholders hear from many organizations every day, see what they have to offer, and have almost limitless opportunities for involvement. What causes stakeholders to say "yes" to some product and causal offerings and "no" to others?

1. Stakeholders are looking for differences among the offerings in the marketplace, particularly in the area of alignment of one's personal values and how they mesh with the values of the organization they are currently attending. The closer the value alignment between organization and stakeholder, the more likely the donation or buying decision will be affected positively.
2. Values are often built around the capabilities an organization holds, the culture it operates from, and how these capabilities and assets are used and promoted in the marketplace.
3. Once internalized by the stakeholder, the competitive difference between one organization and another becomes part of the brand equity of the organization and forms the lens through which the stakeholder views the organization.

Augmenting Success

Most nonprofit organizations can no longer rely solely on one program that differentiates itself from others—in a competitive marketplace there must be more than one offering to the public. In what many call the "synergy tactic" (the whole is more than the sum of its parts), it can become easy for a competitor to mirror an agency's single program but much harder when an organization has multiple offerings that are built on core organizational competencies, are unique, are competitively sustainable, and provide stakeholders with points of differentiation. Organizational synergy is achieved thereby. With programs operating together as opposed to independently, synergy suggests that the responses to multiple programs are not only greater than when programs are run separately, but expenses for the programs might be lower, as will be the initial investment.

In the nonprofit world, synergy often works because of an organization's strong marketplace brand equity, strategic alliances, strong fund-development and marketing capabilities, personnel competency, and location. Here is an example.

> A client in a metropolitan market has a well-known brand name in helping the urban poor. The nonprofit agency has leveraged its brand name and capabilities to expand the number of programs it offers in the fields of education, vocational training, counseling young people, and judicial counseling. Using its vision for the city, available core competencies, established government networks, donors whose values are in alignment with where the organization is going, and its brand strength, the nonprofit agency is using synergy to achieve its mission and improve many lives.

Market Strategies

Markets refer to groupings of men, women, and children who share some common characteristics and common needs. The nonprofit organization that considers employing a market strategy decides it will provide a range of services, causes, or products that fill, or will fill, client, customer, donor, and volunteer needs. In fact, looking for ways to fill this stakeholder need becomes the predominant marketing occupation of the nonprofit agency. Of course, this notion of developing markets to support a cause is very common. Many organizations dream that this will become a reality for them. To achieve this requires the nonprofit organization to have certain capabilities that may not always be readily available. These include

1. Having a system of disciplined, comprehensive, and systematic recordkeeping so an organization knows where it has been and where it wants to go.
2. Identifying the elements through a situation analysis that will shape a strategic plan—in this case, an expansion plan.
3. Looking at a variety of key variables like the seasonality (if applicable) of the offer, all the variables affecting the costs expended on behalf of the expansion, and the expansion vehicle itself. (For example, a nonprofit institution may choose to expand its supportive base through a series of email blasts.)
4. Developing a system that will take care of new donors or customers that come aboard.

One Necessary Commitment and Five Possible Growth Strategies

For a nonprofit organization to prosper in today's economic uncertainty a performance culture with a clearly defined commitment to a core marketing strategy is both needed and required. This commitment can, for example, be a long-term perspective with a clear plan for acquiring new and improving existing organizational capabilities, augmenting the way the agency delivers its value proposition, and aligning the organization with core stakeholders in a new way.

A client decided eight years ago that it wanted to dominate the winter market for camping, not only in his state but in the contiguous states as well. Moving to improve his existing strategy, he listened to his constituents and looked for value alignment, changed his programming team, reworked the infrastructure of the camp to make it supportive of where he was going, continuously improved his site, and rebranded his winter programs.

The strategic plan was perceived by this director as achievable, and he spent years enhancing and improving what he was doing strategically so that he could ultimately enhance his value proposition to those he was marketing to. Although his strategy worked, it was inherently risky. Opportunities could have presented themselves to the organization (and they did) that had short-term payouts and could have been lucrative if they had been pursued. It was not that going with any of these would have been a wrong decision. However, they were not organizational strategies as much as they were organizational opportunities.

How can an organization achieve its growth goals? Five overriding market growth strategies should be considered when an organization looks to strategically expand its boundaries:

1. *Persuading an existing constituency to use a service or product more through more frequent interactions with it (such as giving more frequently) is the most natural step. By becoming more financially involved with an agency such as expanding an individual's average gift size or giving to or purchasing the service more frequently an individual ties their loyalty more closely to the organization.* Most non-profit marketing plans do not allow for upgrading the involvement of donors and customers in the ways just cited. Apart from the increased revenue an organization realizes from this new financial involvement with customers and donors, the organization reduces its competitive exposure because the newfound involvement with the stakeholder makes the organization almost impervious to substitute competitor attacks and provides it with substantial bonding opportunities and the luxury of budgeting on committed dollars.

2. *Allowing the bonding relationship with a market to be reflected in the new product features or the new services the nonprofit organization introduces allows the market to ascertain the agency it has a vested interest in it.* It has been said that marketing is about having customers, not merely acquiring them. Attracting clients, customers, and donors is only the first step in the nonprofit organization's marketing program; maximizing their time with the organization and enabling them to enjoy a long-term, multiple-service relationship with the institution is another and, perhaps, equally important goal of marketing. This is accomplished in various ways—for example, features can be added to existing products and programs to enhance certain constituent members' experience with the organization and to enhance their value equity with the organization.

3. *Expanding into and targeting new audience segments for services or products.* Geographic expansion is now becoming more of an option to those nonprofit agencies that are growing and willing to take on new commitments. Because a number of nonprofit organizations—across industries—are in trouble financially, growth for those agencies that have a strong value proposition may take them to new territories, states, and countries.

4. *Where possible, using vertical integration to move closer to the customer or donor.* For example, a nonprofit organization had a deal with a printing company to have its materials printed by the company; it paid the company a fee and royalties for the privilege of warehousing inventory. The company now uses online publishers who print per piece; it no longer worries about inventory and moves, by its activity pattern, closer to the client, donor, or constituent.

5. *Related diversification and the merger of nonprofit organizations.* Two nonprofit organizations in the same field, often unable to compete effectively with others, may combine their expertise, services, resources, advertising, and fund-development dollars and thereby operate efficiently. Or they may consider merging—often a quick solution to growth problems. Mergers save management and organizational time while allowing an organization to acquire skills and resources not present internally. No doubt the driving force here is either financial stresses on the nonprofit organization or pressure from donors.

Summary

This chapter has focused on the strategic dimensions nonprofit organizations can use to improve performance. In today's uncertain, turbulent, and extremely competitive world, lasting marketing success depends on the quality of strategic thinking used by nonprofit organizations. The overriding question is, How do organizations take strategy that is formulated at the top and translate it into operational reality? The difficulty of imposing strategy and making it work is the subject of Chapter 9.

CHAPTER

9

Winning through Competitive Strategy Options

The young lieutenant of a small Hungarian detachment in the Alps sent a reconnaissance unit into the icy wilderness. It began to snow immediately, snowed for two days, and the unit did not return. The lieutenant suffered, fearing that he had dispatched his own people to death. But the third day the unit came back. Where had they been? How had they made their way? Yes, they said, we considered ourselves lost and waited for the end. And then one of us found a map in his pocket. That calmed us down. We pitched camp, lasted out the snowstorm, and then with the map we discovered our bearings. And here we are. The lieutenant borrowed this remarkable map and had a good look at it. He discovered to his astonishment that it was not a map of the Alps, but a map of the Pyrenees.

Karl E. Weick, "Substitutes for Strategy," in David J. Teece
(ed.), *The Competitive Challenge*
(New York; Harper and Row, 1987), p. 222

In a turbulent and unpredictable environment will any map do when you are lost? Extending the analogy to the issue of strategy, will any strategy do when an organization is unsure which way to go? How does the same organization use strategy, and how does it know which strategy to employ? Should an organization adapt to a given strategy, or should the strategy fit the characteristics of the organization? And given the realities of various competitive situations, are there some organizations for which no strategy will work? This chapter provides answers to these questions.

You cannot separate a nonprofit organization from the strategy it chooses. Using a strategy—even the wrong strategy—can indeed help to focus its purpose for existence through an intensive review of its plans, positions, and perspectives. This analysis is aided by managers using conceptual frameworks that help organizations identify areas of strengths, weaknesses, and particular corporate characteristics (what some call "human dimensions"), necessitating an ongoing, never-ending internal analysis of competencies and strategy desirabilities to ensure a fit between them. Depicting the interaction of organizational components has resulted in many framework models designed by behavioral scientists and consultants to determine whether organizations can support their particular strategies.

Before looking at some of the strategies available to nonprofit managers and leaders, it is important to look at how strategies are interpreted by managers before they are implemented by their organizations and then at how strategies are developed by those who will implement them.

The Nature of Strategy and Its Uses

Given the uncertain economic environment many nonprofit organizations face currently, it is important for a nonprofit manager to be able to align the purposes and goals of his or her organization with the changes the environment may be imposing on the organization. This often necessitates repositioning one's institution in light of an uncertain future and identifying and making the necessary changes within an organization called for by this uncertainty. A nonprofit agency's strategy can ensure that these changes occur as long as the necessary prerequisites are in place.

- The working strategy must be drawn up in light of the institution's major goals and policies.
- The strategy must coordinate and control actions to achieve a few key targets or goals.
- The strategy must take into account both what is known and what is unknown (no analyst can program a strategy as to take into account what will happen once humans get into the act).

- The strategy in question should be supported by other organizational strategies, depending on a company's complexity.

Given the need for a fundamental structure, organizational direction can be changed so that the values and ideals of the non-profit in question can be realized. Furthering this notion, Paul Nutt and Robert Backoff in their book *Strategic Management of Public and Third Sector Organizations* list three ways in which a strategy can be used in light of its environment. They can be summed up as follows:

1. *Strategy as focus.* Because people within organizations have individualistic goals that can both be competitive and at odds with the organization, strategy can serve as a deterrent to disallow personal "fiefdoms" to take root and grow by focusing effort, which, in turn, helps coordinate activity in an agreed-on direction.
2. *Strategy as consistency.* Strategy can reduce uncertainty by offering direction for obtaining what is wanted, thereby satisfying people's needs for order and predictability in their affairs.
3. *Strategy as purpose.* Strategy also provides meaning to those inside and outside the organization by giving them a way to understand what the organization is about and a way to differentiate it from other organizations engaged in seemingly similar activities.[1]

Because there are many uses of strategy within an organization, many authors have written about it, and the lists of its uses seem endless. At base level, strategy seems to have at least six primary uses within a nonprofit institution:

1. Strategy is, or becomes, a plan that takes the organization on some intentional direction.
2. Strategy can also be used to send signals to competitors. In his important book *Competitive Strategy: Techniques for Analyzing Industries and Competitors,* Michael Porter suggests that organizations can give signals that sometimes serve to dissuade another organization from entering the marketplace.[2] For example, if someone runs a food pantry in a town and feels the field is too crowded for others to enter it, he or she might institute strong promotional efforts on television,

through the organization's web site, over the radio, and in print ads to give the impression that the food pantry in question already has the field sewn up, thereby discouraging new attempts at entry.

3. Strategy can be thought of as a pattern connecting the actions that were intended with those that were not originally intended as the environment the organization interacts with changes, thereby forcing new thoughts and discarding old ones as new information surfaces. This type of thinking was summed up by the business executive who said, "Gradually, the successful approaches merge into a pattern of action that becomes our strategy."[3]

4. Apart from being used as a plan, perhaps the most popular use of strategy is to create a market niche. Using an organization's strengths in light of its environment, niche strategies direct organizational resources into areas where there is little competition, thereby protecting the organization from competitors and maximizing an environment's receptivity to its products.

5. While not often discussed in the nonprofit context, strategy can also be thought of as the personality of the organization—what Henry Mintzberg calls "perspective . . . an ingrained way of perceiving the world."[4] Strategy defines how an organization will deal with problems and opportunities. In this light, strategy may also be thought of as the protector of the core values of the organization.

6. Finally, strategy is also used as promotion. By setting out a direction for what the organization hopes to become, strategy begins the process of shaping action towards the organization's long-term aspirations by means of its promotional efforts.

To be successful, strategies must add value for the stakeholder to the organization's presentation; otherwise, there is little need for a strategy to be employed. Real value, perceived by stakeholders to be important, sustainable, and meaningful to them at the moment of decision must be the result of any successful strategy. Value is typically conveyed through the value proposition that the organization uses as part of its strategic mix. This proposition, built around the real or aspirational capabilities and assets of the organization, must be pertinent and believable from the consumer's point of view and must be realizable by the organization. Most importantly, what the organization promises to the stakeholder through the value proposition must be perceived by the stakeholder as different from what competitors are offering. Without this perceived difference, stakeholders see sameness in competing offers and feel free to choose any strategic option, given that all of them appear to be the same.

Environmental Context and Strategic Options

What do the following examples have in common?

- A well-known adoption agency that for years has been placing relatively healthy children from a certain country with appreciative families in the United States, has now been told by that country that mentally and physically healthy children will no longer be available for adoption. The agency can, instead, try to place young children from the same country who have neurological or physical disabilities.
- A Midwestern nonprofit agency spent more than $2.5 million donated dollars building an attraction that it said would have national drawing power and make the nonprofit agency well-known throughout the country. The experiment failed miserably, and the building is currently used as a giant meeting room.
- A large nonprofit agency received almost 22 percent of its donated dollars from executives and agencies that worked in Silicon Valley. Almost all of these donated dollars disappeared after the dot.com financial bust, and the agency has never recovered financially.

In each of these cases, the circumstances and settings in which the nonprofit organizations operated changed. The changes, in turn, had a serious effect on the agencies when they occurred. To deal successfully with these changes would have required different skills, different capabilities, and a change in their strategic vision (in each of these scenarios, the nonprofit agency had to make radical changes in the way it operated). Strategic decisions, an organization's vision, and the tactics it uses depend largely on the agency's ability to understand important trends and critical issues as they relate to an institution. Not being able to do so puts an organization at risk.

Strategic adaptability is required to manage change when context changes. In each of the foregoing cases, the strategic plan that was at work in one context turned out to be the wrong plan in a different context. How does an organization learn to seize important opportunities for its future or avoid investments that will potentially harm it? To do so requires organizational competence in identifying trends that could hurt the institution, identifying vulnerabilities that could put the organization at risk, and having the ability to be strategically adaptable in any situation:

- *Identifying trends through routine assessments.* Marketing texts are filled with the idea of doing routine "situation or market assessments" designed to help an organization to understand what it is facing regarding trends that donors and customers might be evidencing and to understand how to deal with them organizationally. This is a good idea as far as it goes, but it doesn't go far enough for the organization that does this on an annual basis or on a five-year review basis. Trends arrive very quickly, and many managers simply do not have a good understanding of the context their donors and customers act within. Witness the debate today on how best to use—or whether to use—e-mail for solicitation purposes.
- *Force your organization to change and adapt.* Having the ability to adjust a strategy or the way an organization deals with opportunities or vulnerabilities requires a culture and its leaders to adapt aggressively to the contextual changes they face. Whether the issue is an opportunity that can be met through innovation, a change in strategic posture based on trends key donors are showing, or a potential damaging flaw that is uncovered in the organization's mission, each should be met with organizational action and the capability to accommodate the new context.
- *A willingness to do things differently.* It does not matter if one part of the business is succeeding and doing things better if failure in another part of the organizational work could bring the company down or hurt its competitive advantage. There must be a willingness to break the mold of incremental change that so many organizations favor and deliver a "frame change" if warranted by changed circumstances. An institution must

constantly look at its competitive environment and gauge whether its strategies and products will help it achieve a competitive advantage. Without this understanding and constant reading of an organization's context, it is almost impossible to know whether a chosen strategy can deliver the advantage leadership is seeking.

Strategy Frameworks

In building a strategy, sometimes it is helpful to view all of the pieces that constitute the strategy to make better overall judgments concerning resources and tactics. By disassembling and viewing a strategy through a strategic framework, an organization can merge its past performance, present standing, and future strategic goals into a coherent document.

The choosing of a theoretical framework can reveal structural strengths in an organization while matching those strengths to the environment surrounding it. In undergoing this exercise, an organization begins to shape its structure and systems in anticipation of its strategy. The two are not mutually exclusive, nor do they work independent of each other; strategy and organizational structure must exist interdependently.

There are many frameworks that help nonprofit agencies cope with where they are economically and programmatically on a macro level, and how they can compete at the customer and market level. Two of these are discussed in the following sections.

The Balanced Scorecard

Financial and nonfinancial indicators are important to the leaders of nonprofit ventures. The Balanced Scorecard links strategy to all organizational activities, including both day-to-day and long-term activities. It is an integrated framework that translates strategy through the use of linked performance measures in four perspectives: customers, internal processes, employee learning and growth, and finance. Developed by Robert Kaplan, a professor at Harvard and David Norton, a consultant, the framework came out of their search for new methods of performance measurements. Wanting to go beyond exclusively financial measures, Kaplan and Norton developed a framework that captures measures from the entire organization; they summarized their findings in an initial *Harvard Business Review* article and a later book.[5]

In using the Balanced Scorecard for a nonprofit organization, driving strategy and alignment remain central to all the Scorecard system tries to do. Measuring the degree of achievement of the nonprofit organization's mission and serving clients become dominant goals, as opposed to just increasing shareholder value.

The McKinsey 7-S Framework

The 7-S Framework, though one of the older frameworks used for organizational analysis, is still important to a nonprofit strategy discussion for a number of reasons. One critical reason is the Framework's assertion that structure and strategy cannot be discussed sensibly without a review of the people and the skill level of the organization being considered. Many nonprofit organizations enact strategies without first looking at their internal feasibility.

Though developed in the early 1980s, the 7-S Framework gained major recognition through two influential books of the time on strategy, structure, and organizations: *In Search of Excellence* and *The Art of Japanese Management.* Tom Peters and Robert Waterman, authors of *In Search of Excellence,* identified seven independent variables that interact with each other within an organization:

1. Strategy
2. Structure
3. Systems
4. Skills
5. Staff
6. Style
7. Shared values

The first three—strategy, structure, and systems—form the "hardware" of the organization, and skills, staff, style, and shared values form the "software."[6] When they are all joined together, these seven variables create a managerial system that a manager has to balance, each variable being conditioned by the other six.

Strategy Models

While there are literally hundreds of strategies available to profit and nonprofit managers, some schools of thought bear closer scrutiny, which will be discussed.

The first of these is conceptual in nature. The Harvard Policy Model looks at the values and obligations of management along with the capabilities of the organization to find the best strategy fit with the environment that surrounds the company.

The Harvard Policy Model

The Harvard Policy Model is designed to help an organization develop a fit between its own capabilities and resources and the environment it finds itself in.

In formulating its strategy, a nonprofit organization identifies an intended future that matches both its strengths and market opportunities. Perhaps more importantly, this intended future should match senior management's intentions and aspirations. Strategy is formulated through four steps:

1. Analysis of external environment for opportunities and threats.
2. Analysis of internal strengths and weaknesses of the nonprofit agency in question.
3. Analysis of the personal values of the senior management of the nonprofit.
4. Analysis of the responsibility of the nonprofit to the general public.

Fundamentally, the Model identifies the strengths and weaknesses of an institution and its value system and then identifies the threats and opportunities of the environment surrounding the institution, along with the social obligations of the nonprofit. The systematic assessment of the strengths, weaknesses, opportunities, and threats— known as the SWOT analysis—is the primary strength of the Harvard model and is applicable to both profit and nonprofit organizations.

The Harvard model directs managers to first focus on environmental trends (an activity that benefits nonprofit institutions). Looking at economic, political, social, and technological trends forces a nonprofit manager to undertake the following observations:

- *Economic trends*—trends in competition, cost, or donation structure in the causal industry, the seasonality (if applicable) of the nonprofit's clients and donations, and the relationship of the nonprofit agency to the local or national economy.

- *Political trends*—public attitudes towards the cause the non-profit promotes, regulations that will affect how the nonprofit undertakes its daily business now and in the future, and the attitude of elected officials towards what an organization does.
- *Social trends*—the changing buying, loyalty, and donation patterns of certain age categories in relation to the nonprofit agency, as well as changing patterns in the family, income, political identification, and raising of children within the nonprofit's environment.
- *Technological trends*—changes in gathering and retrieving data, the ways new markets are being created through the electronic media, all types of computer technology.

Having looked at trends, a practitioner then looks at

- *Internal strengths.* An organization looks at its internal strengths (and weaknesses) to decide which goals and objectives it is capable of pursuing and which goals and objectives are simply beyond its grasp.
- *Values.* The Model forces managers to ask, What are our values and how do they affect the choices for our future strategy?
- *The general public.* A nonprofit marketing manager should always put clients, customers, donors, and stockholders on the organizational chart first, with everyone else working for this important group listed underneath on the chart.

The Harvard Policy Model has real value to the nonprofit world. The aforementioned SWOT analysis and its strong internal and external focus, which provide a systematic way for managers to ask questions about themselves, their company, and their environment, allow for a balanced strategic approach. In this way, a reasoned approach is prescribed as opposed to a more common entrepreneurial approach. The impact on particular audiences is also of concern in the model, as opposed to the more unilateral approach taken by the entrepreneur.

The Portfolio Framework

Nonprofit organizations that have different divisions, causes, or services still have similar problems across divisions. Each division is managed differently, each division needs differing amounts of cash, and each division differs in its ability to generate clients. In particular, many nonprofit divisions are encouraged to fund their own growth. How does a nonprofit senior manager decide which service, division, or cause is starved for resources (people, equipment, and money) and which division receives the amount it needs? Does the manager make such a decision based on potential, based on loss, based on the need for cash, or based on the division's ability to fund other divisions through its ability to stimulate cash flow?

Portfolio strategies force decisions regarding cash, service, opportunity, and growth strategies for different causes, services, and divisions through an overt analysis as opposed to default decision making. In addition this methodology appraises the financial potential of each division and leads to marketing and management recommendations regarding the future of each division.

There are as many portfolio models to look at as there are reasons why nonprofit and for-profit companies diversify. The focus here is on the Boston Consulting Group's Portfolio and Growth Share Matrix. In a multidivision nonprofit agency, a manager looks at his diversified nonprofit with its various causes, services, and causal products and thinks of it as a portfolio of businesses, with each business having varying degrees of client potential and cash flow. The manager has many options to choose from: he or she can have a different strategy for each division, differing cost expenditures, different and possibly overlapping audiences, and differing expectations (service, financial, and otherwise) for each division.

In 1979, Bruce Henderson postulated a relationship known as the experience curve, and from this postulate grew the Boston Consulting Group matrix, outlined in his book *Henderson on Corporate Strategy*.[7] Henderson said that any business could be categorized into one of four types:

1. High growth/high market share businesses, which he called "stars," generate substantial cash but also require large investments to maintain their share of market or to increase it. For a nonprofit agency, these are causes or divisions that are in a growth mode and in a strong competitive position. Normally, they have a strong experience curve and are able to generate sizable sums of money. These "star" divisions are

generally self-supporting and are usually capable of commanding resource infusions from management.

2. "Cash cows" are low-growth/high-share businesses that not only generate large cash flows but require low investments and generate profits that can be used elsewhere in the business. In a nonprofit organization, a "cash cow" normally represents a mature cause or service and client and donor market, with the "cash cow" division requiring little in the way of cash infusion from the corporate office.

3. Low-growth/low-market share businesses, called "dogs," produce few clients and little cash and offer little prospect that their market share will increase. Because they are presumed to be weak in their experience curve, divisions that are classified as "dogs" are often seen as "bottomless pits" for cash and usually represent both a management and financial drain on the nonprofit.

4. A high-growth/low-market share business, called a "question mark" by Henderson, normally requires substantial investment to become a "star" or "cash cow"; therefore, their future is often undecided. If they continue to need heavy cash infusions they will become "dogs," whereas if they show promise and their market position can be changed, these "question marks" can become "stars."

Many nonprofit companies today consist of multiple causes or services that are only marginally related, primarily because of entrepreneurism on the part of the founder or institution. One nonprofit I am aware of works with one multimillion-dollar company that has more than 40 divisions, some of which are only slightly related to the purpose of the organization.

On a daily basis, some nonprofit managers make decisions about allocating resources to different causes or services, usually through hunches or personal favoritism but not through strategic portfolio models. The strength of the portfolio method is that it provides a means of measurement against dimensions of strategic import.

The Forces of Competition

Professor Michael Porter's first major work, *Competitive Strategy: Techniques for Analyzing Industries and Competitors* (New York: Free Press,

1980) identifies five key industry forces—the relative power of buyers, substitutes, suppliers, industry competitors, and potential entrants—which, depending on their intensity, serve to drive industry profitability either up or down.[8]

A manager's job (nonprofit and otherwise) is to pay close attention to the five forces that govern the industry; strategy's "job" is to allow the organization to find a position where it can defend itself against these forces or turn them in an institution's favor. Let's consider each force.

Relative Power of Buyers

By "buyers," Porter means "clients and customers," and his sense is they are not all alike. An example from the nonprofit world illustrates this.

> The marketing director for a publishing house knows that selling books to individuals is a very different proposition from selling them to bookstore chains. An individual usually buys one book from the bookstore shelf at the retail price. The bookstore chain, on the other hand, is in a better position to negotiate price because it purchases so many books in volume. In fact, when there are substitute products available from several publishing houses, the bookstore chain negotiates among several publishers for the best prices. It has strong buying power as compared with the individual buyer.

Buying power is usually most significant for standard or undifferentiated products—products for which many substitutes can be found. Extending the publishing example, consider publishers of Bibles. There are literally hundreds of different Bible publishers in operation, with most products being substitutes for each other. In this example, buyers constitute a major force because of the sameness of the product and the ability of the buyer to shop around for the cheapest product.

Relative Power of Suppliers

Suppliers provide the means for an organization to continue. They include anyone from financial institutions to dealers in material goods. In the for-profit world, suppliers exert pressure on an industry by raising prices or reducing the quality of goods. Thus, they can literally squeeze the profit out of some industries. On face value, Porter's supplier group may not seem to have much to offer the nonprofit world. Consider, though, donors for one second. A number of nonprofit agencies are dominated by just a few donors, whose gifts the institution relies on heavily. Even though some nonprofits resent being dependent on just a few individuals or foundations, they have very little choice but to continue. Nonprofits in this situation typically don't make a concerted effort to find new donors, which would reduce their reliance on the few. The psychological and pragmatic cost of undertaking such a task is too great. (In the for-profit world, these costs would be called "switching costs." In the nonprofit example, the switching costs are too high.)

Threat of Substitute Products

In many nonprofit situations, more than one cause or service may perform the same function for the client. The presence of substitute causal products limits the amount of service or profits a causal industry can enjoy along with the potential. A nonprofit example explains Porter's notion.

> The children's camping industry has numerous competitors, and many of the camps are roughly the same size and have the same disposition. Industry growth is slow, and many of the camps lack any differentiation; to build camp traffic, they often resort to cutting prices. Unfortunately, for many camps fixed costs are also high, and because their debt load can be high as well, leaving or exiting the business may not be an option in spite of earning low or negative returns.

Industry Competitors

Rivalry in a causal industry is usually a function of a number of factors including competitors that are equally balanced, slow causal industry growth, a large number of substitute services or products within the industry for clients and buyers with little differentiation among them, and high strategic stakes. Rivalry intensifies when one of the competitors senses the need to seize an opportunity or feels under pressure from other areas of expense within its own organization. Such rivalry often leads to new marketing moves and retaliation by other members of the causal industry.

A move by a city mission to start working among women on the street prompts the other three mission competitors in town to start working with women. A church starts a day care service to attract new members, and other churches in the area start the same type of service. Each action by one organization creates a response by another.

Potential Entrants

The key to understanding how potential entrants come into an industry is to understand what Porter calls "entry barriers." These barriers serve to prevent new competitors from entering and then succeeding in an industry. Porter identifies seven barriers that limit industry access by for-profit companies, some of which very much apply to nonprofit organizations.

1. *The lack of strong economies of scale.* Some nonprofits simply cannot afford to enter some causes even if they feel strongly about them.
2. *Product differentiation.* By this, Porter means that some existing products within the industry enjoy high degrees of customer loyalty. While there are many organizations involved in building affordable housing, Habitat for Humanity enjoys a high degree of client, volunteer, and donor loyalty.
3. *Capital requirements* (especially when they are large and risky). By some estimates, it can cost close to ten million dollars to build a youth camp. Not many nonprofits can afford this.
4. *Lack of access to distribution channels.* Small, independent publishers often have a problem getting their books to a buying public.
5. *Switching costs.* These are absorbed by a company in moving from one industry to another, or when investing in new equipment or new training programs for employees.
6. *Cost disadvantages.* These may arise if competitors enjoy either proprietary product technologies or are receiving sizable

subsidies from some entity. For example, a nonprofit counseling center can offer its seminars cheaply because a donor and client endowed the organization's marriage seminar division.

7. *Government policy.* Whether through licensing or regulation, it may limit certain types of organizational operations. Some nonprofit work has been put at risk by government regulations.

The identification of these seven industry forces and their comparative strength is key in determining an agency's strengths and weaknesses in relation to other competitors within the same causal industry. By knowing an institution's strengths and weaknesses, a marketing manager can then establish a strategy position with respect to each of the industry forces.

Porter's Three Competitive Strategies

It is not the causal industry your nonprofit finds itself in that defines your marketing strategy; instead, Porter suggests, you have to decide where you want to compete with respect to the forces.

The structural analysis of an industry and its forces is Porter's first major thesis; his second is the notion that there are three generic competitive strategies that can be applied as a way of coping or in response to the industry forces. These three strategies are mutually exclusive, and, according to Porter, an institution cannot pursue more than one at the same time for the same product or service and still succeed. Nevertheless, Porter's three strategies— overall cost leadership, differentiation, and focus—are useful to nonprofits to think through.

- *Overall cost leadership.* Many agencies try to gain leadership by managing expenses closely. As a result the agency (1) can sometimes remain profitable when rival organizations trim both expenses and margins, (2) can remain more competitively flexible even though costs of providing services may increase, (3) can deter other nonprofits from entering an industry (i.e., put up "entry barriers") by not allowing them to achieve sufficient economies of scale, and (4) can allow the nonprofit in question to compete with other nonprofits that might also produce substitute or similar products.

- *Differentiation.* Michael Porter's second generic strategy is to differentiate an agency's product or service so that it is perceived industry-wide as being unique. Differentiation is valuable to an agency because (1) it isolates the institution from other competitors by developing loyalties between the service or causal product and clients, based on the product's differentiation; (2) such a loyalty creates an entry barrier for a new nonprofit trying to enter the same causal field; and (3) if the differentiation is successful in a client's or donor's eyes, the product's parent is able to charge higher fees for its purchase as customers become insulated from substitutes, or to raise more dollars as donors become less sensitive to the cost of the service being provided.
- *Focus.* The goal of a focus strategy is to serve a particular group very well; in thus serving this strategic target, the institution can typically operate more efficiently and effectively for a particular group than an organization with an industry-wide focus. Potentially, the nonprofit that runs a focus strategy can often achieve above-average financial returns because it offers its market superior client and donor service, as well as producing specialized services and causal products that meet specialized needs.

So far our focus has been on strategy models that assume a basic status quo in nonprofit operations and the environment they operate in. The previous models have not been specifically designed to accommodate new trends in the environment or the emergence of new ideas and groups. The governing assumption for the previous strategy models has been that the rules are the same for everyone in the causal industries they operate in and that these rules are relatively stable. What happens when this is not the case?

We now move into a final strategy model, which is really not about strategy at all. It is called the Planning Process Framework.

The Planning Process Framework

If a nonprofit has an annual plan or if it develops a strategy, it usually perceives that it is developing one along the lines of the Planning Process Framework. For many nonprofit mangers, strategy and planning are interchangeable concepts. By planning, you achieve or derive a strategy.

The executive director of a nonprofit likened his job to that of a conductor leading a large orchestra. In speaking to the staff, he would say that his job was to get the various parts of the orchestra functioning in a like-minded, sequential way. The audience or environment was not as important to the end result as was the interconnection between the parts of the orchestra.

Even if the audience for this hypothetical orchestra did not enjoy the music or got up from their chairs during its performance, the music (i.e., the functioning of the various institutional parts) could still be accomplished in a relatively controlled manner.

The main idea behind the Planning Process Framework is that the most important part of any strategy is the way or process by which decisions are implemented. In this framework, managers make, implement, and control decisions across various functions and levels within a nonprofit. Planning process systems typically address four questions:

1. Where are we going (mission)?
2. How do we get there (strategies)?
3. What is our blueprint for action (budget)?
4. How do we know whether we are on track (control)?[9]

The key idea in the Planning Process Framework is to link mission, strategy, resources, and direction so that their interconnection can be identified and carefully managed. There is logic to this process; for most managers it makes sense to concentrate on the core mission of the organization, acknowledging where it is going, how it is getting there, and whether it is accomplishing its mission while correcting any performance that does not contribute to the overall mission.

Some organizations operate this way, but many don't. As a result, a great number of nonprofit planning systems typically focus on a few areas of concern, rely on a decision-making process in which organizational history and/or politics plays a major role, and control something other than program outcomes—budget expenditures, for example.

Organizations operating this way often use a linear strategy, employing checklists and step-by-step procedures; strategies that might have emerged because of competitors' moves are all but ignored. Strategic effectiveness here really depends on how well managers can devise and carry out procedures for fitting their organizations into the environment that surrounds them.

The Framework's obvious strength is its intended purpose of controlling the outcomes of many systems and functions across an organization. A tremendous benefit is provided to nonprofit executives and managers; having well-defined responsibilities enables them to think through and consider strategic questions. Further, should an organization contemplate a change in its operations or experience a change in its environment that is both complex and larger than normal, formal planning systems are useful.

The profound weakness of the System is that in rigid organizations with strong centralized authority, strategy can be lost, as can attention to mission. In fact, strategy is treated quite differently in this framework, as opposed to the strategy models we previously looked at. Strategy is only incidental in the Planning Process Framework. The Planning Process is centrally concerned with its own maintenance as a process, not the strategy produced by the process.

Typically, formal planning as part of the Framework is done in a planning cycle, usually addressing five issues:

1. Set objectives.
2. Generate alternative strategies for achieving objectives.
3. Analyze the pros and cons of each alternative.
4. Select the best strategic alternative.
5. Prepare appropriate plans, budgets, cash flow statements, and so on.

While there are literally hundreds of different formal planning frameworks, all tend to work in a linear manner, building on the answers to specific questions until a full-fledged strategy has evolved. Following this path, a nonprofit loses its ability to act quickly or take advantage of economic opportunities because of its commitment to the "system."

Summary

The reader has now looked at a number of strategy models. We next consider taking the strategy to the public and the advantages that branding provides an organization competitively. These issues are discussed in Chapter 10.

CHAPTER

10

Creating a Competitive Image and Brand

A nonprofit organization can produce an extremely satisfying array of programs for its clients that both helps and satisfies them; it can have excellent relations in its work force; it can even have a strong and successful marketing and fund-raising program; but if it fails to communicate this information on a regular basis to the various stakeholders who constitute its support base, the nonprofit organization's management and marketing team is making an error that could hurt the organization long-term.

Barry McLeish at the McConkey/Johnston client
conference, Colorado Springs, CO, 2009

No discussion of marketing for nonprofit organizations can be complete without addressing the large—and often overlooked—topic of managing the external (and internal) image of the organization. The "brand management," "public relations," or "image management" function serves to let the public know of the nonprofit's successes; the way it differs from competitors; its reliability, goodwill, and sustainability; and the way it handles its finances. Though the term is no longer new, image management grew out of nonprofit organizations' realization that they could no longer afford to assume that good performance with clients would automatically generate resources and the support of certain audiences.

In the current times of hyper-competition and donor, customer, and volunteer skepticism, a nonprofit marketing manager must be sure that potential supporters know the exact purpose of the organization, its works, its integrity, its reputation, and its ability to survive, especially if a high percentage of money is directly applied to a specified cause.

Brand Formulation

The need for a good nonprofit image or identity is one of the most generally agreed-on but least understood aspects of nonprofit marketing strategy. At its most simplistic, a nonprofit's organizational image is seen as its logo or the way its stationery or brochure is designed. At the other end of the organizational image spectrum is the idea that a nonprofit's image is best understood in light of its branded communication strategies, the nomenclature it uses, its relationship with donors and volunteers, its programmatical implementation, and the way it carries on its affairs differentiated from those it competes with.

Yet many nonprofit executives believe that the way a nonprofit organization projects its image is little more than a "cosmetic" issue, something that is done to dress up the agency for public consumption. Some of these executives think an agency has little to gain from a thought-through sustained organizational branding campaign. In fact, image management is usually regarded as a series of tactics rather than a strategy to be implemented.

However, to many other nonprofit marketers a nonprofit organization's image and brand is not only a very positive representative tool but "is" the organization. These thoughtful managers have three overriding concerns when it comes to their organization. First, they want to retain their donors and customers for as long as possible. Second, they want to differentiate themselves from the pack and their competitors. And third, they want to dominate in their category of service.

This projected "brand" is a sophisticated way to both speak to and hear from an organization's constituency. The thoughtful organization starts from its objectives and reason for being as it thinks through how it would like to be known. From this starting point, the strategy is developed and implemented, taking into account all the nonprofit organization's programs, services, and operations and the way these are portrayed to the public through the organization's communication tools. Over time, a nonprofit organization's images slowly begin to impress themselves on its various constituencies, building an awareness that results in attitudes, positive or negative, being formed towards the organization. The end result is an "image" or "brand" that is associated with the organization and allows it to represent its value proposition and all the assets and capabilities that are linked to it. In doing so, an agency begins to differentiate itself from other agencies trying to undertake similar programming.

To be effective, an institution's brand and branding program has to create value for its internal and external stakeholders. It has to be planned for and should include one or more of the following attributes:

- Through its branded image the nonprofit organization needs to educate or inform its supportive publics and constituencies regarding the organization's goals, objectives, and role in the community or communities in which it operates.
- An organization's brand is designed to build up the nonprofit agency and to garner favorable opinions about its work, service, and community relationships; in so doing, it begins to differentiate itself from others that are attempting to deliver similar objectives.
- Given the skepticism of donors, customers, and volunteers, a nonprofit organization's brand should project confidence in how the organization spends its money, uses its resources, and takes care of its clients.
- The nonprofit organization's reputation as a result of its image should convey the idea that the organization is a good place for volunteers to work, as well as for qualified individuals who may be contemplating long-term employment.
- The brand of the organization should suggest that the agency is strategic and visionary, willing to be long-term in its orientation and principled in its pursuit of its objectives.

Basically an institution needs to view its brand as a major resource and asset. As such, it needs to be carefully planned for, developed, nurtured, and controlled.

The Advantage of Focus and Differentiation

North American donors and nonprofit customers have a stunning array of options and programs from which to choose. This over-abundance of choice has led the average stakeholder to a perception of sameness regarding many of the programmatic options he or she faces. This phenomenon is called "parity" or "commoditization" by marketers, and many organizations, in spite of marketplace conformity, spend little or no time on sustainable differentiation of their institution from others. Unfortunately, it is these discussions about donors and customers and how to use an agency's communication systems, programs, reach, and solicitation strategies that connect a cause to its brand. Peter Sealey, in his book *Simplicity Marketing*, observed,

> *[I]n the context of too much choice, brand becomes the shortest, most efficient path to potential satisfaction and tension release. Brands are playing a bigger role as the exasperated consumer's simplified shortcut to a purchase decision.*[1]

The goals of a branding program are often muddled into an all-encompassing, unfocused organizational "good image." A focused branding campaign, coordinated with all organizational media on-line and off-line, is often an important tactic for combating commoditization. By integrating how an agency operates with a strong brand strategy, an organization can effectively win the battle for stakeholder loyalty, even in a crowded marketplace.

There are three primary reasons for a nonprofit organization to focus strongly on a strategic branding goal in developing its program:

1. *First*, a nonprofit organization must decide how it wants to "be seen" by the consumer. To "be seen" means that individuals begin to develop a sense of familiarity and recall regarding the organization. In addition, it means that the organization signals to competitors regarding its intentions and commitment of being in a particular market. Having created a goal allows the organization to monitor all of its external operations and communications in the light of this goal. Each element must contribute to the whole. There are always

pressures within an agency to change the way it presents itself to the public. However, by not complying with this goal a nonprofit organization often presents a fragmented image to the public.

2. *Second*, a branding goal allows a nonprofit organization to avoid the inefficiencies and confusion that often result from a fragmented image. Because stakeholders are deluged daily with various marketing messages and humanitarian causes, building awareness and a branded presence in the market-place around a particular set of messages allows an organization to fight clutter and fragmentation in the stakeholder's mind regarding organizations within a particular causal industry. In particular, there are benefits gained in the promotional arena from allowing various publics to know precisely who the organization is and what it stands for—and, therefore, what they are responding to.

3. *Third*, a focused image and brand also facilitate growth in a nonprofit organization by projecting a presence that is memorable and distinctive, thereby encouraging stakeholder loyalty and preference for the organization while creating a competitive advantage over agencies that have a fragmented and unsustainable image.

Merging Brand and Strategy

How do you connect the strategy around a brand to an organization's operational strategy? Both are obviously important, and their merger involves a number of steps.

> *Stakeholder modeling.* Because a brand strategy is necessarily long-term in nature, it must not be equated with an advertising strategy. Sometimes the two become caught up in the conflict over immediate short-term, quarter-to-quarter pressures versus longer-term concerns. In fact, branding really starts with an organization's knowing the type of person it wants as a stakeholder, what stakeholders consider of value, and the alignment that can be gained between the competencies of the organization and the interests of the individual. Stakeholder modeling is more than a strong segmentation strategy. How these target individuals think, what they consider

of value within the cause being represented, how they make gifts to a cause or become involved, and how a cause fits into a typical worldview are all important concerns. Great benefits occur to the organization (and the stakeholder) when branded alignment occurs between the agency and the individual in the following ways:

- Organizations with strong brands often raise more money and have stronger return on investment.
- Strong nonprofit brands often encourage continuity of support for the organization.
- Strongly branded organizations often have an easier time introducing new causal products because of the aligned relationship between individual and agency already built.
- Stakeholders aligned with brands often willingly tell their circle of friends about the cause.
- Strong brands can often charge their customers a premium price for their product offers.

Building awareness. The more stakeholders are aware of a brand and what it stands for, the more this familiarity becomes a form of commitment and sustained interest, sometimes proving impervious to competing claims. Given the aforementioned fragmentation and clutter in the nonprofit industry, awareness can become preference, and in any nonprofit agency, groups of men and women who show a preferred interest in a particular cause and sponsoring agency become an enormous strategic advantage. To be category loyal or cause loyal means that from an agency's point of view, stakeholders are easier to hang on to as donors or customers. They are more willing to speak their minds regarding the future direction of the agency and their personal satisfaction levels, and they stand as a deterrent— or barrier to entry—to competitors. What's more, stakeholders who are in the process of becoming loyal to an agency do two very important things:

- They help an agency weather crises or emergencies that threaten it by giving at above-average levels and supporting the agency with all manner of help.
- In times of hyper-competition and organizational stress they do not abandon ship, allowing the agency time to

reconfigure how it wants to compete in the particular product category.

Distinguishing a position. What should the brand stand for? What competencies and disciplines should an agency build its brand around? These are important questions, because the more in agreement and in alignment a stakeholder is with an organization, the more loyalty is instilled in the individual towards the organization and stakeholders, in turn, are more inclined to refuse competitor substitutions:

> In a study for a camp client, it was found that young people who were turned away when certain weeks were sold out did not choose to go to other camps; rather, they chose not to go to camp at all.[2]

Distinguishing features from rational and emotional benefits and ensuring differentiation from competitors, what the organization offers the public must be seen by the target audience as relevant and compelling. The "face" the organization puts on must closely match the face the stakeholder wants to see on the organization. There are obviously many options regarding features and competencies that an organization can promote in hopes of providing face characteristics similar to the ones the stakeholder wants to see. In one study, researchers Michael Treacy and Fred Wiersema looked at leading market companies and concluded that successful organizations excel at delivering one of three distinct value types to their customers: best product, best total cost, or best solution. They then focus, build, and allocate their organization's resources around one of the value types.[3] Rather than seeking equilibrium and well-roundedness, successful companies differentiate themselves and focus on one key aspect of their organization.

Core brand elements. As part of developing an organizational brand, the agency must decide what the core elements of the brand are to be. These essential elements become the primary scaffolding of the brand-building program and ultimately the foundation on which organizational decisions as to program and service compatibility are based. As such, these elements must

 ◆ Be perceived by core stakeholders as being in alignment
   with their values.
 ◆ Be strong enough differentiators that competitors cannot
   easily mimic the elements or claims.
 ◆ Create a summation point that reflects the core strategy
   and reason for the cause that is easily remembered.

Looking across the organization. Obviously, to arrive at the goal of
   having a strong brand, the nonprofit marketing director
   must first look at the strengths of the organization and determine what would encourage a potential donor or volunteer to donate either time or money. Second however,
   managers in medium-sized and larger nonprofit agencies
   must look across the entire organization and be prepared to
   manage multiple stakeholder relationships, diverse growth
   expectations, and program interconnections through multiple brands or subbrands.

   Obviously, a single brand identity may not easily apply to
   multiple programs or causes. Managers must consider how
   the brand might be adapted to multiple viewpoints. Segmented audiences within nonprofit agencies having multiple
   causes and representing different lifestyles and value systems
   require these institutions to manage a portfolio of brand
   relationships across these audiences. This does not usually
   happen organically inside a nonprofit agency as much as it
   happens strategically, with the organization controlling
   expenditures and initiatives across each brand in order to
   gain competitive differentiation. Since not every cause attracts
   donations and service at the same rate, an organization may
   venture into causal areas for which it lacks the necessary skills
   and competencies to compete effectively. The net effect can
   be brand erosion and, in the worst cases, a feeling on the part
   of stakeholders that their gifts and support are being wasted.

Maintaining brand context and relevance. For a brand to be important to an organization, it must be relevant to the stakeholder. And yet there is nothing simple about maintaining
   relevance to stakeholders over long periods of time, given
   that personal value systems routinely change. This sense of
   institutional diligence is extremely critical when a brand is
   ''working'' for an organization and there is a danger of

organizational apathy and a willingness to sit back. Agencies working hard to ensure that their brand efforts are in alignment with their constituents often coordinate and systematically employ some of the following tactics to ensure that both parties have similar expectations:

- ◆ Ensure an organizational culture of collaboration so that both the organization and the stakeholder gain by their mutual participation.
- ◆ Ensure that retention of stakeholders is one of the most important strategies the organization is concerned with.
- ◆ Routinely conduct interviews with former donors, volunteers, and customers to seek out reasons for their exit and to uncover areas of vulnerability.
- ◆ Measure the loyalty and satisfaction of existing donors and customers through programs such as Donor Value Mapping and the like.
- ◆ Force synergy in the organization's media mix by ensuring that those in charge of all communication options—Internet, direct mail, inbound and outbound telemarketing, customer service people, field representatives—are skilled in delivering and listening through ongoing communication programs.
- ◆ Routinely look at ongoing donor and customer analytics to measure donor movement and specifics such as donor lifetime value.

The "experience" one has in relation to a nonprofit organization also directly contributes to feelings of loyalty, relevance, and alignment towards the sponsoring organization. Stakeholder experience is a dominant concern for for-profit organizations such as Nordstrom, Amazon, and Starbucks. It is equally important in the nonprofit world—though it is not often strategically talked about—and includes touchpoint issues such as being thanked promptly for one's gift through a receipt that accurately records the transaction and correctly spells the donor's name, ensuring that online questions are answered quickly, training organization telemarketers to be gracious, and not sending out multiple copies of the same e-mail solicitation to the same individual. Stakeholders' feelings, thoughts, and perceptions all reside in the experiential contact they have with an agency they are interested in.

Using the Brand Strategically

The message an organization chooses to communicate to a target audience represents the brand position the organization is taking. This position can interact with a marketplace in a variety of ways and can be dynamic. Consider the organization in the following example (whose real name is masked), which is national in scope and is trying to decide how to build its brand position.

The Help Young People Nonprofit

The organization's goal is to work with young people of high school age who are in crisis. In more than 180 areas around the country, its program directors have studied the needs of young people and their families, and they have developed programs for ages 13 through 19. They are market driven and routinely look at the needs and wants of the communities they serve and develop programs to fit these needs and wants. Examples include programs aimed at teen parents, programs for young people who are incarcerated or on parole, and programs for urban youth.

In addition, the directors train their staff thoroughly to deal effectively with young people in a loving and educationally sound manner. Staff must also deal with the ups and downs of managing their high school groups and student leaders and interfacing with a very large volunteer labor force. Their duties include mentoring adults, community leaders, donors, and volunteer boards of directors. In particular, volunteers are targeted for special service and consideration, because their numbers determine to a large measure how many young people can be served, not to mention the enormous financial savings these volunteers contribute to the organization.

Finally, this high standard of operation is communicated to the public through local events such as banquets and rallies, through a relatively strong communication program, and through the organization's constant emphasis on a quality operation, which involves interfacing with the communities and places of worship from which it draws its clients and volunteers.

In addition, the organization would like to partner with some corporate sponsors to help its client population and to benefit from the joint efforts of nationally recognized corporations.

Consider the possible strengths a nonprofit organization such as this could communicate to its various publics about its programs and how those strengths might be reflected in a branding initiative. The possible benefits include

1. Recent recognition or rewards.
2. Favorable financial ratings or results.
3. The benevolent programs the organization runs for young parents, their families, and those incarcerated, where no charge for services is imposed.
4. The programs it runs in various ethnic environments, aimed at their particular population.
5. The high school equivalency programs and adult mentoring programs it offers to young people.
6. The leadership training it provides.
7. The ethnic diversity of its current leadership.
8. The nature of its volunteer programs, the type of volunteer it attracts, the benefits the programs bring to the lives of young people, and the benefits the volunteers receive themselves.
9. The possibility of being a part of corporate sponsored events that could benefit young people from all walks of life.
10. The nature of the organization's volunteer boards.
11. Current American leaders who have benefited from agency programs.
12. The urban city programs, particularly the ones that benefit entire communities.
13. The skills that are taught to young people through the broad diversity of the programs the agency offers.
14. The public events the organization sponsors, which mix races, income strata, and young people and adults.

The fourteen listed strengths of the Help Young People nonprofit (Exhibit 10.1) can be translated into potential branding positions through which the agency's image branding program could be enhanced. As can be seen, by taken the strengths an organization has to offer, a nonprofit marketing director or manager has, in written form, a number of possibilities that he or she can begin to develop as brand positions.

Exhibit 10.1   Strengths of the Help Young People Program Developed into 14 Goal Statements for a Branding Program

1. *A recent public recognition or reward* can be announced to the national electronic and print media, and the coverage can present the organization in a good light. In addition, awards can be posted on the organization's web site as part of its communication program, and the news should be distributed throughout the organization's staff, volunteers, and student groups.

2. *Favorable programmatical results* can become a means to achieving the organizational goal of attracting new volunteers and/or donors who desire to be involved with a program that gets results. These results can be used to differentiate the organization from other groups that do not achieve similar results from their programs.

3. *In showing that certain programs run at no charge*, the nonprofit organization can be seen as being caring and compassionate and desiring to be differentiated from organizations that may be perceived as always having their hand out.

4. *Demonstrating ethnic programming* positions the organization as one that is not interested in cookie-cutter programs but seeks to treat each person as an individual and cares for all young people, regardless of position or economic circumstances.

5. *High school equivalency and mentoring programs* are exceptionally strong tools in demonstrating that the organization is seriously interested in issues of morality and the social concerns of this country and not only has goals in these areas but has programs that are achieving results.

6. *If the Help Young People's leadership training programs are strong*, they can demonstrate to the general public that the organization is concerned about this country's future and is willing to do something about it by training its future leadership. Because this organization works with a large number of young people of various ethnic backgrounds, a brand position that claims it is training ethnic leadership could also be very attractive.

7. *Ethnic diversity of current leadership* supports the brand position stated in item 6 in that the Help Young People agency believes in promoting individuals based on their abilities and talents regardless of background and lives what it preaches throughout the organization itself.

8. *Detailing the nature of the nonprofit organization's volunteer programs* allows the agency to develop goals of attracting more competent volunteers and can serve to show potential donors how the organization runs while positioning itself as cost conscious. The presence of many volunteers establishes the organization's brand as one that is interested in attracting outside help and collaboration.

9. *If the Help Young People organization were a part of ongoing corporate involvement*, a possible branding goal could be demonstrating that the

organization is not only well thought of by corporate partners but collaborates with them and is viewed by the financial community, investors, and corporate employees as a legitimate force for good.

10. *Showing the Help Young People's volunteer board of directors* establishes that the organization is well managed and aims to gather the best community minds and put them in positions of leadership to further the organization's goals in a disciplined and thoughtful way.

11. *Showing current national and community leaders who have benefited from the nonprofit organization's training* may enable Help Young People to convince its constituency that it has strong leadership programs designed for young people and that they actually work.

12. *By detailing the outcomes of its urban programs, the depth of the programs, and community endorsements,* the Help Young People organization establishes the branding goal of being seen as an urban, community-wide operation.

13. *Pointing out skills that it teaches young people* can help brand the nonprofit organization by demonstrating the competency and outcomes of its programs and its teachers, as well as its willingness to see more individuals receive help through its programs.

14. *Events that have multi-ethnic participation* position the organization as one that marches to a different drummer racially; views all individuals as contributing, important, and necessary; and stresses the importance of being collaborative.

Reaching the Branded Goals of the Campaign

Nonprofit management has the obligation to communicate regularly with its various constituencies. An ongoing managed branding program results in a stronger bond between the organization and these same constituencies. The nonprofit organization's management must always remember that even the smallest financial donor and the least willing volunteer still own a part of the nonprofit organization in their minds and will remain loyal as long as the agency shows it cares for them. It does this not only by communicating with them in a manner they prefer but by reminding them that their choice of becoming involved with the organization was the right choice when they made it and is still the right choice today. There are obviously some strategy questions that must be answered at the very beginning of branding discussions, the answers to which help determine the direction the campaign is going to take:

- What are the goals and objectives for the branding campaign?
- Are we changing our brand image from what it is today, aligning ourselves with the marketplace, or trying to be something different?
- What are our strengths and weaknesses as compared with the marketplace when we look at our competitors?
- Are we relevant to our stakeholders?

Putting a brand into action can be strategically important to the organization and can make a profound difference as long as seven overriding rules are followed in its development. These rules are presented in the following sections.

Rule 1: Know Who the Intended Audience Is

The first rule is to know to whom the branding campaign is to be directed and whom it should influence. Is it aimed at particular market segments that are important today or at those that will be tomorrow? What is the best way to reach them? For organizations that do not listen to their supportive constituencies on a regular basis, it is doubtful that a strong brand can be developed without prior research into the opinions and values of these constituencies and their attitudes towards the organization.

There are various ways to collect this information, including

1. Online and off-line surveys along with telephone surveys.
2. Enclosing a questionnaire in an organization's annual report or donor or volunteer publication, or posting the questionnaire on its web site.
3. Undertaking the survey with appropriate constituents face to face.

What is the information a marketing manager needs to have in order to develop a sound branding program? Some possible items are

1. Personal data regarding the average age, education level, income level, and years of supporting the nonprofit organization.
2. Opinions about and knowledge of programmatical aspects of the organization.

3. The needs the organization's mission must address this year and during the next two years.
4. The areas of most satisfying involvement for the constituent at this point in his or her life.
5. The extent of involvement of the constituent in the organization (a) as donors, (b) as volunteers, (c) as both, (d) whether they recommend the organization to others, and (e) whether they attend organizational events.
6. What the organization does or provides for the constituent that is most helpful.
7. The most significant obstacles to the organization in accomplishing its goals during the next three years.
8. The three major strengths of the organization in the constituent's mind.
9. The three major weaknesses of the organization in the constituent's mind.
10. The information that the organization sends that constituents see.
11. The values they hold that are also held by the nonprofit organization.
12. The brands are they familiar with in the industry and how they become familiar with these brands.

Rule 2: Know How You Are Going to Touch Them

Nonprofit organizations recognize intuitively that there are numerous ways for an individual to come in contact with their organization. These contact points are called brand "touchpoints." Every action, tactic, contact point, field representative, donor service agent, or piece of communication matters in running a branding campaign. There are four distinct categories of touchpoints that an organization needs to be concerned *with*.

1. *Pre-donation or pre-purchase touchpoints*. These involve the advertising a nonprofit agency might undertake to influence public opinion, the way the organization's web site is flagged for potential donors, the direct mail campaign that is currently running, the public service spots airing on the local radio station. These are all are designed to help move a

potential stakeholder into a position of donating, buying, or volunteering.

2. *Purchase or donation touchpoints.* These include all the brand touchpoints that move a stakeholder into actually giving or buying, such as contact from a field representative, a phone call, an event solicitation, or an Internet site.

3. *Post-purchase or post-donation touchpoints.* It is important to re-inforce a purchase or donation decision through such tactics as a prompt thank-you letter, donor satisfaction surveys, im-mediate acknowledgment of a gift by the agency, and a highly personalized communication effort.

4. *Influencing touchpoints.* These include all of the indirect touch-points that help make an impression on stakeholders (e.g., an agency annual report, routine special reports, question-naires, status phone calls).[4]

Rule 3: Determine Who Is in Charge

Who should be involved in the branding initiative, and what is the role of each person? In some organizations, this role falls naturally to the marketing manager, development director, or resources man-ager. In some smaller nonprofit organizations, this job falls to the members of the management team. To help achieve the necessary effectiveness, particularly in public situations, a spokesperson should be chosen who will appear to be credible and can be seen as a suitable representative of the organization.

Rule 4: Define What You Need Your Brand Strategy to Achieve for the Organization

Many branding programs have gone wrong because those who initi-ated the programs loaded in too many expectations at the begin-ning of the process, thereby causing it to fail. Agencies need to know how their brand is currently performing in the marketplace to determine what they need to correct and what they need to do stra-tegically over the long term. For example:

- Does your organization need brand awareness and recognition? This is really a question about your current mar-keting tactics. Are you marketing programs that allow individ-uals to find out about your organization Do they know you exist and why or why not? Does your marketing strategy need to be retooled to increase the chances that your target audience will put your cause in their deliberation index?

- Does your organizational have a need for differentiation in a crowded marketplace? Is what your organization is promising to deliver similar to what other competitors are promising? If so, can individuals determine the differences within each organization, or are all the competitors—including your organization—being lumped together?

- Is your organization's cause—and its programs response— perceived as relevant? How meaningful is what you are doing in meeting problems head on, confronting issues, and providing solutions? Is there value alignment between what your constituents feel is important and what your organization believes is important? (This is a particularly important question for agencies that have enjoyed success and have not spent much time changing their program line-up recently.)

- Is your organization's cause preferred by many in the marketplace? If this is the case, you must find out why to understand what parts of your programs and communication are most satisfying to those you have talked to and to find out what other organizations are doing in their marketing strategies.

- For existing customers and donors, you need to know whether what your organization is doing in delivering a brand promise and communicating that promise is living up to people's expectations. How satisfied are individuals with the performance of the brand? This is first and foremost a strategy for retaining existing donors and customers.

Rule 5: Determine an Appropriate Brand Strategy

Based on your marketplace needs and recognizing the strengths and limitations your organization brings with it, you are at a place of deciding what brand strategy to follow. The following list contains 10 generic branding campaigns that many nonprofit organizations have implemented, depending on their corporate goals.

1. "You may not know us, but you know the services we help provide for this community."

This brand position is a favorite of nonprofit organizations, one that serve as an umbrella for many nonprofit initiatives. The best example of using this approach is United Way, which has a multiplicity of programs under its umbrella. The goal of this branding strategy is to promote recognition for both the individual initiatives and the parent company.

2. "Look what we're doing for our city!"

Some nonprofit organizations believe it is important to spend their time, money, and effort to be loved by a community. Although this strategy might appear to be self-serving, it is sometimes helpful for a nonprofit organization anxious to broaden its constituency. An ideal candidate for this strategy would be an old-line nonprofit organization that has done very little advertising of its services in the past, even though it has provided strong programs. This approach would be a way for the organization to gain recognition from the community.

3. "Here's what we ought to do on behalf of ___"

Advocacy campaigns can work very well, particularly in donor and supporter recruitment. This type of brand image campaign is successful only up to the level of interest in the particular subject matter the community at large has. A secondary goal in this endeavor is to have new supporters become advocates and spokespersons on behalf of the issue.

4. "Here's why we're in the news."

News can be potentially the most interesting thing you can offer to a reader or prospective supporter. While it is hard to plan when the media will run a newsworthy piece about your organization, this type of branding image campaign can be quite persuasive to newspaper, magazine, and Internet readers as well as television viewers. It is particularly successful when the crisis the nonprofit agency is dealing with will require a long period of work and healing. A successful offshoot of this approach can occur if the organization has won some civic or national award that the nonprofit can promote heavily.

5. "Meet the new nonprofit organization."

Perhaps this is better titled, "Here are the steps we have taken since dealing with our problems." This scenario is really about re-branding an organization. Unfortunately, some organizations go through crises and have to try to recover from them. Constituents are fans of improvements, efficiency, and new developments. This brand strategy is meaningless unless you can demonstrate to your audience that by rebuilding your organization, you will provide better services, help more people, spend the donors' dollars wisely, and try to ensure that whatever happened to the nonprofit in the past will not happen again.

6. "Have you seen our new services?"

The inherent advantage of this type of brand is that people are intrinsically interested in new products and services. This interest allows a nonprofit organization to present its new services as benefits to the user of the services and to the supportive constituency that will fund the services. Ideally, this type of campaign will not only detail the new services but will do so in light of the characteristics of the organization that is bringing the new services to the public.

7. "Have you met the individuals who are our donors, customers, and volunteers?"

This type of brand campaign supports the interests of an organization's donors and volunteers and shows itself to be solidly on their side. This campaign is an ideal opportunity for a nonprofit organization to advertise for individuals who fit the organization's profile of donors, customers, and volunteers by showing them profiles through character portrayals in the campaign.

8. "By using this celebrity spokesperson, we hope you feel us to be a credible organization."

Though not as popular as it once was, the obvious goal in this type of branded campaign is for the credibility of the spokesperson to be transferred to the organization. Indeed, a well-known face may attract some attention to the organization.

9. "Given the stature of our board chairman or chief executive officer as spokesperson for this organization, we hope you will feel more trust in putting your faith—and hopefully resources—in us."

Some causes have used very high-profile individuals—such as former presidents—to convey credibility for a very serious cause. Perhaps the need is to discuss a new building program or the influx of clients that are straining an organization's budget. The goal here is not to convey that the organization is in trouble but that the issue is serious and warrants the readers' or listeners' attention.

10. "Meet one of our employees."

Many nonprofit agencies like to be seen as "one of the boys." Featuring one or more employees can often be a better strategy than using an outside spokesperson, especially if the employee represents the message. For example, a city mission could feature individuals who have been rehabilitated and now work in some capacity at the mission.

Rule 6: Be Proactive

The single most important marketing issue in brand management is to be proactive. Successful brand management can provide growth and can energize a dormant organization by giving it direction and a renewed reason for being. It can also prepare an organization to enter new markets and can become a leverage point through which the agency can introduce new programs and products.

All of this can happen if the marketing director is proactive in spotting trends that are affecting the institution's constituents, sensing when organizational programs are faltering and not delivering what was promised, and asking the right questions. Essential items that must be thought through by the marketing director for any type of branding campaign are specified in the following list.

- Organizational goals for each service or product, including geographic distribution, increases or decreases in the use of the service by clients, and the future importance of the service to the nonprofit organization.
- Trends for each service or product, including a recent history of the service or product, its markets and users, competitors to the product or service, and expected demand for the product or service in the future. (In addition, note any expected new product or service introduction by the nonprofit organization in the near future.)
- The reputation of the nonprofit organization in relation to its competitors, vendors, donors, volunteers, and clients.

- Significant achievements by the nonprofit organization or achievements by its management or client alumni.
- Important donors, volunteers, alumni, board members, customers, or advocates.

Rule 7: Write It Down

The writing of your brand plan (which encompasses a great deal of your marketing strategy) is an important task. Management and all members of the branding team need to have access to it so that they can evaluate its progress. The written plan ought to include some basic items.

Current situation. This takes into account any marketing research the organization has gathered specifically on behalf of the plan and should appear at its beginning. Using all relevant information, this section's goal is to let management know the reasons "why" regarding the campaign, what market research information has shown the organization concerning the attitudes of its supportive communities, and the generally expected timing and results of the proposed campaign.

Program objectives. Once the "current situation" has been described, "program objectives" are presented. This section can be divided into "immediate" and "long-range" objectives. This division of objectives is important, because the net effect of a branding campaign is most likely cumulative. Objectives can be as simple as the following:

1. Heightening the credibility of the organization's programs.
2. Increasing the awareness of the agency.
3. Building the donor base.

Rationale. Following the "objectives" portion of the plan, it is essential to state why the particular brand approach is being recommended at all. Many nonprofit organizations do not see the need to spend much time building a brand or creating a difference between one organization and another. The purpose of this section is, in part, to point out what will be accomplished over and above the normal marketing programs of the nonprofit agency by pursuing a branding initiative. Issues that are sometimes important are the potential cost-effectiveness of the campaign, its ability to reach certain key audiences, the credibility of its message and its brand position, and the possible long-term effects it will have in reaching new donors, volunteers, and interested parties.

Vehicles. The final section of the plan—the section that can appear before the closing statements—deals with the campaign itself. This section details the media vehicles to be used and their function in the campaign. How each fits into the strategy should be detailed. It is often helpful to divide this section into sub-units such as "Internet," "Direct Mail," "Formal Presentations," "Events," and "Advertising."

Summary

As the reader has seen, having a great strategy is only part of the equation in building a strong nonprofit organization. The concept of an organization's brand and the messaging around it are also critical to its acceptance within various constituencies. The Epilogue speaks to the nonprofit marketing practitioner about how to think strategically while implementing strategic choices.

Rethinking How We Do Nonprofit Marketing

"[W]e stumble from crisis to crash program, lurching into the future without a plan, without hope, without vision."
Alvin Toffler, *The Third Wave*
(New York: William Morrow, 1980), p. 18

"Where are the donors?"
Barry McLeish, Client, Conversation, January 2010

Nonprofit marketing was once relatively simply. You created programs on your own, composed fund-development and advertising messages in which you explained the features of the programs in terms of the benefits they provided to donors and other groups, and you spoke in a unidirectional manner, in control of the context, the media, and the message. Obviously much has changed. Now there is an overabundance of nonprofit agencies, imitating most of their competitors' messaging and causing product and program life cycles to denigrate far more quickly than ever before. This creates immense pressure on program leaders to innovate quickly to create new value, and on marketing directors to generate stakeholder collaboration through their marketing strategies as well as to provide new donor and customer experiences through their strategies and tactics.

The "we are competent to receive your gift" messaging to anonymous donors and customers and the sense that "they work for us" has been replaced, now that stakeholders have access to near-faultless information about virtually any agency and have the ability to send and receive messages through any media they choose. Most stunningly and importantly, consumers have reversed the answer to "who works for whom." In many situations, traditional marketing approaches can no longer safely be recommended; nonprofit marketing is being reborn with consumers in control.

Given the overabundance of nonprofit options and the sameness of their messages, the need for branding and agency differentiation has never been more important. This has also led to a change in the nature and tone of donor and customer relationships. Stakeholders communicate with agencies through more than one medium, and they are now more demanding and insightful. Some want mutual agency/stakeholder collaboration and also want a say in how agencies fulfill their mission. The good news is that new media options have allowed organizations to go deeper with stakeholders than ever before. However, many individuals want a relationship and an experience with the nonprofit brands they choose to support, thereby creating some difficulties with organizations that have been used to providing only functional benefits. As a consequence, many organizations now are rapidly adding digital content to their media mix, including e-newsletters, interactive web sites, social media programs, and increased focus on face-to-face interaction, all in an attempt to stay relevant and appear competent.

In all of this, it is important to remember that many successful agencies must now live in two worlds—the worlds of the new media and the old media. Both are remarkably important; one has not eclipsed the other. For many organizations the fund-development "ask" is still bound to traditional media such as face-to-face contact, direct mail, events, and campaigns. For other organizations, the new media are facilitating stakeholders' demands for greater involvement, openness, collaboration, and brand transparency.

While the need for marketing has never been greater, increasingly many nonprofit agencies are cutting back on their marketing functions. Even though virtually every nonprofit marketing seminar speaks of the benefits of relationship marketing, whole groups of donors are feeling increasingly disaffected. Most significantly, chief executive officers and some marketing officers do not see important discussions about nonprofit branding and cause or product differ-entiation as producing measurable results. These efforts, spelled out in this book, are therefore lost as tactical strategies.

The issues facing marketing officers—donor fragmentation, causal commoditization, developing social media strategies, and dealing with vocalized stakeholder demands—have hurt many programs. The big marketing issues such as donor retention and loyalty and all that goes along with them, including value align-ment and delivery of benefits to stakeholders, have also suffered in the process.

When Nirmalya Kumar speaks of a CEO marketing manifesto in his book, few nonprofit marketing officers can relate, never having been given a set of transformational initiatives to implement by their senior leaders other than, "Don't spend too much on the mar-keting programs."[1] What marketing initiatives might a marketing officer undertake that could transform his or her nonprofit agency and help ensure its strategic readiness?

A correct response to that question goes beyond buzzwords and into the notion of strategic tactics. Some of these tactics appear in the following list.

1. *Competitive benchmarking.* Are there better ways to run your organization and produce your programs, services, and products? For many nonprofit marketers and programmers, the answer is often "Yes!" For years the best run nonprofit agencies have looked within their industries and searched out their competitors, investigating how they produce their programs and products and how they run their service sys-tems. The concept of "benchmarking" (the technique of searching out the best in competitor processes and systems and then emulating them, regardless of how painful such emulation is) has become extremely important and is a means whereby some institutions attempt to "catch up" in their fields.

   Identifying superior performance in particular functions, whether personal or corporate, requires nonprofit agencies to rely not only on trade journals, company publications, an-nual reports, consultants, and professional presentations, but to visit other nonprofit agencies to find out how they engage their various environments strategically. Societal needs are now so great that our country can't afford nonprofit institutions that operate on fewer than "all eight cylinders."

> *If you want to maintain the status quo, then don't benchmark. If you want to remain where you are, secure in the knowledge that you're doing the best you can, don't benchmark. Benchmarking will open the organization to change, and to humility. . . . Benchmarking provides the stones for building a path toward competitive excellence and long-run success.*[2]

2. *Increased emphasis on stakeholder listening.* Over the years, market research has been used by the for-profit sector as a primary means of learning about their customers. Rather than adopting this practice, much of the nonprofit world has chosen to ignore it.

   The future growth of the nonprofit sector requires a renaissance in this area. Branding depends on it, agency differentiation depends on it, astute programming depends on it, and the very survival of many organizations depends on a change in how we listen to those we serve and those who support us. Whether we agree with it or not, hyper-competition within the nonprofit world forces to offer a differentiated, value-laden message to a well-defined audience using the right media to deliver it. These decisions are often made without knowing our audience and without really knowing what to do. Many nonprofit agencies have simply forgotten how to win with their donors and customers.

   Too often measurement is applied to many variables but little is gained from the process. This is not helpful research. There are three areas that, for those starting out, must be looked at constantly:
   - Donor, client, and customer satisfaction levels
   - Employee satisfaction levels
   - The way the agency spends its cash

   New media have made market research and stakeholder listening easier. In real time an agency can change its marketing posture based on what stakeholders are saying. Online communities can help agencies connect on a deeper level with those who have the potential to be the best donors or customers. Smaller agencies can now find advantages formally found only in larger nonprofit organizations, regardless of location, through stakeholder partnerships, collaboration, and interaction.

3. *The absolute necessity of focusing on clients, customers, and donors.* If the value of market research pertains to the methodology of obtaining information on clients, customers, and donors, then the nonprofit focusing on these same groups must start with some conformance of client, customer, and donor requirements. They must become central to all that the organization hopes to accomplish. For this to happen, there has to be an organizational culture of dialog, relevance, collaboration, and accountability inside the leadership. In other words, they must want this to happen. It does not happen on its own.

   Nonprofit agencies need to learn to develop deep knowledge about their constituents. Using the information that the organization gathers on its constituency, it must be able to target both individuals and the mass market using a variety of media platforms. The conveyance of value to the stakeholder must dominate any discussion of marketing and fund development and must be elevated to the primary goal of organization–constituent transactions.

   Many nonprofit donors and customers are routinely reevaluating their support of nonprofit organizations. Some are cutting the amount of dollars they spend with nonprofit organizations; others are narrowing their focus to two or three nonprofits and going deeper with these groups relationally and financially. Still others are in a wait-and-see mode. Shouldn't agencies get to know these individuals better, in order to serve them better and allow them to serve the nonprofit better?

4. *Know how to differentiate yourself from your competitors.* Getting control of a marketing strategy doesn't involve a lot of "what if" scenarios. A good marketing strategy often starts by looking at what competitors are doing and the type of value they are offering their constituents. It continues with an intense evaluation of what they are doing right and what they are doing wrong. It examines their programs and marketing team. It looks at their online and off-line literature, networks, advertising, volunteers, and solicitation strategies to benchmark

their organization against those items and to also find areas of vulnerability that an agency's ability and expertise will allow it to exploit in the marketplace.

Frederick the Great said, "It is pardonable to be defeated, but never to be surprised."[3] A nonprofit's marketing strategy makes sense only in light of what its competitors are doing and how the organization differentiates itself from them.

Competitor differentiation must become a priority for nonprofit marketing managers, especially in light of hyper-competition and developing strategies aimed at gaining market share. In theory, differentiation is an organization's primary defense against commoditization. And yet, given the speed in which competitors match new programs, meaningful differentiation often cannot be sustained. What should a marketer do? Somehow branded agencies need to produce programs and appeals that move potential stakeholders out of their doldrums into becoming identified with the brand. They must become value aligned and differentiated in a way that allows them to separate themselves from other causes around them.

5. *The economy will continue to affect everything negatively.* This will be felt in a number of ways, including

   • *Slow growth.* Slow growth may be a condition some nonprofit agencies will experience for a very long time. As the availability of financial resources constricts, nonprofit managers will have to change their operating style. One consequence will be felt in the area of experimentation; the lack of "venture dollars" drastically limits the margin of error managers can make. Slow growth amplifies the painful consequences of strategic mistakes. Suddenly the market no longer forgives errors of judgment. Market and stakeholder analysis, strategic thinking, and an unwillingness to do things simply because they have always been done that way must become central to the marketing manager's thinking.

   • *Strategic stalemate.* Some nonprofit markets have reached maturity. Their market share has become fixed, as has their competitors', and their strategy has become stalemated. It becomes hard for a nonprofit to stimulate new demand in this situation; change also is hard and usually expensive.

- *There are options to overcome a stalemate.* The first option is to ensure that the nonprofit organization has done a good job of differentiating itself in the marketplace through its branding strategies. Since few nonprofit agencies avail themselves of this option, it can be a very strong tactical weapon. A second option is for the nonprofit to consider diversification of its programming into areas that competitors are not at work in. There is also the increasingly popular option of merger.
- *Uneven distribution of resources.* Nonprofit organizations have differing supplies of labor, land, resources, materials, and technology. Not every program can be made successful; nor can every competitive strategy have the resources it needs for market domination. Nonprofit strategists have to decide which programs will provide the greatest boost to their nonprofit's overall effort and which will not. Without doing so, allocations of resources and materials often take on a bureaucratic nature, with little regard to the overall balance of a nonprofit's goals and opportunities.

6. *New tactics.* Nonprofit institutions have to move faster these days because the life cycle of so many of their causal services and products is shorter. Service and product development must be shorter, competitor information must be more factual, and service and product launches and introductions must be carefully crafted. Needless to say, an institution's services and products need to be of the highest quality, because fixing or correcting them in a crowded marketplace usually dooms the service or product and is next to impossible to accomplish.

   - Tracking the relationship and continuity of clients, service users, customers, and donors is not optional. In fact, marketing and development managers need to be obsessed with what is happening with their key donors and customers.
   - Nonprofit leaders have to stop assuming they can keep from evaluating their organization's performance. "The majority (of nonprofits) still believe that good intentions and a pure heart are all that are needed," wrote management expert Peter Drucker in the *Wall Street Journal.* "They

do not yet see themselves as accountable for performance and results.''[4]

Leaders and managers of all types of institutions face violent upheaval around them. Demographic changes, the shift in the United States's value structure, the decline of organizational and product loyalty, the reduction in federally funded programs, a shift in spending priorities by both public and private sector companies, and the obsolescence of international boundaries have all contributed to this volatility.

This increased uncertainty and ambiguity of roles and borders requires nonprofit organizations to think and act quite unlike the way they have in the past. For some institutions, this means employing a strategy to help reach the end goals that their organizations have put forth—a strategic effort that is disciplined and designed to produce fundamental decisions and actions that ultimately will help guide the leadership into becoming the institution it envisions for itself.

Serious questions still remain for marketing directors to sort through, such as, How should marketing directors think about their nonprofit's long-term direction? and Is a marketing strategy an essential part of this thought process?

A good marketing strategy is often the essential or critical ingredient to an organization's goal realization. A marketing strategy takes an organization's goals, policies, and action sequences and helps the agency allocate the resources—time, people, and money—towards achieving its goals.

In 1960, Theodore Levitt wrote a classic article in the *Harvard Business Review* entitled ''Marketing Myopia.'' One statement in this article was, ''We've forgotten the needs of our customers. We must get back in touch with them.''[5] What was true then is true now. In a world that is desperate for solutions, the use of a simple tool such as a marketing strategy will allow hundreds, if not thousands, of nonprofit agencies to improve their performances and their services at a time when both are more desperately needed than ever.

Notes

Preface

1. Margaret J. Wheatley, *Finding Our Way* (San Francisco: Berret-Koehler Publishers, 2005), 2.
2. Nirmalya Kumar, *Marketing as Strategy* (Boston: Harvard Business School Press, 2004), 4.
3. Dev Patnaik with Peter Mortensen, *Wired to Care* (Upper Saddle River, NJ: FT Press, 2009, 23.
4. William Foster, and Gail Fine, "How Nonprofits Get Really Big," *Stanford Social Innovation Review* (Spring 2007), 46–55.
5. Reuters, "World's Wealth Surges; Giving Doesn't," *The Orange County Registrar,* June 20, 2007 cited in Wesley Willmer, *Revolution in Generosity* (Chicago: Moody Publishers), 26.
6. Paul Postma, *The New Marketing Era* (New York: McGraw-Hill, 1999), 11.
7. Steve Lohr, "Is Windows Near End of Its Run?" *New York Times*, October 14, 2006, C3.
8. Akin Arikan, *Multichannel Marketing* (Indianapolis: John Wiley & Sons, 2008), 4.
9. Larry Johnston, "The Relentless Pursuit of Donor Delight," lecture given in Colorado Springs, CO, 2009.
10. Kumar, 5.

Chapter 1 A New Way of Doing Business for the Nonprofit Organization

1. Barry McLeish, *The Donor Bond* (Rockville, IL: The Taft Group, 1991).
2. Herbart Rowen, "Japan's American Prophet," *The Washington Post Weekly Edition,* July 29–Aug. 4, 1991, vol. 8, no. 39, 5.
3. Philip Kotler, "Strategies for Introducing Marketing into Nonprofit Organizations," in *Strategic Marketing for Nonprofit Organizations: Cases and Readings,* 3rd ed., ed. Philip Kotler, O.C. Ferrell, and Charles Lamb (Englewood Cliffs, NJ: Prentice Hall, 1987), 5.
4. This section adapted from the following articles: Benson S. Shapiro, "Marketing for Nonprofit Organizations," *Harvard Business Review*, Sept.–Oct., 1973, and Siri N. Espy, "Corporate Identity and Directions," taken from David L.

Gies, J. Steven Ott, and Jay M. Shafritz, *The Nonprofit Organization* (Pacific Grove, CA, Brooks/Cole Publishing, 1990), pp. 143–155.

5. Thomas Wolf, *Managing A Nonprofit Organization* (New York: Simon & Schuster, 1990), 126.
6. Armand Lauffer, *Marketing for Not-for-Profit Organizations* (New York: Free Press, 1984), 20.
7. Ibid, 18.
8. Benson S. Shapiro, "Marketing for Nonprofit Organizations," *Harvard Business Review*, 263.
9. The author recommends the following books on nonprofit resource attraction: Barry McLeish, *Yours, Mine, and Ours: Creating a Compelling Donor Experience* (Hoboken, NJ: John Wiley & Sons, 2007) and Leslie R. Crutchfield and Heather McLeod Grant, *Forces For Good* (San Francisco: Jossey-Bass, 2008).
10. Houston G. Elam, and Norton Paley, *Marketing For Nonmarketers* (New York: AMACOM, 1992), 7.

Chapter 2 The Development of a Marketing Strategy

1. Barry McLeish, client file 2009.
2. Ibid.
3. Ibid.
4. David L. Gates, Steven J. Ott, and Jay M. Shafritz, *The Nonprofit Organization* (Pacific Grove, CA: Brooks/Cole Publishing, 1990), 138.
5. John M. Bryson, *Strategic Planning for Public and Nonprofit Organizations* (San Francisco: Jossey-Bass, 1988), 4.
6. Ibid., 1.
7. Kathryn Rudie Harrigan, *Strategic Flexibility* (Lexington, MA: Lexington Books, 1985), 3.

Chapter 3 The Phased Strategic Marketing Plan

1. Cited at the McConkey/Johnston client conference in Colorado Springs, CO in 2009.
2. Geraldine Larkin, *12 Simple Steps to a Winning Marketing Plan* (Chicago: Probus Publishing, 1992), 4.

Chapter 4 External Analysis: Client, Donor, Volunteer, and Competitor Research

1. Thomas H. Davenport and John C. Beck, *The Attention Economy* (Boston: Harvard Business School Press, 2001), 6.
2. John Lyons, *Guts* (New York: AMACOM, 1987), 10.
3. Melinda Cuthbert, "All Buyers Not Alike," *Business 2.0*, December 26, 2000.

4. David A. Aaker, *Strategic Market Management*, 7th ed. (Toronto: John Wiley & Sons, 1984), 70.

5. David A. Aaker, *Strategic Market Management*, 8th ed., (Hoboken, NJ: John Wiley & Sons, 2008), 57.

Chapter 5   Researching Your Nonprofit Organization's Environment

1. David A. Aaker, *Strategic Market Management* (Toronto: John Wiley & Sons, 1984), 70.

2. Peter F. Drucker, *Managing the Nonprofit Organization* (New York: Harper-Collins, 1990), 17.

3. Ibid. 10–11.

4. Michael E. Porter, *Competitive Strategy* (New York: Free Press, 1980), 7.

5. J. Donald Weinrauch, *The Marketing Problem Solver* (New York: John Wiley & Sons, 1987), 25.

6. Theodore Levitt, *Marketing for Business Growth* (New York: McGraw-Hill, 1974), 152–153.

Chapter 6   Competition and Internal Marketing Analysis

1. Faye Rice, "What Intelligent Consumers Want," *Fortune*, December 28, 1992, 57.

2. Christopher Locke, Rick Levine, Doc Searls, and David Weinberger, *The Cluetrain Manifesto: The End of Business as Usual* (Cambridge, MA: Perseus Publishing, 2001).

3. Alvin Toffler, *The Third Wave* (New York: William Morrow, 1980), 27.

4. "Unit of One: Sales School," as quoted in Anna Muoio, ed., *Fast Company*, November, 1998, 108.

5. Nirmalya Kumar, *Marketing as Strategy* (Boston: Harvard Business School Press, 2004), 84.

6. James C. Collins and Jerry I. Porras, *Built to Last: Successful Habits of Visionary Companies* (New York: HarperBusiness, 1994), 212–218.

Chapter 7   Value Propositions and Marketing Objectives

1. John O. Alexander, "Planning and Management in Nonprofit Organizations," in *The Nonprofit Organization*, ed. David L. Gates, J. Steven Ott, and Jay M. Shafritz (Pacific Grove, CA: Brooks/Cole Publishing, 1990), 160.

2. Though it is an older book, nonprofit executives would do well to revisit Tom Peters and Nancy Austin's book, *A Passion for Excellence* (New York: Random House, 1985), and in particular Chapter 12, "The Smell of Innovation."

3. Thomas E. Broce, *Fundraising* (Norman, OK: University of Oklahoma Press, 1986), 20.

4. Peter Drucker, *People and Performance: The Best of Peter Drucker* (New York: Harper's College Press, 1999), 119.
5. J. Donald Weinrauch, *The Marketing Problem Solver* (New York: John Wiley & Sons, 1987), 28.
6. Parts of this section are adapted from Barry McLeish, *Yours, Mine, and Ours: Creating a Compelling Donor Experience* (Hoboken, NJ: John Wiley & Sons, 2007), Ch. 6.
7. George H. Peeler, *Selling in the Quality Era* (Cambridge, MA: Blackwell Business, 1996), 8.
8. Parts of this section are adapted from Barry McLeish, *Yours, Mine, and Ours; Creating a Compelling Donor Experience* (Hoboken, NJ: John Wiley & Sons, 2007), Ch. 6.
9. Philip Kotler, O.C. Ferrell, and Charles Lamb, eds., *Strategic Marketing for Nonprofit Organizations: Cases and Readings*, 3rd ed. (Englewood Cliffs, NJ: Prentice Hall, 1987), 5.

Chapter 8 Creating Competitive Advantage

1. Theodore Levitt, M*arketing for Business Growth* (New York: McGraw-Hill, 1974), 8.
2. George Labovtz and Victor Rosansky, *The Power of Alignment* (New York: John Wiley & Sons, 1997), 16.
3. Regis McKenna, *Relationship Marketing* (New York: Addison-Wesley, 1991), 57.
4. David A. Aaker, *Strategic Management*, 8th ed. (Hoboken, NJ: John Wiley & Sons, 2008), 120.
5. Rich Horwath, *Deep Dive* (Austin, TX: Greenleaf Book Group Press, 2009), 39.

Chapter 9 Winning through Competitive Strategy Options

1. Paul C. Nutt and Robert W. Backoff, *Strategic Management of Public and Third Sector Organizations* (San Francisco: Jossey-Bass, 1992), 58–61.
2. Michael E. Porter, *Competitive Strategy; Techniques for Analyzing Industries and Competitors* (New York: Free Press, 1980).
3. Henry M. Mintzberg, "The Strategy Concept I: Five Ps for Strategy," *California Management Review*, Fall, 1987, 12.
4. Ibid., 16.
5. Robert S. Kaplan and David P. Norton, "The Balanced Scorecard—Measures That Drive Performance," *Harvard Business Review*, Jan–Feb, 1992, 71–79.
Robert S. Kaplan and David P. Norton, *The Balanced Scorecard* (Boston: Harvard Business School Press, 1996).
6. Thomas J. Peters and Robert H. Waterman, *In Search of Excellence* (New York: Harper and Row, 1982).
7. Bruce D. Henderson, *Henderson on Strategy* (Cambridge, MA: ABT Books, 1979).
8. Michael E. Porter, *Competitive Strategy Techniques for Analyzing Industries and Competitors* (New York: Free Press, 1980).

9. John M. Bryson, *Strategic Planning for Public and Nonprofit Organizations* (San Francisco: Jossey-Bass, 1988), 32.

Chapter 10 Creating a Competitive Image and Brand

1. Peter Sealey, *Simplicity Marketing*, as quoted by Scott M. Davis and Michael Dunn in *Building the Brand-Driven Business* (San Francisco: Jossey-Bass, 2002), 21.
2. From Barry McLeish client files, 2009.
3. Michael Treacy and Fred Wiersema, *The Discipline of Market Leaders* (New York: Addison-Wesley, 1995).
4. Scott M. Davis and Michael Dunn, *Building the Brand-Driven Business* (San Francisco: Jossey-Bass, 2002).

Epilogue

1. Nirmalya Kumar, *Marketing as Strategy* (Boston: Harvard Business Press, 2004), 9.
2. Jesse Cole, "Bettering the Best," *Sky*, January 1993, 22.
3. Richard S. Teitelbaum, "The New Race For Intelligence," *Fortune*, May 17, 1993, 55.
4. Beth Spring with Thomas Giles, "Battle for the Bottom Line," *Christianity Today*, April 16, 1992, 67.
5. Theodore Levitt, "Marketing Myopia," *Harvard Business Review*, July–Aug., 1960.

References

Atkin, Douglas. 2004. *The culting of brands.* New York: Portfolio.

Barna, George. 1990. *The frog in the kettle.* Ventura, CA: Regal Books.

Drucker, Peter. 1964. *Managing for results.* New York: Harper.

Earls, Mark. 2002. *Welcome to the Creative Age: Bananas, Business and the Death of Marketing.* West Sussex, UK: John Wiley & Sons.

Godin, Seth. 2007. *Meatball Sundae: Is Your Marketing out of Sync?* New York: Portfolio.

Hamel, Gary, and Bill Breen. 2007. *The Future of Management.* Boston: Harvard Business School Press.

Kelly, Kevin. 1998. *New Rules for the New Economy.* New York: Penguin Books.

Pascale, Richard Tanner, and Anthony G. Athos. 1981. *The Art of Japanese Management.* New York: Warner Books.

Pine, Joseph and James Gilmore. 1999. *The Experience Economy.* Boston: Harvard Business School.

Popcorn, Faith and Lys Marigold. 1997. *Clicking.* New York: HarperCollins.

Surowiecki, James. 2004. *The Wisdom of Crowds.* New York: Doubleday.

Yastrow, Steve. 2007. *We.* New York: SelectBooks.

About the Author

Barry McLeish, M.A., is the International Vice President of McConkey/ Johnston International, Inc., a fundraising and marketing management consulting firm specializing in nonprofit organizations and associations. Before joining McConkey/Johnston, McLeish was a development director for a $22 million nonprofit organization. He is a published author and a frequent and popular speaker and seminar leader, having spoken at numerous conventions in the United States and Canada on brand management, major donor campaigning, market planning, and fund-development tactics for nonprofit and for-profit organizations. He has led large marketing seminars for many organizations, including Merrill Lynch, the American Association of Manufacturers, and The Salvation Army. He works throughout the United States, Canada, and Great Britain.

Index

Aaker, David A., 87–88, 94, 106
Adaptability, importance of, 191–193
Akin, Douglas, xxvii
Anderson, Chris, xxx
Art of Japanese Management, The
   (Waterman), 194
Associated costs, exchange theory and,
   17–18
Atikan, Akin, xxiv–xxv
Audience, brand development and,
   220–221. *See also* Stakeholders

Backoff, Robert, 189
Balanced Scorecard, 193–194
Ballmer, Steven A., xxiv
Barna, George, 40
Benchmarks, performance evaluation
   and, 132, 231–232
Benefits, exchange theory and, 17–18
Boston Consulting Group, 197
Brand, 207–228
   attributes of, 209
   focus and differentiation and,
      210–211
   formulation of, 208–209
   need for, 230
   rules for developing of, 219–228
   steps in merging with strategy,
      211–215
   using strategically, example of,
      216–219
Brand loyalty:
   dynamic variables and, 79
   internal analysis and, 132–134
Breen, Bill, 39
Bridgespan Group, xxii

Broce, Thomas, 154
Bryson, John, 33
Budgets, marketing strategy and, 37–38
Buyers, relative power of, 199

"Cash cows," experience curve and,
   198
Causal industry:
   adapting to changes in, 7–8
   competition and, 89–90
   marketing strategy and, 39
   stakeholders and, xxvi
Causal industry, researching of
      environment for, 93–117
   delivery of services, 106–107
   differentiation, 113–117
   environment's size, 96–98
   environment's structure, 98–102
   external analysis and competitors,
      95–96
   growth potential, 109–110
   how to enter, 103–106
   nature of environment, 94–95
   product life cycles, 111–113
Clicking (Popcorn and Lys), 90
Clients. *See also* Stakeholders
   assessing long-term relationships
      with, 141–143
   competitive advantage and, 181
   as constituents, 20
   describing for market research,
      81–82
   dynamic variables and, 78–79
   external-analysis phase and, 52–54,
      72–73
   focus on, 233

Clients. *See also* Stakeholders
(*Continued*)
  future trends and organization's
    objectives, 150
  growth and upgrading involvement
    of, 184
  motivations of, as dynamic variable,
    79–80
  objectives and excellence in
    marketing, 154
  organization's self-image and,
    133
  place in structure of causal industry,
    101–102
  pricing and, 25
  as stakeholders, 5–6
Commitment, of management, 38
Commodity listening and research,
  68–69
Communication:
  assessing of stakeholder retention
    and, 138–140
  as marketing tool, 22–24
  in strategic plan, 126
Competencies, as marketing tool, 14,
  26–27
Competitive advantage, 167–185
  aligning with correct market, 176
  assessing strengths and weaknesses
    of, 140–141
  creating sustainable advantage,
    178–181
  marketing strategy and, 36–37
  objectives and, 165–166
  strategic postures, 172–176
  strategy options, 168–172
  strategy's importance to, 168,
    182–185
  success augmentation and, 181–182
  tactics for achieving, 177
Competitive Strategy (Porter), 99–102,
  189, 198–203
Competitive strategy, steps to, 47–48
Competitors. *See also* Competitive
    advantage
  areas of nonprofit competitions,
    88–91

decision to enter causal industry and,
    105–106
  differentiation from, 113–117
  external-analysis phase and, 54–55,
    84–87, 95–96
  forces of competition, 198–202
  marketing strategy and, 36, 189
  new marketing orientation and, 4–5
  as operational constraint, 44
  organization's self-image and, 133
  place in causal industry's
    environment, 8, 99–100
  potential, 100, 201–202
  relative power of, 200–201
Consistency, as marketing strategy, 189
Constituencies. *See also* Stakeholders
  assessing long-term relationships
    with, 141–143
  as definer of markets, 46
  describing for market research,
    81–82
  dual nature of nonprofits and, 20
  external-analysis phase and, 52–54,
    72–73
  listening to needs of, 11–12
  marketing culture and, 130
  organization's self-image and, 133
  as stakeholders, 5–6
Conversational marketing, 126
Costs:
  cost and performance analysis as
    measures of success, 143–144
  cost leadership as competitive
    strategy, 201–202
  exchange theory and, 17–18
  objectives and "profit"
    measurement, 157–158
  strategy and, 171–172
Crisis, strategy determined by, 170
Culting of Brands, The (Akin), xxvii

Data. *See* Information systems
Day-to-day marketing, 23–24
Dean, Dizzy, 84
Deming, W. Edwards, 10, 158
Demographics:
  as enduring variable, 74, 76–77, 82

future trends and organization's
objectives, 151
performance measurement and, 128
trends in, and marketing strategy,
41–42, 108
Development survey. *See* Internal
analysis
Differentiation:
advantages to brand, 210–211
as competitive strategy, 201, 203
importance of, 233–234
need for, 230
organizational environment and,
113–117
Distance listening and research, 70
Distinctive competencies, as marketing
tool, 14, 26–27
Diversification, as possible growth
strategy, 185
Donation touchpoint, 222
Donors/supporters. *See also*
Stakeholders
assessing long-term relationships
with, 141–143
competitive advantage and, 181
as constituents, 20
describing for market research,
81–82
external-analysis phase and, 52–54,
72–73
focus on, 233
future trends and organization's
objectives, 150–151
growth potential and, 109–110, 184
motivations as dynamic variable,
79–80
objectives and excellence in
marketing, 154
organization's self-image and, 133
pricing and, 25
reciprocity and marketing strategy,
40–41
as stakeholders, 5–6
Drucker, Peter, 46–47, 94–95, 156–157,
163, 235–236
Dynamic variables, in market research,
75, 78–80

brand loyalty and monthly partners,
79
heavy users/major donors, 78–79
stakeholder motivations, 79–80

Earl, Mark, 41–42
Economic trends:
effect of, 234
Harvard Policy Model and, 195
marketing strategy and, 108
organization's objectives and,
151–152
Einstein, Albert, 158
Elam, Houston, 22
Enduring variables, 74–80
demographics, 74, 76–77
geography, 74, 77
psychographics, 74, 77–78
Environment. *See Organizational
environment entries*
Environmental audit. *See* Internal
analysis
Environmental responsibility,
stakeholders and organization's
objectives, 151
Exchange theory (self-interest), 12, 13,
15–18
Experience curve, 197–198
Experience Economy, The (Pine and
Gilmore), xxv
Experts (new), marketing strategy and,
39, 44–45
External-analysis phase, of marketing
plan, 52–56, 63–91
areas of nonprofit competition,
88–91
competition analysis, 54–55, 84–88,
95–96
differentiation and, 113–117
flexibility and, 71–72
focus and, 68–71
industry analysis, 55–56
listening and analysis, 65–66
listening and analysis, objections to,
66–67
segmentation and, 73–74
segmentation variables and, 74–80

External-analysis phase, of marketing
    plan (*Continued*)
  stakeholder analysis, 52–54, 72–73
  stakeholder descriptions, 81–82
  strategies following segmentation,
    83–84
  understanding "the Market,"
    87
External world, marketing to, 10

Financial activity, of donors, 82
Financial resources, objectives and
    "profit" measurement, 157
Flexibility:
  balancing with tradition, 48
  in external marketing research,
    71–72
Focus:
  advantage to brand, 210–211
  as competitive strategy, 203
  importance in marketing plan
    research, 68–71
  as marketing strategy, 189
  necessity of, 233
Focus groups, 77
Ford, Henry, 74
For-profit vs. nonprofit organizations,
    difference and marketing tasks,
    18–19
Frederick the Great, 234
Frog in the Kettle, The (Barna), 40
Future of Management, The (Hamel and
    Breen), 39

Geography:
  as enduring variable, 74, 77
  growth and expansion of service area,
    184
Gilmore, James, xxv
Goal of organization. *See also* Objectives
    of organization
  brand development and, 222–223
  internal analysis and, 124
  marketing culture and, 130
  marketing imperatives and,
    xxvi–xxvii
Godin, Seth, xxi

Growth:
  objectives and "profit"
    measurement, 157
  possible strategies for, 183–185
  potential for, 109–110
Growth stage, in product life cycle, 111,
    112
Guts (Lyons), 68

Hamel, Gary, 39
Harrigan, Kathryn Rudie, 34
Harvard Policy Model, 195–196
Henderson, Bruce, 197–198
Henderson on Corporate Strategy
    (Henderson), 197–198
High growth/high market share
    businesses, experience curve and,
    197–198
High growth/low market share
    businesses, experience curve and,
    198
Homogenous segmentation strategy, 83
Hope, strategy of, 169–170
Human factor, as marketing
    imperative, xxv
Hyper-competition, for stakeholders'
    interest, 6–7

Image. *See* Brand
Industry analysis, in marketing plan,
    55–56
Influencing touchpoints, 222
Information systems:
  collection and, 164–165
  critical measures of, 162–164
  processing of information about
    stakeholders, xxiii–xxv
In Search of Excellence (Peters), 194
Intangible objectives, 160–162
Internal analysis, 119–145. *See also*
    Objectives of organization
  assessing strengths and weaknesses,
    137–141
  cost and performance analysis, 143–144
  elements of, 123–124
  importance of, 119–122
  internal audits and, 144–145

managing long-term relationships, 141–143
performance measurement and, 122, 124–132
as phase of marketing plan, 52, 56–57
uncovering strategic problems and uncertainty, 132–137
Internal audits, organizational assessment and, 144–145
Internal operations/internal productivity, objectives and "profit" measurement, 157
Internet:
changes in social engagement with stakeholders, xv–xvi
stakeholder research and, 69
Intervening objectives, 160–162

Johnston, Larry, xxv

Kaplan, Robert, 193
Kelly, Kevin, xxiv
Kotler, Philip, 11, 164
Kumar, Nirmalya, 231

Larkin, Geraldine, 57
Lauffer, Armand, 17
Leadership:
brand development and, 222
strategic plan and, 126
strategy and, 59–60
Levitt, Theodore, 112, 175, 236
Life cycles, of products, 111–113
Lifestyle changes, marketing strategy and, 41–42
Listening and analysis, in marketing plan research:
addressing objections to, 66–67
focus and, 68–71
importance and goals of, 65–66
need for emphasis on, 232–233
objectives and, 164
Listening grid, 69
Location, performance measurement and, 127–128
Long-range planning:
adverse effects on strategy, 169

effect of new environment on, 7
Long-term relationships, assessing of, 141–143
Long Trail, The (Anderson), xxx
Low growth/low market share businesses, experience curve and, 198
Lyons, John, 68

Managerial commitment, marketing strategy and, 38
Managing for Results (Drucker), 46–47
Marigold, Lys, 90
"Market, the":
aligning with correct, 176
exchange theory and, 16–18
positioning to understand, 87
Market decline stage, in product life cycle, 111, 113
Market-development phase:
of marketing plan, 52, 57–58
in product life cycle, 111–112
Marketing:
defined, 10–13
four Ps approach to, xxi
imperatives of, xxv–xxvii
importance of tracking history, 135
marketing campaign, 23–24
"marketing concept," 103–104
Marketing audit. *See* Internal analysis
Marketing culture, performance measurement and, 128–132
Marketing for Nonmarketers (Elam and Paley), 22
Marketing functions, changes in, 3–27
definition of marketing, 10–13
distinctive competencies, 14, 26–27
external world, 10
marketing tasks, 12, 14, 18–22
nonprofit organization changes, 5–10
outline of marketing strategies, 13–18
Marketing plan, 51–60
external-analysis phase, 52–56
internal-analysis phase, 52, 56–57
market-development phase, 52, 57–58
plan presentation, 52, 59–60
strategy-selection phase, 52, 59

Marketing strategy, 29–49, 187–205.
    See also Marketing plan
  competitive forces, 198–202
  competitive strategies, 202–203
  developing outline for, 13–18
  environmental context and strategic
    options, 191–193
  examples, 29–31
  future trends and organization's
    objectives, 150–152
  importance and benefits of, 31–33
  importance to competitive
    advantage, 182–185
  nature of, 188–189
  new reality and, 9–10
  objectives and major tasks of
    organization, 153–154
  operating environment's effect on,
    38–47
  planning process framework,
    203–205
  portfolio framework, 196–198
  process of, 31
  steps in defining, 33–38
  steps in merging with brand, 211–215
  steps to competitive, 47–48
  strategy frameworks, 193–194
  strategy models, 194–196
  tradition and flexibility, 48
  uses of, 189–191
Marketing tasks, 14, 18–22
  for-profit versus nonprofit, 18–19
  nature of constituencies and, 20
  profit motive and, 19
  resource attraction and, 20–22
Marketing tools/marketing mix, 14,
    22–26
  communication program, 22–24
  distribution channels, 22, 26
  pricing, 22, 25–26
  programming, 22, 26
Market niche, strategy and, 190
Markets, organization's self-image and,
    133
Market signals, 114–117
Market trends, taking advantage of,
    90–91

Maturity stage, in product life cycle,
    111, 112–113, 234–235
McKinsey 7-S Framework, 194
McLinden, Jeff, 115
Meatball Sunday (Godin), xxi
Media:
  new and old, 230
  objectives and "profit"
    measurement, 157
Merger, as possible growth strategy, 185
Mintzberg, Henry, 190
Mission, marketing strategy and, 13,
    14–15
Mission statement:
  marketing objectives and, 149
  marketing strategy and, 34–35
Momentum, maintaining of, 9
Monthly partners:
  dynamic variables and, 79
  growth potential and, 109–110
Motivational hierarchy, 80
Motivations, dynamic variables and,
    79–80, 82

Nelson, Lloyd, 158
Networks, changes in usefulness of, 6
New experts, marketing strategy and,
    39, 44–45
New Marketing Era, The (Postma), xxiii
New Rules for the New Economy (Kelly),
    xxiv
Nonprofit Organization, The, 32
Nonprofit organizations, changes in,
    5–10
  adaptation to new reality, 9–10
  as businesses, 45
  causal business and change
    management, 7–8
  hyper-competition, 6–7
  marketing strategy and changes in
    organizational environment, 38–47
  network reliability, 6
  no longer culturally favored, 45–46
Norton, David, 193
"No strategic change" posture,
    173–174
Nutt, Paul, 189

Objectives of organization, 147–166
  defined, 167
  developing of, 148–153
  information-gathering process and,
    162–165
  intervening and intangible objectives,
    160–162
  marketing excellence and, 153–155
  performance measurement and,
    155–165
  "profit" measurement, 156–158
  remaining competitive, 165–166
  success and failure measurement,
    158–159
Online communication, elements of, 24
Opportunity analysis. *See* Internal
  analysis
Organizational environment,
    marketing strategy and, 38–47
  constraining operating conditions,
    43–46
  individuals and reciprocity, 40–41
  institutional turmoil, 42–43
  lifestyle and demographic trends,
    41–42
  stakeholder focus, 46–47
  strategic options and, 191–193
Organizational environment,
    researching of, 93–117
  competitive environment's size,
    96–98
  competitive environment's structure,
    98–102
  delivery of services, 106–107
  differentiation, 113–117
  entry into causal industry, 103–106
  external analysis and, 95–96
  growth potential, 109–110
  nature of, 94–95
  product life cycles, 111–113
Outsourced listening and research,
    69–70

Paley, Norton, 22
Patnaik, Dev, xxii
Perceptual map, of environment,
    109–110

Performance benchmarking, 231–232
Performance measurement, 122,
    124–132
  location issues, 127–128
  marketing culture and, 128–132
  objectives and, 155–165
  plan evaluation, 125–127
  "profit" measurement, 156–158
Personality of organization, strategy
    and, 190
Peters, Tom, 194
Physical plant, objectives and "profit"
    measurement, 157
Pine, Joseph, xxv
Planning:
  balancing with operating, 130–131
  defined, 168
Planning Process Framework, 203–205
Policy, defined, 168
Political trends, Harvard Policy Model
    and, 196
Popcorn, Faith, 90
Porter, Michael, 99–102, 189, 198–203
Postma, Paul, xxiii
Post-purchase/post-donation
    touchpoint, 222
Potential competitors:
  place in causal industry's
    environment, 100
  relative power of, 201–202
Pre-donation/pre-purchase
    touchpoint, 221–222
Presentation, of marketing plan, 52,
    59–60
Pricing, as marketing tool, 22,
    25–26
Product distribution, as marketing tool,
    22, 26
Products:
  future trends and organization's
    objectives, 151
  life cycle of, 111–113
  mix of, 13
  objectives and "profit"
    measurement, 157
  substitute, 101, 200
Product strategy posture, 174–176

Profit:
  for-profit versus nonprofit, 18–19
  objectives and measurement of,
    156–158
  profit motive and, 19
Programmatical superiority, competing
  with, 88
Programming, as marketing tool, 22,
  26
Promotion, strategy and, 190
Prospects:
  exchange theory and, 16–18
  internal analysis and discovering of,
    135–137
"Prosumers," 131
Psychographics, as enduring variable,
  74, 77–78
Public relations. *See* Brand
Purchase touchpoint, 222
Purpose, as marketing strategy, 189

Quality of programs, competing with,
  89–90

Reciprocity, individuals search for,
  40–41
Research, benefits of, 13
Resource attraction:
  issues of, 21–22
  marketing tasks and, 20–22
  paths of, 20–21

Sealey, Peter, 210
Segmentation:
  external audit and, 83–84
  market research and, 73–74
  variables and, 74–80
Self-image of organization, assessing of,
  133–134
Self-interest. *See* Exchange theory
Sequencing of gifts, 154
Services:
  assessing delivery of, 137–138
  competitive advantage and, 180–181
  cost and performance analysis,
    143–144
  delivery of, 106–107

  measuring level of services provided,
    101–102
  need for and decision to enter causal
    industry, 104–105
  substitute, in environment, 101, 200
Simplicity Marketing (Sealey), 210
Social media:
  competitors and, 140–141
  marketing culture and, 131–132
Social trends, Harvard Policy Model
  and, 196
Stakeholders:
  brand and, 211–215
  causal marketing and, xxvi
  centrality of and value attainment,
    xv–xvii
  communication and retention of,
    138–140
  focus of, as operational constraint,
    46–47
  groups comprising, 5–6
  imperative of finding right, xxvi
  importance of internal analysis and,
    120–125
  importance of processing
    information from, xxiii–xxv
  internal analysis and satisfaction of,
    132–134
  marketing culture and, 129
  marketing strategy and value, 35
  mistrust of and marketing strategy,
    42–43
  new means of social engagement
    with, xvii–xviii
  organizational mission and, 14–15
  perceptions of strategic success,
    159
Status quo, strategy and, 170–171
Strategic Flexibility (Harrigan), 34
Strategic listening and research, 70
*Strategic Management of Public and Third
  Sector Organizations* (Nutt and
  Backoff), 189
*Strategic Marketing for Nonprofit
  Organizations* (Kotler), 11
*Strategic Marketing for Not-for-Profit
  Organizations* (Lauffer), 17

Strategic Planning for Public and Nonprofit Organizations (Bryson), 33
Strategic plans, internal analysis of, 125–127
Strategic problems, internal analysis and dealing with, 132–137
  failure to consider stakeholder satisfaction, 132–134
  marketing history, 135
  prospect discovery, 135–137
Strategic stalemate, 234–235
Strategy, defined, 168
Strategy-selection phase, of marketing plan, 52, 59
Strengths and weaknesses, assessing of, 137–141
  communication, 138–140
  competitive advantages, 140–141
  organization's objectives, 152–153
  service delivery, 137–138
Substitute causes/services/products:
  in environmental structure, 101
  relative power of, 200
Success:
  augmenting for competitive advantage, 181–182
  cost and performance analysis and, 143–144
  objectives and measurement of, 158–159
Suppliers:
  in organization's environment, 102
  relative power of, 199–200
Support services, competing with, 90
Surowiecki, James, 70
Sustainable competitive advantage, 178–181
SWOT analysis, 195–196
"Synergy tactic," for competitive advantage, 181–182

Technological superiority, competing with, 88
Technology trends:
  Harvard Policy Model and, 196
  marketing strategy and, 108

organization's objectives and, 152
Third Wave, The (Toffler), 131
Toffler, Alvin, 131
Top Management Strategy (Tregoe and Zimmerman), 168
Touchpoints, categories of, 221–222
Tregoe, Benjamin B., 168
Trends:
  demographic, 41–42, 108
  economic, 108, 151–152, 195, 234
  Harvard Policy Model and, 195–196
  market, 90–91
  marketing strategy and, 192
  objectives and planning for uncertain future, 150–152
  in organizations' environment, 107–108
  political, 196
  social, 196
  technological, 108, 152, 196
12 simple Steps to a Winning Marketing Plan (Larkin), 57
"Two-product" pricing policies, 25–26

Uncertainty. *See* Strategic problems
User groups, identifying of, 97–98, 135–137

Vaill, Peter, 8
Value proposition. *See also* Objectives of organization
  competitive advantage and, 179–181
  marketing strategy and, 35
  organizational mission and, 15
Vertical integration, as possible growth strategy, 185
Volunteers. *See also* Stakeholders
  assessing long-term relationships with, 141–143
  competitive advantage and, 181
  as constituents, 20
  describing for market research, 81–82
  external-analysis phase and, 52–54, 72–73

Volunteers. *See also* Stakeholders
(*Continued*)
objectives and excellence in
marketing, 154
as stakeholders, 5–6

Waterman, Robert, 194
We (Yastrow), xix
Welch, Jack, 139

Welcome to the Creative Age (Earl),
41–42
Wheatley, Margaret J., xviii
Wholly segmented strategy,
83–84

Yastrow, Steve, xix

Zimmerman, John W., 168